# THE LAW AND
# YOUR LEGAL
# RIGHTS

## A Bilingual Guide to
## Everyday Legal Issues

### JESS J. ARAUJO, ESQ.

D1364692

A FIRESIDE BOOK
PUBLISHED BY SIMON & SCHUSTER

FIRESIDE
Rockefeller Center
1230 Avenue of the Americas
New York, New York 10020

Copyright © 1989 by Lic. Jesus J. Araujo
Copyright © 1998 by Jess J. Araujo

This publication contains the opinions and ideas of its author and is designed to provide useful advice in regard to the subject matter covered. The author and publisher are not engaged in rendering legal, accounting, or other professional services in this publication. Laws vary from state to state, as do the facts and circumstances of various legal situations, and this publication is not intended to provide a basis for action in particular circumstances without consideration by a competent professional. The author and publisher expressly disclaim any responsibility for any liability, loss, or risk, personal or otherwise, which is incurred as a consequence, directly or indirectly, of the use and application of any of the contents of this book.

All rights reserved including the right of reproduction in whole or in part in any form.

FIRESIDE and colophon are registered trademarks of Simon & Schuster Inc.

Book design by Pagesetters/IPA
Manufactured in the United States of America

10 9 8 7 6 5 4 3 2 1

Library of Congress Cataloging-in-Publication Data
Araujo, Jess J.
The law and your legal rights : a bilingual guide to everyday legal issues / Jess J. Araujo.
p.   cm.
Includes index.
Added title page title: Ley y sus derechos legales.
1. Law—United States—Popular works. I. Title. II. Title: Ley y sus derechos legales
KF387.A68   1998
349.73—dc21
98-21982
CIP

ISBN 0-684-83970-9

*To Donna Marie Araujo, my remarkably gifted and exceptionally loving wife, who has been a constant source of comfort, inspiration, motivation, and energy in my life.*

*To my children, Jess J. Araujo, Jr., and Kristina Araujo Massa, whose love and support exemplify the significance of familia.*

*To my father, Juan Araujo, for having had confidence in my abilities and for treating me like a man since age fourteen.*

*To my beloved mother, Dolores Gómez Araujo, who single-handedly made sure that I learned the finest aspects of the Mexican culture and traditions, as well as the Spanish language.*

# Contents

## 3. SMALL CLAIMS COURT    40

## 4. CONTRACTS    51

## 8. BANKRUPTCY   88

## 9. WILLS, TRUSTS, AND PROBATE   97

## 10. EMPLOYEE AND EMPLOYER RIGHTS IN THE WORKPLACE   102

## 11. LANDLORD–TENANT LAW 121

## 12. FAMILY LAW: MARRIAGE, DIVORCE, CHILD CUSTODY, DOMESTIC VIOLENCE, ADOPTION, AND PARENTAL RESPONSIBILITY    133

## 13. MOTOR VEHICLES    160

14    *Contents*

# Foreword
# by Ricardo Montalbán

America's heritage has long borne the nickname the Melting Pot. Often new arrivals to the United States sought comfort in their new land by settling together with those who spoke the same language, further seeking reassurance in a community with a common cultural background while they learned the ways of a vast new land governed by new laws and a unique political structure. Oftentimes those who arrived came to escape the harsh political and economic climates of their native lands. Others came hoping to reap the bounty of the "land of opportunity." For whatever reasons, all who arrived in the United States were awed by its enormous size and power and the promise of a fair and just legal system that would allow average people to work and prosper.

It is not surprising that a substantial portion of those living in America today learned Spanish as their first language, since Spanish is the most common mother tongue in the Western Hemisphere.* This book is dedicated to those people living in America who speak Spanish as their first language.

I am honored to tell you about this book, written by my close friend Jess Araujo. Jess is an attorney who is renowned in the United States and who retains strong ties to his Hispanic heritage. Throughout a highly successful career he has demonstrated over and over again his understanding of the issues that face the non-English-speaking American. As founder of LAVA, the Latin American Voters of America, Jess has led a national movement to encourage Hispanics to become active in the political process at all levels. He has been at the forefront in

---

*1995 *World Almanac*. Mandarin (No. 1) and Hindi (No. 2) have the greatest number of speakers in the world. Spanish is No. 3 and English, No. 4. In the Western Hemisphere, it would follow, Spanish is the first language of more people than any other, including English. English is spoken by more people than Spanish, but the reasons for this seem to be the frequency with which native speakers of other languages learn English, often to be able to participate in international business.

strengthening relationships within the Hispanic legal community through participation in the Hispanic Bar Association.

Jess devotes a great deal of his time and energy to ensuring that the Hispanic community is a cohesive and supportive entity whose strength and power form a visible presence in the greater community of America.

On a personal level, Jess has been an inspiration and mentor to many. He speaks to us not as an authority but as one who comes from the common roots that bind us. Jess understands the issues facing the Spanish speaker who may be unaware of the responsibilities each of us has to know the law and to follow its mandate.

In addressing those needs, Jess has written this book to help us understand the laws that govern our daily lives. He has patiently and thoughtfully taken the often confusing words of the lawmakers and transformed them into examples that show us how the law works in our everyday relationships. He shows us the reasons behind the laws and demystifies the legal process. He also offers invaluable advice on how to prevent problems from arising by pointing out misconceptions that many of us have brought with us from the legal systems of our native countries.

Jess Araujo has given the Spanish-speaking community a great gift through this book. He has made it easy for anyone who reads Spanish or English to understand the law and to enjoy the benefits it offers. In the pages of this book, even those who seem hopelessly intimidated by the law will come to see the reason and order upon which the laws of the United States are based, and fortified with that knowledge, they will be able to go forth, armed with a tool against fear borne of ignorance.

*The Law and Your Legal Rights (La ley y sus derechos legales)* should be in the library of every home and business in which Spanish is spoken.

# Preface

The attainment of adequate knowledge and information can often be the difference between success and failure in practically any situation. The lack of adequate knowledge and/or information can be and, all too often, is costly, painful, embarrassing, and even fatal. Whether you are trying to determine why your car will not start or trying to decide whether you should attempt mouth-to-mouth resuscitation on an unconscious person in a public place, the amount of appropriate knowledge and information you possess will have a very drastic effect on the ultimate results.

Because so many aspects of our lives are complex and technical, it is extremely difficult for us to adequately master all of the subjects that must be mastered in order to enjoy and experience the maximum benefits available. That is why doctors, lawyers, electricians, and hundreds of other specialists identify an area of information, become thoroughly knowledgeable in that area, and then proceed to sell their knowledge in order to help solve your problems in that area. They realize, as you do, that it is simply not possible for everyone to go to law school just to be able to personally resolve one or two legal problems that may arise in a lifetime. It is much more practical to pay a fee to an attorney on those rare occasions when a legal need arises. Add to this that not everyone possesses the necessary aptitude, motivation, and financial resources to successfully obtain a legal education, and you can readily understand why hiring a lawyer often is the only practical solution to resolving a legal problem.

In the legal profession, however, as in any other service-oriented industry, there is a wide range of variables that will determine the nature and quality of the service and results you will receive. The service and results you receive will be greatly dependent on the personal and professional qualities of the lawyer you hire.

Having practiced law for over twenty years and having represented literally thousands of clients, I have, on many occasions, advised people who had previously consulted with or hired a lawyer to assist in resolving one or more legal matters. As a result, I have concluded that many people either wait too long after a problem arises before seeing a lawyer, go to the wrong lawyer, or unwisely fire a good lawyer who is doing a good job. Most people simply do not know enough about how routine legal matters are handled or about how basic laws affect even the most common situations.

This book is designed to provide very basic and general information about the laws and legal procedures that regulate everyday life. Areas such as employer and employee rights in the workplace, small claims court, motor vehicle laws, drunk driving laws, wills, bankruptcy, and divorce law are but a few of the subjects covered in the following pages.

Of the hundreds of legal subjects and topics that constitute our "body of law," I have carefully selected only those that I believe are likely to be of interest to and frequently affect the "average person." (While I totally appreciate the extremely imprecise nature of such a term, I am confident that most readers will indulge my use of it and allow themselves to benefit from the concept it is designed to identify.)

This book is not a substitute for an attorney. Nor is it a complete treatment of every legal aspect of any subject or any specific legal situation. An attorney should be consulted with respect to specific legal problems or situations since laws often vary from state to state and the federal system and are frequently changed and/or repealed.

I have attempted to use nontechnical language, where appropriate, in order to avoid confusion and to maximize understanding, especially when describing the basic rights and responsibilities of individuals. Where use of a technical term is necessary, it is defined or explained.

Because of my belief that the information in this book is uniquely useful to immigrants in general and Spanish-speaking immigrants in particular, I have provided a Spanish translation to the text. Since some of the concepts in Latin American countries are significantly different from those I have described in the U.S. legal system, I have added explanatory notes in the Spanish version only.

It is my intent and sincere desire that this book provide useful and necessary information in a manner that is straightforward and easy to understand.

# Acknowledgments

My thanks to:

Ricardo Montalbán for having taken the time from an extremely busy schedule to read and discuss the manuscript and for writing the introduction as only Ricardo could have.

Betsy Amster, my literary agent, whose careful criticism, valuable suggestions, and effective representation produced an enjoyable, productive, and profitable result.

Professor Lee Ramírez for having contributed so much to the writing style, grammatical content, and proofreading process of this book (as he did for my previous book).

Andrew J. "Andy" DiMarco, Esq., Steven J. DiMarco, Esq., and John A. Montevideo, Esq., my law partners and colleagues, for having believed in this book and for having exercised exceptional flexibility in our professional lives in order to accommodate the intense schedule required of me during the writing of this book.

Dr. José L. Santana, who exercised primary responsibility for the Spanish-language version of the text.

Teresa Calhoon, Irma Gómez, Estuardo Méndez, Germán Sánchez, and Ricardo Sandoval for providing additional Spanish-language translation and expert collaboration in the preparation of the Spanish text.

Gary H. Manulkin, Esq., for editing and enhancing the chapter on immigration law.

José "Joji" Gutiérrez, who provided excellent and unique computer-related services throughout the development of numerous versions of both languages of the text.

Farid H. Sarah, my *compadre* and mentor, whose creativity and insight helped to develop several key themes in the book.

Lucy Araujo, my beloved sister, whose keen understanding of two cultures, two languages, and legal principles contributed greatly to the final product.

# 1

# Introduction to the Legal System

## THE SUPREME LAW OF THE LAND

In the United States of America the United States Constitution is the supreme law of the land. No state may pass any law that would contradict the Constitution, and no court may rule against the Constitution.

## DRAFTING THE CONSTITUTION

The original thirteen colonies were governed by the Articles of Confederation, but no provision was made for a judicial system. Without a judicial system, there was no branch of government to interpret the laws. To correct that situation, the Constitution was drafted. It was adopted by the members of the Constitutional Convention in 1787 and became effective in 1789.

## THE PREAMBLE TO THE CONSTITUTION

The Preamble to the Constitution reads as follows:

We the People of the United States, in Order to form a more perfect Union, establish Justice, insure domestic Tranquility, provide for the common defense, promote the general Welfare, and secure the Blessings of Liberty to ourselves and our Posterity, do ordain and establish this Constitution for the United States of America.

## THE THREE BRANCHES OF GOVERNMENT

The Constitution provides for three branches of government: the legislative branch, which makes laws; the judicial branch, which interprets the laws; and the executive branch, which administers the laws. Each branch of the government is independent, creating a system of checks and balances, which prevents any one branch from having greater power than the others. The executive branch has power by which it can veto a law passed by the legislative branch. The legislative branch may overcome an executive veto by having two-thirds of its members vote for a law. The judicial branch can rule that a law passed by the legislative branch and signed by the executive branch is unconstitutional and cannot be enforced.

### ARTICLE I: CREATING THE LEGISLATURE

Article I of the Constitution provides for the legislative branch, also called the Congress. The federal Congress is called bicameral, which means that it consists of two parts: the House of Representatives and the Senate. Members of Congress are elected by the people. Each state elects two senators, and senators serve terms of six years. Representatives, as the members of the House of Representatives are known, are elected by federal legislative districts and serve two-year terms. The number of federal legislative districts in each state is determined by the population of each state. (Sparsely populated states have few federal congressional districts. New Mexico has only three, and Arizona has six, while more densely populated states have greater numbers. California has fifty-two, New York has thirty-one, Texas has thirty, Florida has twenty-three, and Illinois has twenty.) The members of Congress are responsible for writing and enacting the statutory laws that govern those aspects of life with which the federal government is concerned.

### ARTICLE II: CREATING THE EXECUTIVE BRANCH

Article II provides for the executive branch, which includes the offices of the president and the vice president. The Constitution broadly defines the powers and limitations of the offices of the executive branch.

## ARTICLE III: CREATING THE JUDICIAL BRANCH

Article III provides for the judicial branch. It establishes the federal Supreme Court and makes a provision for Congress to create the lesser federal courts. It also defines the powers of the federal courts and delineates which matters shall be heard in the federal courts and which in the courts of the individual states. It is the duty of the judiciary to interpret the laws made by Congress and to rule, when asked, on whether a law made by Congress violates the U.S. Constitution.

## THE BILL OF RIGHTS

To provide for the rights and liberties of individuals, the first ten amendments to the United States Constitution were adopted in 1791. These ten amendments, known as the Bill of Rights, are the cornerstone of a free and independent society. A summary of the most significant provisions of the Bill of Rights follows.

**Amendment I** provides for personal liberties, including freedom of speech, religion, and assembly; a free press; and the right to seek legal remedy for violation of those rights.

**Amendment II** allows the people to bear arms and form a militia to protect the nation.

**Amendment III** prohibits the military from occupying any person's home without his or her consent.

**Amendment IV** prohibits unreasonable searches and seizures.

**Amendment V** guarantees individuals the right against self-incrimination, to due process of law, and prohibits double jeopardy.

**Amendment VI** states the rights of anyone accused of a crime, including the right to trial by jury.

**Amendment VII** provides for trial by jury in noncriminal cases.

**Amendment VIII** prohibits the government from levying excessive bail or fines or administering cruel and unusual punishment to individuals.

**Amendment IX** provides that certain rights are retained by the people.

**Amendment X** proclaims that those powers not specifically reserved by the federal government shall be the domain of the individual states.

## AMENDMENTS: CHANGING THE CONSTITUTION

The Founding Fathers, who wrote the Constitution, knew that the country would grow and change over the years, so they provided a way for amendments to be added to the Constitution. There are now twenty-seven amendments, and others can be added when the people believe it is necessary.

## RIGHTS OF THE STATES

In addition to the powers the Constitution gives the federal government, the states, under the Tenth Amendment, have powers of their own. Each state has the right to make its own laws, so long as they are not in violation of the U.S. Constitution, and to provide for the rights of individuals within that state. For the most part, we shall limit our discussion to state laws and use the relevant laws of those states with significant Hispanic populations, which are Arizona, California, Florida, Illinois, New Mexico, New York, and Texas.

# 2

# Understanding the Court System

## Two Court Systems: Federal and State

In the United States all courts belong either to the federal court system or to the individual state court systems.

### Federal Courts

Federal courts hear cases that involve federal laws, the U.S. Constitution, matters in which the U.S. government is named, matters that involve individuals or groups from different states or from other countries, and maritime laws. The courts of general jurisdiction in the federal system are the federal district courts, the federal courts of appeal, and sometimes the Supreme Court. There are several courts of limited jurisdiction in the federal system, including courts that handle only patent and copyright matters and bankruptcy courts, among many others.

### State Courts

State courts hear cases that involve state laws, state constitutions, and cases in which the state is named. At the state level some courts of limited jurisdiction are municipal courts, justice courts, small claims courts, traffic courts, and juvenile courts. In each of these cases, the court in question can hear only those matters specifically delegated to it by law. State courts also have courts of limited jurisdiction to handle particular criminal and civil cases and courts of general jurisdiction such as superior courts and appeals courts.

## JURISDICTION

*Jurisdiction* is a court's legal and geographic area of authority to hear a case.

## CIVIL AND CRIMINAL LAWS

Federal and state courts handle both criminal and civil cases.

*Criminal laws* define conduct or acts that are considered crimes or wrongs against society, also called the State.

*Civil laws* involve noncriminal matters, including the private or personal wrongdoing between individuals or between individuals and businesses or governments.

## COURTS OF ORIGINAL JURISDICTION: THE TRIAL COURT

Nearly all cases begin at the *trial court* level, which is also called the court of original jurisdiction. That a case is heard in trial court does not necessarily mean a jury will be used; sometimes a judge alone will hear the case. Trial courts decide the facts in a dispute and determine how the law should be applied to those facts. In criminal cases, trial courts determine the guilt or innocence of the accused. If the accused is found guilty, the trial court judge determines the penalty and pronounces the sentence of the court.

At the federal level the trial court is usually the U.S. district court for the geographic area where the case has been filed. Each state has at least one federal judicial district, and the number of districts is determined by the population and geographic size of the state.

In the state court system the trial court is usually the superior court, although for some cases the lower courts of limited jurisdiction may be the trial courts (see state court system, page 25).

## APPEALING THE TRIAL COURT'S DECISION

The losing party is often entitled to appeal the decision of the trial court. When a decision is appealed, the legal issues in the case are reexamined by a higher court.

At the federal level the immediate appellate courts are the U.S. courts of appeals. There are thirteen federal courts of appeals, each of which covers a particular geographic area known as a *circuit* (See Figure 2-1: The Thirteen Federal Judicial Circuits, page 29). At the state level cases subject to appeal are sent to the state appellate courts and ultimately to the highest court in each state, usually called the state supreme court (See state court system diagrams on pages 31 to 39).

Appellate courts, either federal or state, review the case to see if relevant points of law were correctly applied by the trial court. *Appellate courts do not reevaluate the facts found by the trial courts.* In California the final appellate court is the California Supreme Court. At the federal level the final appellate court is the United States Supreme Court.

## CREATING LAWS

Each of the three branches of government, at the federal and state levels, can create "laws," but each uses a different device in doing so.

*Statutory law* is created by the *legislative branch* through bills that become law when signed by the chief executive (the president at the federal level or the governor at the state level). Sometimes the president declines to sign a bill approved by the Congress through the executive power of the veto. Congress can override a presidential veto and pass the bill, however, if two-thirds of the legislators in both houses of Congress vote in favor of the law. Comparable provisions in state constitutions apply when governors veto bills approved by state legislatures.

*Administrative law* consists of the rules and regulations issued by the various administrative agencies. At the federal and state levels, administrative agencies are part of the *executive branch.* Some agencies like the Federal Reserve Board, which controls the nation's money supply, are independent agencies and are allowed to set their own rules without interference from the legislative branch, the executive branch, or the judicial branch. Other administrative agencies are not independent but report directly to the president of the United States. An example is the Department of State, which handles foreign affairs.

*Common law,* also known as *case law,* comes from the *judicial branch* of government and results from court decisions in particular cases. Common law is based on **precedent,** meaning that a previously decided similar case becomes the authority for future decisions in such cases.

However, these precedents change over time to accommodate the new demands of our society. Whenever the court does not apply a traditional precedent to a case, with the purpose of implementing a new ruling, it is said that the court has established a new law, which will become a new precedent to be used by the court.

## VENUE

Once a court has jurisdiction of a case, *venue* must be established. Venue is the actual building or courthouse where a case is properly filed. While *jurisdiction* is the court's inherent power and authority to decide a case, *venue* designates the particular place in which a case can be filed.

## DECISIONS OF THE COURT

Once a case has been heard and a decision has been reached, the court will issue a *judgment.* This is the court's final decision on a case and will state the rights and obligations of the parties that have been involved.

## PARTIES TO A LEGAL ACTION

As an example, the following hypothetical civil case illustrates the parties to a case: José owes Rubén one thousand dollars but refuses to pay him. Rubén files a lawsuit in which he asks the court to issue a judgment against José for the one thousand dollars. In this case Rubén is the *plaintiff,* and José is the *respondent* or *defendant.* If the court determines that Rubén, the plaintiff, is entitled to the money he says José owes him, it will issue a judgment stating that José, the defendant, must pay Rubén one thousand dollars. The plaintiff, Rubén, then becomes the *judgment creditor,* and the defendant, José, becomes the *judgment debtor.*

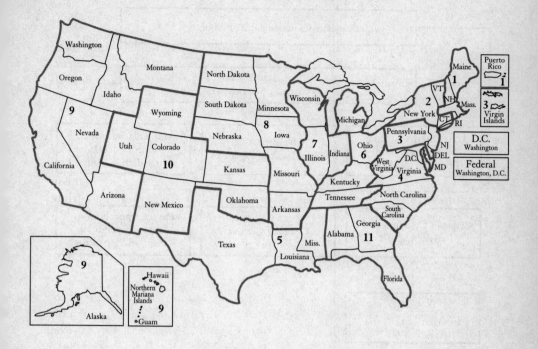

**FIGURE 2-1: THE THIRTEEN FEDERAL JUDICIAL CIRCUITS**

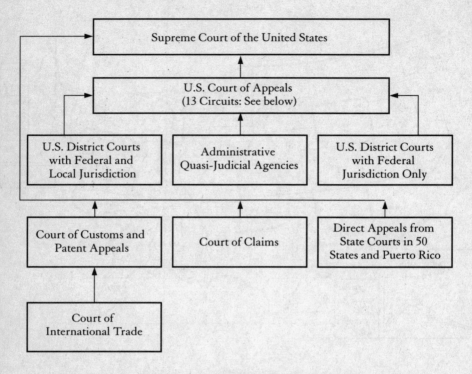

UNITED STATES COURTS OF APPEALS FOR THE THIRTEEN CIRCUITS

| First Circuit | Second Circuit | Third Circuit | Fourth Circuit | Fifth Circuit | Sixth Circuit |
|---|---|---|---|---|---|
| Maine | Connecticut | Delaware | Maryland | Louisiana | Kentucky |
| Massachusetts | New York | New Jersey | North Carolina | Mississippi | Michigan |
| New Hampshire | Vermont | Pennsylvania | South Carolina | Texas | Ohio |
| Rhode Island | | Virgin Islands | Virginia | | Tennessee |
| Puerto Rico | | | West Virginia | | |

| Seventh Circuit | Eight Circuit | Ninth Circuit | Tenth Circuit | Eleventh Circuit | District of Columbia Circuit |
|---|---|---|---|---|---|
| Illinois | Iowa | Alaska | Colorado | Alabama | Washington, D.C. |
| Indiana | Minnesota | Arizona | Kansas | Florida | |
| Wisconsin | Missouri | California | New Mexico | Georgia | |
| | Nebraska | Hawaii | Oklahoma | | |
| | North Dakota | Idaho | Utah | | Federal Circuit |
| | South Dakota | Montana | Wyoming | | Washington, D.C. |
| | | Nevada | | | |
| | | Oregon | | | |
| | | Washington | | | |
| | | Guam | | | |

FIGURE 2-2: FEDERAL JUDICIAL SYSTEM FLOW CHART

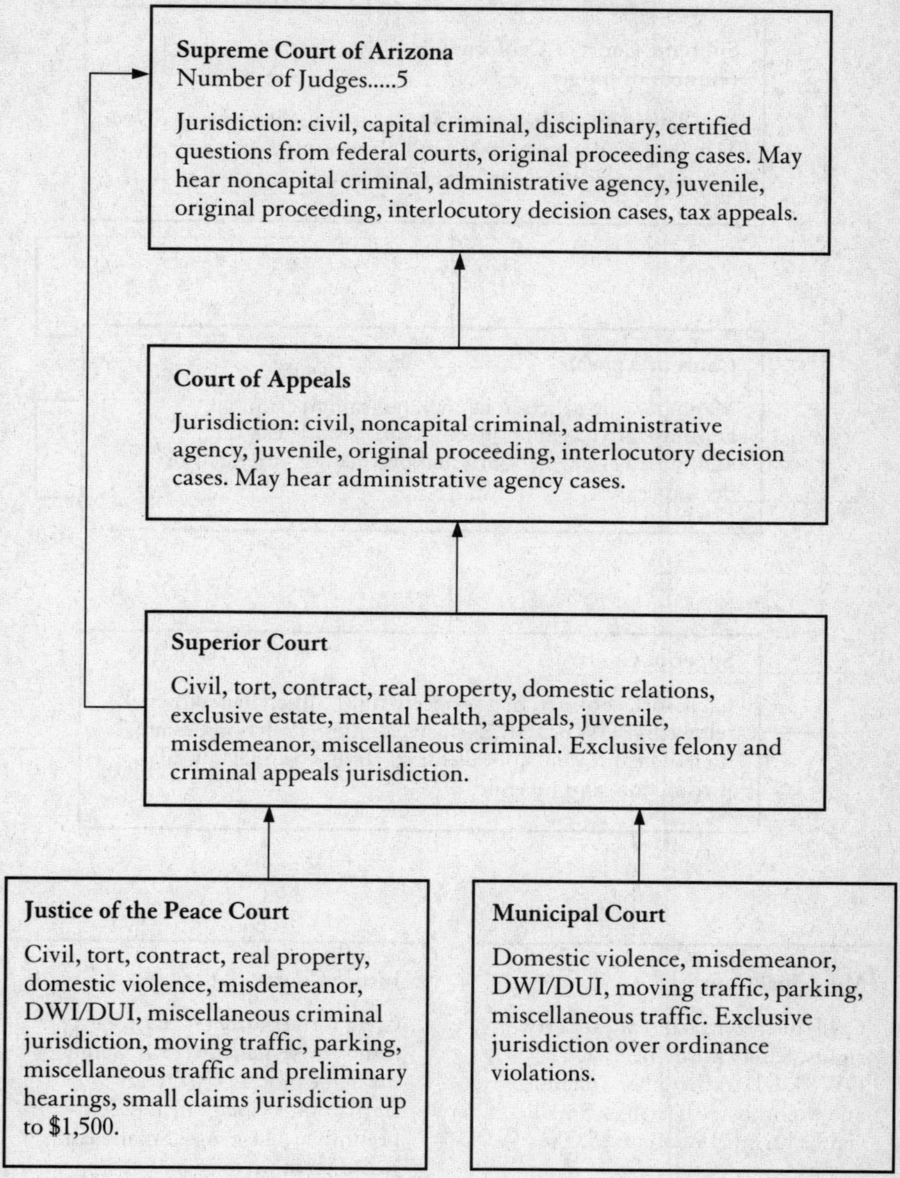

**Supreme Court of Arizona**
Number of Judges.....5

Jurisdiction: civil, capital criminal, disciplinary, certified
questions from federal courts, original proceeding cases. May
hear noncapital criminal, administrative agency, juvenile,
original proceeding, interlocutory decision cases, tax appeals.

**Court of Appeals**

Jurisdiction: civil, noncapital criminal, administrative
agency, juvenile, original proceeding, interlocutory decision
cases. May hear administrative agency cases.

**Superior Court**

Civil, tort, contract, real property, domestic relations,
exclusive estate, mental health, appeals, juvenile,
misdemeanor, miscellaneous criminal. Exclusive felony and
criminal appeals jurisdiction.

**Justice of the Peace Court**

Civil, tort, contract, real property,
domestic violence, misdemeanor,
DWI/DUI, miscellaneous criminal
jurisdiction, moving traffic, parking,
miscellaneous traffic and preliminary
hearings, small claims jurisdiction up
to $1,500.

**Municipal Court**

Domestic violence, misdemeanor,
DWI/DUI, moving traffic, parking,
miscellaneous traffic. Exclusive
jurisdiction over ordinance
violations.

FIGURE 2-3: ARIZONA COURT SYSTEM FLOW CHART

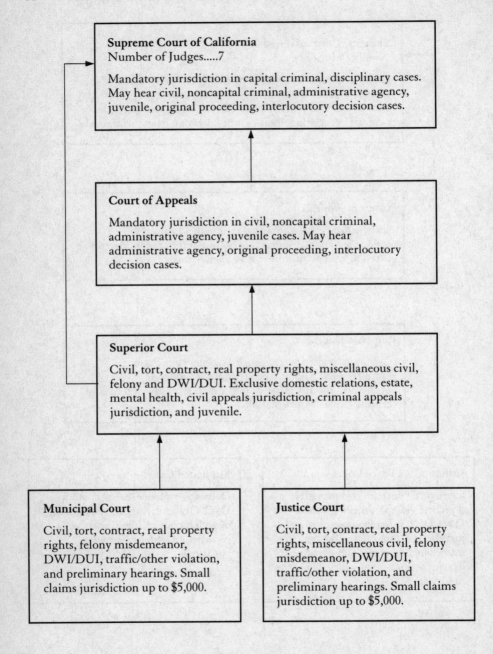

**Supreme Court of California**
Number of Judges.....7

Mandatory jurisdiction in capital criminal, disciplinary cases. May hear civil, noncapital criminal, administrative agency, juvenile, original proceeding, interlocutory decision cases.

**Court of Appeals**

Mandatory jurisdiction in civil, noncapital criminal, administrative agency, juvenile cases. May hear administrative agency, original proceeding, interlocutory decision cases.

**Superior Court**

Civil, tort, contract, real property rights, miscellaneous civil, felony and DWI/DUI. Exclusive domestic relations, estate, mental health, civil appeals jurisdiction, criminal appeals jurisdiction, and juvenile.

**Municipal Court**

Civil, tort, contract, real property rights, felony misdemeanor, DWI/DUI, traffic/other violation, and preliminary hearings. Small claims jurisdiction up to $5,000.

**Justice Court**

Civil, tort, contract, real property rights, miscellaneous civil, felony misdemeanor, DWI/DUI, traffic/other violation, and preliminary hearings. Small claims jurisdiction up to $5,000.

**FIGURE 2-4: CALIFORNIA COURT SYSTEM FLOW CHART**

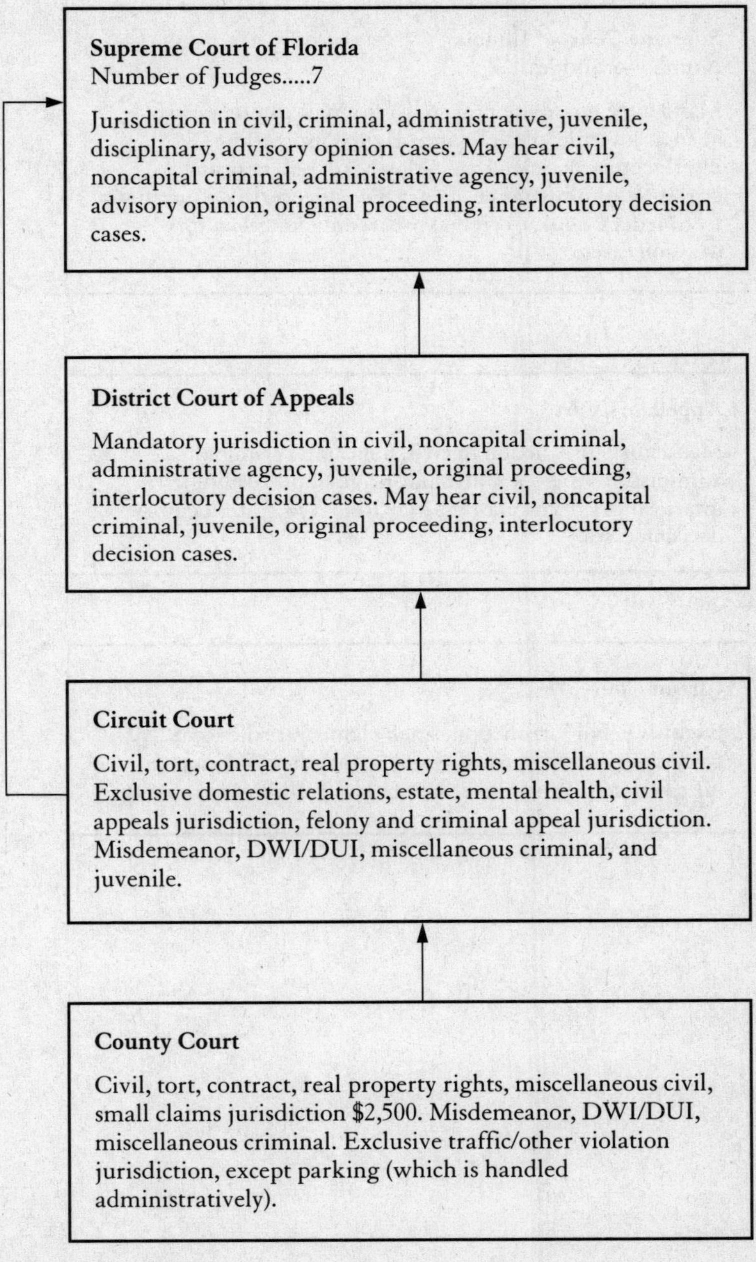

**Supreme Court of Florida**
Number of Judges.....7

Jurisdiction in civil, criminal, administrative, juvenile, disciplinary, advisory opinion cases. May hear civil, noncapital criminal, administrative agency, juvenile, advisory opinion, original proceeding, interlocutory decision cases.

**District Court of Appeals**

Mandatory jurisdiction in civil, noncapital criminal, administrative agency, juvenile, original proceeding, interlocutory decision cases. May hear civil, noncapital criminal, juvenile, original proceeding, interlocutory decision cases.

**Circuit Court**

Civil, tort, contract, real property rights, miscellaneous civil. Exclusive domestic relations, estate, mental health, civil appeals jurisdiction, felony and criminal appeal jurisdiction. Misdemeanor, DWI/DUI, miscellaneous criminal, and juvenile.

**County Court**

Civil, tort, contract, real property rights, miscellaneous civil, small claims jurisdiction $2,500. Misdemeanor, DWI/DUI, miscellaneous criminal. Exclusive traffic/other violation jurisdiction, except parking (which is handled administratively).

**FIGURE 2-5: FLORIDA COURT SYSTEM FLOW CHART**

**Supreme Court of Illinois**
Number of Judges.....7

Mandatory jurisdiction in civil, criminal, administrative agency, juvenile, disciplinary, original proceeding, interlocutory decision cases. May hear civil, noncapital criminal, administrative agency, juvenile, certified questions from federal courts, original proceeding, interlocutory decision cases.

**Appellate Court**

Mandatory jurisdiction in civil, noncapital criminal, administrative agency, juvenile, original proceeding, interlocutory decision cases. May hear civil, interlocutory decision cases.

**Circuit Court**

Exclusive civil jurisdiction, small claims jurisdiction $2,500. Exclusive criminal jurisdiction, traffic/other violation jurisdiction, juvenile jurisdiction, and preliminary hearings.

FIGURE 2-6: ILLINOIS COURT SYSTEM FLOW CHART

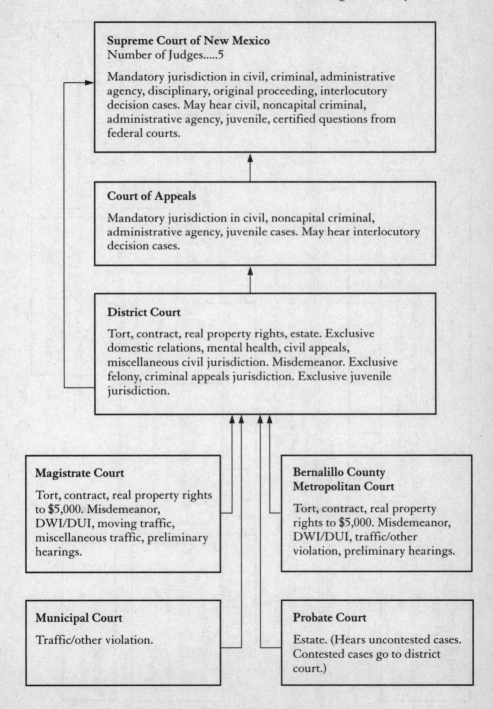

**Supreme Court of New Mexico**
Number of Judges.....5

Mandatory jurisdiction in civil, criminal, administrative agency, disciplinary, original proceeding, interlocutory decision cases. May hear civil, noncapital criminal, administrative agency, juvenile, certified questions from federal courts.

**Court of Appeals**

Mandatory jurisdiction in civil, noncapital criminal, administrative agency, juvenile cases. May hear interlocutory decision cases.

**District Court**

Tort, contract, real property rights, estate. Exclusive domestic relations, mental health, civil appeals, miscellaneous civil jurisdiction. Misdemeanor. Exclusive felony, criminal appeals jurisdiction. Exclusive juvenile jurisdiction.

**Magistrate Court**

Tort, contract, real property rights to $5,000. Misdemeanor, DWI/DUI, moving traffic, miscellaneous traffic, preliminary hearings.

**Bernalillo County Metropolitan Court**

Tort, contract, real property rights to $5,000. Misdemeanor, DWI/DUI, traffic/other violation, preliminary hearings.

**Municipal Court**

Traffic/other violation.

**Probate Court**

Estate. (Hears uncontested cases. Contested cases go to district court.)

**FIGURE 2-7: NEW MEXICO COURT SYSTEM FLOW CHART**

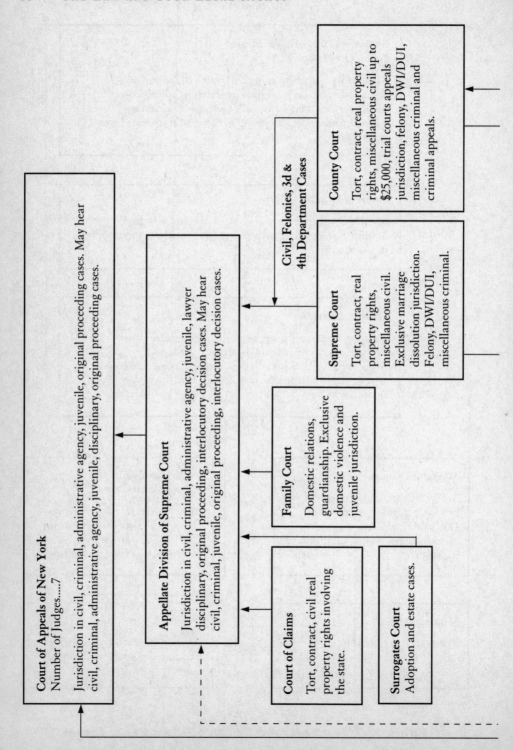

**Court of Appeals of New York**
Number of Judges.....7
Jurisdiction in civil, criminal, administrative agency, juvenile, original proceeding cases. May hear civil, criminal, administrative agency, juvenile, disciplinary, original proceeding cases.

**Appellate Division of Supreme Court**
Jurisdiction in civil, criminal, administrative agency, juvenile, lawyer disciplinary, original proceeding, interlocutory decision cases. May hear civil, criminal, juvenile, original proceeding, interlocutory decision cases.

Civil, Felonies, 3d &
4th Department Cases

**County Court**
Tort, contract, real property rights, miscellaneous civil up to $25,000, trial courts appeals jurisdiction, felony, DWI/DUI, miscellaneous criminal and criminal appeals.

**Supreme Court**
Tort, contract, real property rights, miscellaneous civil. Exclusive marriage dissolution jurisdiction. Felony, DWI/DUI, miscellaneous criminal.

**Family Court**
Domestic relations, guardianship. Exclusive domestic violence and juvenile jurisdiction.

**Court of Claims**
Tort, contract, civil real property rights involving the state.

**Surrogates Court**
Adoption and estate cases.

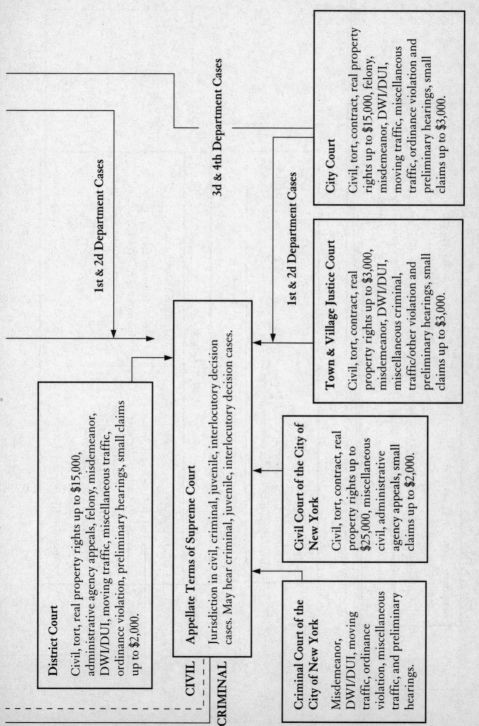

**FIGURE 2-8: NEW YORK COURT SYSTEM FLOW CHART**

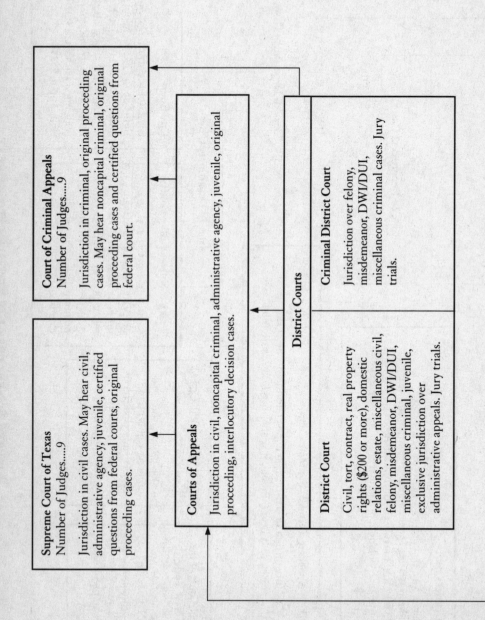

**Supreme Court of Texas**
Number of Judges.....9

Jurisdiction in civil cases. May hear civil, administrative agency, juvenile, certified questions from federal courts, original proceeding cases.

**Court of Criminal Appeals**
Number of Judges.....9

Jurisdiction in criminal, original proceeding cases. May hear noncapital criminal, original proceeding cases and certified questions from federal court.

**Courts of Appeals**

Jurisdiction in civil, noncapital criminal, administrative agency, juvenile, original proceeding, interlocutory decision cases.

**District Courts**

**District Court**

Civil, tort, contract, real property rights ($200 or more), domestic relations, estate, miscellaneous civil, felony, misdemeanor, DWI/DUI, miscellaneous criminal, juvenile, exclusive jurisdiction over administrative appeals. Jury trials.

**Criminal District Court**

Jurisdiction over felony, misdemeanor, DWI/DUI, miscellaneous criminal cases. Jury trials.

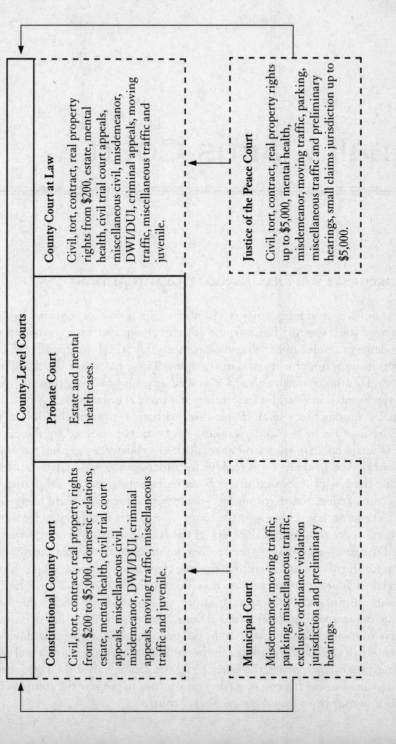

**County-Level Courts**

**Constitutional County Court**

Civil, tort, contract, real property rights from $200 to $5,000, domestic relations, estate, mental health, civil trial court appeals, miscellaneous civil, misdemeanor, DWI/DUI, criminal appeals, moving traffic, miscellaneous traffic and juvenile.

**Probate Court**

Estate and mental health cases.

**County Court at Law**

Civil, tort, contract, real property rights from $200, estate, mental health, civil trial court appeals, miscellaneous civil, misdemeanor, DWI/DUI, criminal appeals, moving traffic, miscellaneous traffic and juvenile.

**Municipal Court**

Misdemeanor, moving traffic, parking, miscellaneous traffic, exclusive ordinance violation jurisdiction and preliminary hearings.

**Justice of the Peace Court**

Civil, tort, contract, real property rights up to $5,000, mental health, misdemeanor, moving traffic, parking, miscellaneous traffic and preliminary hearings, small claims jurisdiction up to $5,000.

**FIGURE 2-9: TEXAS COURT SYSTEM FLOW CHART**

# 3

# Small Claims Court

## REQUIREMENTS FOR FILING A SMALL CLAIMS ACTION

Small claims court in most states is a part of a state municipal or other limited-jurisdiction court system. The purpose of small claims court is to provide a way for residents to resolve minor disputes promptly, fairly, and inexpensively. Each state sets its own rules for small claims actions. Those rules may include a maximum dollar amount one can sue for as well as prohibitions against any party being represented in court by an attorney at a small claims action.

Usually a judge hears small claims cases without a jury and decides the case on the basis of his or her understanding of the facts presented by the parties. Often when people are successful at small claims court, they get judgments for the money owed to them or to recover for other damages they have suffered.

While the law prohibits attorneys from representing any of the parties in a small claims action, the parties may consult with attorneys before filing small claims actions or before appearing in court. The papers necessary to file a small claims action are simple, and the clerk of the court can assist in completing the form. If the party initiating the action does not understand the law, he may seek help. In California the state requires that the clerk advise anyone who is filing a small claims action that an adviser may be contacted at no charge. The state maintains a list of such volunteers as attorneys, law students, and paralegals to assist the public in filing small claims actions. The state is interested in ensuring a successful small claims system that the public has access to, since any claim that is filed in small claims court reduces the potential burden on the municipal court. By using small claims court, the party filing the action, called the petitioner or plaintiff, can also save the cost of paying an attorney to prepare the complex documents that may be required for municipal court.

## STATUTE OF LIMITATIONS

The *statute of limitations* refers to the time limit allowed for filing a lawsuit. If a suit is not filed before the statute of limitations expires, the plaintiff may be denied an award of damages even if he can prove that the defendant caused the damages and was negligent. Different matters have different limitation periods.

## SMALL CLAIMS: BREACH OF CONTRACT, TORT CLAIMS, AND STATUTE VIOLATIONS

A claim filed in small claims court cannot exceed the jurisdictional maximum amount in each state plus filing fees. Claims may be filed in person or by mail and may seek actual and punitive damages for breach of contract, a tort or civil wrong, or violation of a law or statute. A tenant may sue in small claims court to have his security deposit returned after he vacates an apartment or may sue the landlord and ask for damages if the landlord fails to correct a health or safety violation in the apartment (see multistate compendium on small claims jurisdictional amounts on page 50).

## VENUE AND JURISDICTION

Small claims courts are usually divisions of municipal or superior courts. For a particular court to have jurisdiction over the claim, the lawsuit must be filed in the proper court. To locate the proper small claims court, a plaintiff should contact his local municipal courts. Under most state laws, a plaintiff may file his claim in any of the following judicial districts:

1. Where the defendant resides
2. Where the injury to persons or property occurred
3. Where a contract was signed
4. Where the business in question is located

*Venue* refers to the geographical location where a lawsuit may be filed. In most states the venue requirements for small claims court are the same as those for municipal court. Consumer protection laws contain special venue requirements in contract actions against consumers in order to protect consumers from merchants who might want to file an action in a court that is difficult for the consumer to get to, thus allowing of the consumer's inability to appear in court. In California the Unruh Act and the Rees-Levering Motor Vehicle Sales and Financing Act protect consumers from having to defend themselves in courts a long distance from where they live or work, even if the business might have the apparent legal basis to file in an out-of-the-way court.

## MATTERS THAT CAN AND CANNOT BE HEARD IN SMALL CLAIMS COURT

Some matters cannot be heard in small claims court even if the amount in controversy is within the monetary limits. Issues pertaining to collection of past due child or spousal support, a worker's compensation claim, an unlawful detainer action brought by a landlord against a tenant, an action that requires only equitable relief, such as an injunction, and an action involving an out-of-state defendant who cannot be served in the state are all matters that cannot be heard in small claims court.

An example of a typical small claims action might involve an agreement whereby Tom has agreed to care for Susan's house and dog for one month for $250. After Tom has performed as promised, Susan refuses to pay him. Tom can bring a suit against Susan for the money she promised to pay him. This is an example of breach of contract and is subject to legal action. Whether the contract was written or oral, Tom has the right to bring suit for the money owed to him since he has fulfilled his part of the contract.

A tort action may be filed in small claims court too. *Tort* is defined as "a private or civil wrong or injury. It is a wrong not involving a contract. There must always be a violation of a duty which arises by operation of general law. And there must always be damages which are proximately caused by the tortuous conduct."* Robert was stopped at a traffic light when another motorist hit the rear of his car. Robert can file a claim for damages to his car, for any personal injury he suffered, and for loss of earnings resulting from the accident. If the total of the damages that Robert wants to recover does not exceed the state's statutory limit, he may sue in small claims court. The advantages to Robert are these:

1. He can file a simple form without having to hire an attorney to represent him.
2. His case can be heard and decided quickly.
3. The other party is not entitled to engage in the expensive and time-consuming process of *discovery*, which can involve burdensome paperwork and costly investigations.

However, Robert may get less even if he wins in small claims court because he did not consult with an attorney and did not fully understand his rights, the value of his claim, or how to prove his case.

*Henry Campbel Black, *Black's Law Dictionary, 4th ed*. St. Paul, Minn.: West Publishing Co., 1968.

## ACTUAL DAMAGES AND REALISTIC VALUATION

A party to a small claims suit can recover as actual damages only what an item is worth at the time of damage. He will not recover the replacement value of a new car, his original purchase price, or the amount he owes on the car if that amount exceeds the fair market value. Before filing in small claims court, a prospective plaintiff should determine whether there really is liability on the defendant's part. *Liability* is the legally enforceable responsibility of one person to pay damages to another person. Damages are awarded to one person in a lawsuit because of the other person's negligence or unlawful conduct. The fact that a loss has occurred does not in and of itself establish liability. The plaintiff must establish that the defendant caused his injury or loss. If the plaintiff cannot prove in court that the defendant is liable, no damages will be awarded even though the plaintiff proves he was injured.

## SUING A MINOR

If someone finds it necessary to file suit against a minor—that is, any person under the age of majority—he should also name the minor's parent(s) or guardian(s) as defendants. There are a few exceptions such as a minor on duty with the armed forces, a legally married minor, or one who has been emancipated by court order. Minors who fall into one of these classifications are not considered *minors* and are treated as adults for all legal proceedings.

It is very difficult to sue minors for breach of contract because minors can rescind, or back out of, any contracts they have signed prior to reaching the age of majority. A plaintiff can sue for damages to himself or his property caused by a minor's negligence, but he may not be able to collect once the court issues a judgment because minors seldom have much money. It is often better to settle out of court unless the case is one of blatant willful misconduct for which a parent or guardian can be held liable. Willful misconduct means that the minor intentionally caused the damages. Normally, if the parents are to be held liable, the plaintiff must prove willful misconduct on the part of the minor. Even when parents are held liable, state laws often limit the dollar amount they can be required to pay. In many states parents can be held liable for auto accidents involving their minor children if the parents authorized the minor to drive and especially if they signed for their child's driver's license.

## FILING THE SMALL CLAIMS LAWSUIT

To begin a case in small claims court, the plaintiff, or petitioner, should go to the small claims court clerk's office, fill out the form called the plaintiff's statement, return the form, and pay the filing fee. The clerk then types out an official plaintiff's claim and order to defendant form and assigns the case a number. One copy of this form goes to the judge, and another is served on the defendant. The clerk also assigns a court date.

## SERVING THE DEFENDANT

A small claims complaint is not complete until the defendant has been officially served with a copy of the plaintiff's claim and order to defendant. Each defendant listed in the claim must be properly served. Even if the two defendants are married to each other, each must be served. The court will not issue a judgment against anyone not properly served.

For the most part, there are four legally accepted methods of service:

1. Personal service
2. Substituted service
3. Service by mail
4. Service by publication

### PERSONAL SERVICE

*Personal service* is made when the plaintiff's claim and order to defendant is handed directly to the defendant. This type of service requires the plaintiff to know where the server can find the defendant. Any adult except the person bringing the suit can serve papers on a defendant. The plaintiff may have a friend or relative serve the defendant or may hire the county sheriff or marshal or a private process server to serve the defendant.

If the defendant refuses to accept the papers, the process server should leave the documents close to the defendant and leave peaceably. If the person serving the papers does not know the defendant on sight, the server must make sure he is serving the correct person.

### SUBSTITUTED SERVICE

If the defendant is difficult to serve in person or if a corporation or agency is named as a defendant, the plaintiff may have the papers served by *substituted service.* In this case the papers are given to a representative or agent of the defendant. The representative must be an adult.

Following delivery by substituted service, the plaintiff must mail a copy of the claim of plaintiff to the defendant at the same address where the papers were left.

## SERVICE BY MAIL

In most states today the plaintiff can serve the plaintiff's claim and order to defendant by *certified mail.* However, the service is valid and binding only after the defendant has signed for the mail. If he refuses the mail, the court assumes he was never properly served. In some jurisdictions the clerk of the court will do the mailing for the plaintiff. The receipt that is returned with certified mail goes directly back to the clerk of the court. The plaintiff should contact the court a few days before the court date to make sure the service of process has been completed.

## SERVICE BY PUBLICATION

In some cases, the court will allow *service by publication.* To have an effective service by publication, a notice of the proceedings must be published in a newspaper approved by the court and must run for a period of time specified by law. Service by publication is designed to resolve issues when the defendant cannot be located.

## FILING A PROOF OF SERVICE WITH THE COURT

After the papers have been served, the plaintiff must file a *proof of service* with the court. In the case of substituted service, the proof of service must be signed by the person who actually served the papers on the defendant's representative.

## THE COURT HEARING

In small claims court the judge usually begins by asking the plaintiff to state his case. The defendant is then allowed to answer the charges and explain his side of the story. The judge will often ask both the plaintiff and the defendant a few questions. Witnesses will be allowed to testify, and evidence can be presented at this time.

If a witness is not willing to appear at the hearing, the plaintiff or defendant may ask the clerk of the court to issue a subpoena. A *subpoena* is a court order that requires the witness to go to the trial. If one of the parties needs papers to prove his case, he may ask the clerk of the court to issue a *subpoena duces tecum,* a court order requiring that certain papers be brought to the hearing.

The purpose of *evidence* is to prove the existence or nonexistence of a fact. Evidence exists in a variety of forms including oral evidence, such as the testimony of a witness; written evidence such as handwriting and documents, and other physical evidence such as real or personal property and photographs.

The law makes a distinction between original evidence and duplicate evidence. *Original evidence* means the first form of the writing. An original of a photograph includes the negative and any prints. If material is stored in a computer, any accurate and readable printout is considered an original. Any material that has been accurately reproduced is considered duplicate evidence.

Depending on the case and the evidence being offered, the court may invoke the best evidence rule, which requires that none other than the original of a writing is admissible to prove the content of that writing.

## DIRECT EVIDENCE, CIRCUMSTANTIAL EVIDENCE, AND HEARSAY EVIDENCE

*Direct evidence* is that which directly proves a fact and conclusively establishes that fact. *Circumstantial evidence* is indirect evidence. There are two kinds of circumstantial evidence: *certain,* from which a conclusion follows, and *uncertain,* from which a conclusion does not necessarily follow. *Hearsay evidence* refers to any statement made by someone other than the witness who is testifying and is offered to prove the truth of the statement. *Relevant evidence* is that which has any tendency to prove or disprove any disputed fact that could affect the outcome of the case, including evidence that demonstrates the credibility of a witness.

## THE BURDEN OF PROOF

Evidence itself is not proof. Proof is the establishment by evidence of a necessary degree of belief concerning a fact. The *burden of proof* is the obligation of a party to establish that degree of believability.

## INADMISSIBLE EVIDENCE

Parties are often surprised to learn that evidence that they have brought to court is inadmissible. There are strict rules that regulate what will and will not be admitted as evidence in court. Evidence laws are usually contained in the evidence codes of the various states. For the most part, however, small claims courts do not strictly apply the rules of evidence in their proceedings.

The court may exclude evidence that would take up too much time or would confuse the issues. It may also exclude any evidence that would result in undue prejudice.

## PROOF BY A PREPONDERANCE OF THE EVIDENCE

In civil cases the burden of proof is established by a *preponderance of the evidence.* If one party's evidence is more convincing than his opponent's evidence, the party with the more convincing evidence will win.

## BUSINESSES REQUIRING A LICENSE

In small claims actions involving a business, many states require the business to prove it is properly licensed in order to defend against a claim or prosecute to collect a judgment. Businesses that require licenses include, but are not limited to, contractors, manicure and hair salons, auto repair facilities, securities dealers, and pawnshops.

## THE JUDGE'S DECISION

After the judge has heard from both parties, he renders a decision on a form called the *Notice of Entry of Judgment.* Sometimes the decision is given in the courtroom, and sometimes the judge takes a little more time to review the case and issues his decision by mail. This usually requires only a few days, and the notice of entry of judgment is mailed to both parties.

If the defendant fails to appear on the original court date, the plaintiff may be awarded a *default judgment.* This means the plaintiff wins automatically because the defendant failed to show up in court. The defendant then has a short time, usually thirty days, to set aside the default judgment. If the defendant can prove that his absence was unavoidable, the judge may order that the parties appear at another hearing.

## APPEALING A SMALL CLAIMS DECISION

In small claims court the plaintiff usually cannot appeal the judge's decision. The defendant is the only party that has the right to appeal. Small claims court appeals are often filed in superior court in the same county as the small claims court. On appeal, the appellate court will hear the case from the beginning and will either uphold or reverse the decision of the small claims court. Usually appeals must be filed within twenty days of the trial court's decision. Enforcement of the judgment is postponed until the time for filing an appeal has expired or until after the appeal is decided.

## COLLECTING THE JUDGMENT

If a plaintiff files a suit against someone for running into his car and he wins the case, the court issues a judgment in his favor. He then becomes *the judgment creditor*, and the losing party becomes *the judgment debtor*. Once a party has been awarded a judgment, it is his responsibility to collect the money from the judgment debtor. If the judgment debtor accepts the court's decision and pays the judgment debtor promptly, the judgment creditor must then file a form called *Satisfaction of Judgment* with the court. This form indicates to the credit bureau, as well as to the court, that the debtor has met his obligation.

If the judgment debtor does not willingly pay, the creditor may have to take additional steps to collect the judgment. The court does not collect the money for the prevailing party. Once the time limit for filing an appeal has expired, the judgment creditor may attempt to collect the judgment by first sending the debtor a letter requesting him to pay. If the creditor has not received payment after ten days, he should contact the court and request a *writ of execution*. The form for this writ may be obtained from the small claims court clerk and must be served by the sheriff or marshal of the county where the debtor's assets are located.

## GARNISHING WAGES AND ATTACHING BANK ACCOUNTS OF JUDGMENT DEBTOR

If the judgment creditor knows where the debtor works, the writ of execution can be used to have a portion of the judgment debtor's wages garnished. *Garnishment* means a portion of his wages can be withheld to pay off his debt. The sheriff or marshal can "levy" on the debtor's bank account and attach whatever money is in the account if the name and location of the judgment debtor's bank are known. *Attachment* means that the money is seized and is used to pay the debt.

There are many exceptions regarding which types of funds may be attached to pay judgment debts. Social Security, federal government payroll checks, and pension and retirement benefits may not be garnished or attached to satisfy small claims court judgments.

## SELLING ASSETS TO SATISFY THE JUDGMENT

It is often difficult to satisfy a judgment with personal assets because of the exemption laws and the financial limit imposed for a suit in small claims court. Sometimes personal property can be seized by writ of execution and sold to pay the debt. Again there are exceptions that limit what may be seized. For example, the debtor is allowed an exemption (twelve hundred dollars in California) in equity on motor vehicles. That means if the debtor has a car worth four thousand dollars and he owes the finance company three thousand dollars, his equity in the car is only one thousand dollars and therefore exempt. If the vehicle is used in the debtor's line of work, it is exempt. For example, if the debtor is a gardener and owns a truck that he uses to carry his tools, the truck is considered exempt and cannot be taken away or sold to pay debts.

## The Judgment Debtor's Statement of Assets

The law provides means of collecting a judgment, but the party attempting to collect is required to proceed within the framework allowed for judgment collection. If the collecting party suspects that the debtor has viable assets but does not know their location, that party may be able to track them down. There are laws that require a judgment debtor to fill out a form called *Judgment Debtor's Statement of Assets*. This form must be sent to the judgment creditor within a specified period (usually thirty days) of the date the judgment becomes effective except when the debtor pays the debt, files an appeal, or makes a motion to set aside, or vacate, the judgment.

If the debtor does not fill out this form, the creditor can ask the court to issue a *declaration and order of examination*. This order requires the debtor to appear in court and answer any questions about his assets. If the debtor fails to appear, the judge can issue a bench warrant for his arrest. A *bench warrant* is an order from the court authorizing the police to seize a person and have him brought before the court.

When the debtor appears at the order of examination hearing, the creditor can levy any cash in the debtor's personal possession and apply that toward the debt. If the debtor does not answer questions about his assets truthfully, he may be held in contempt of court or prosecuted for perjury.

## Provisions for the Hearing- and Vision-Disabled

In most states courts are required to provide, at no charge, an assistive listening or computer-aided transcription to a plaintiff or defendant who needs it. The person must request the assistance in advance of the hearing.

## Interpreters for Non-English Speakers

Small claims courts usually make reasonable efforts to maintain, and make available upon request, a list of interpreters who will interpret, at no charge or for a minor fee, for all non-English-speaking plaintiffs, defendants, and witnesses.

### Table 3-1: Small Claims Courts Limits

#### MAXIMUM AMOUNT SMALL CLAIMS COURT

| | |
|---|---|
| Arizona | $2,500 |
| California | $5,000* |
| Florida | $2,500 |
| Illinois | $2,500 |
| New Mexico | $5,000 |
| New York | $3,000 |
| Texas | $5,000 |

*No person may file more than two small claims actions in which each amount exceeds $2,500 anywhere in the state, unless it is brought by the city, county, school district, or public entity.

# 4

# Contracts

Historically the laws governing contracts and consumer rights gave little protection to the consumer. At one time the concept of caveat emptor ("let the buyer beware") dominated contract and consumer law. Under that system the buyer bore the responsibility for the quality, safety, and usability of any product he purchased. Changing social and economic times have led to major changes in the laws so that today the burden has shifted to the seller and manufacturer of goods and services.

## DEFINITION OF A CONTRACT

A contract is an agreement between two or more parties to do or not to do something. Some contracts must be in writing to be enforceable, while others can be oral or even understood as long as both parties understand the same thing. A contract can be very simple, such as an agreement to pay a neighbor one dollar for a bag of oranges, or very complex, such as the purchase of a house or business, which may require several separate but related contracts.

## ELEMENTS OF A CONTRACT

A valid contract is formed when two or more parties enter into an agreement that consists of an offer by one party, acceptance of the offer by the other party, and the exchange of something of value, which is called a *consideration*. A party to a contract may be a natural person such as Joe or Sue or a legal person, which is what a business entity such as a corporation is called.

The elements of a contract are important because if any of the essential elements is missing, the contract is not valid or enforceable. All parties to a contract must have the same understanding of what the agreement requires of each party, and they all must enter into the agreement willingly.

In a simple contract transaction Mary *offers* to pay Sue one dollar if Sue will give Mary a bag of oranges. If Sue agrees, she *accepts* Mary's offer, and they exchange the dollar for the bag of oranges. The *consideration* in this exchange is money and oranges, each of which has some value.

## CONSIDERATION

One of the essential elements of a contract is the consideration. This is something of value. It may be money, a tangible object, or just a promise to do or not to do something. To be valid, the consideration that each party contributes to a contract must be something new. Something of value that was part of an earlier agreement cannot be used as a consideration to create a new contract.

For instance, if Joe agrees to paint Jim's house for five hundred dollars, and that is the entire agreement between them, Joe's consideration in the agreement is his promise to paint the house, and Jim's consideration is his promise to pay five hundred dollars. If, however, Jim asks Joe to paint his house because Jim paid Joe four hundred dollars to landscape his yard the previous year, Jim is not providing any additional consideration on his part. Consequently there is no contract even though Joe may agree to paint Jim's house without further payment. Neither party is bound by a contract since Joe's promise is a gift, not a contractual obligation.

## THE ESSENTIAL ELEMENT OF GOOD FAITH

All contracts must be based on *good faith*. This abstract concept describes the state of mind of a person who is honest in his purpose, has no intent to defraud another, and is faithful to his obligation or duty. If one party can prove that the other party, in entering into the contract, was dishonest in his purpose, intended to defraud the first party, or did not intend to assume his obligation or duty under the contract, the injured party may ask the court to declare the contract void because the essential element of good faith was lacking when the contract was formed.

## ACCEPTANCE, COUNTEROFFER, REJECTION, AND REVOCATION

Agreements are often arrived at after considerable negotiation which may involve one or more counteroffers.

When Mary offers Sue one dollar for a bag of oranges, Mary has made an offer. If Sue responds by saying, "I'll sell you the bag of oranges, but you'll have to pay me a dollar and a quarter for them," Sue has made a counteroffer. Mary can then accept Sue's counteroffer, make a counteroffer to Sue, or reject Sue's counteroffer. While this is an elementary concept, it becomes important in determining *who can accept an offer* and *when an offer terminates* and can no longer be accepted.

## Who May Accept an Offer

An offer is specific and can be accepted only by the person to whom it is addressed.

If Joe offers to paint Jim's house for four hundred dollars, only Jim can accept Joe's offer. If Jim accepts Joe's offer, they have entered into a contract. If Jim says to Joe, "No, I don't want you to paint my house," Jim has rejected Joe's offer, and *the offer ceases to exist*.

What if Jim does not respond to Joe's offer? How long can Jim "think about it" before Joe is no longer obligated to live up to his offer? One way to terminate the offer is for Joe to revoke his offer by telling Jim the offer is withdrawn. Joe can also stipulate a time period within which Jim must accept the offer. If Jim fails to accept Joe's offer within the stipulated time period, the offer automatically expires.

If Joe does not revoke the offer or set a time limit, the offer terminates after a reasonable period of time. If Joe's offer to Jim is made in a face-to-face meeting or on the telephone, the offer terminates when the meeting or phone conversation ends unless Joe agrees to a time limit within which Jim may accept the offer.

In most states Joe's revocation must be communicated to Jim before it becomes effective. Some states, including California, Montana, North Dakota, and South Dakota, have laws making a revocation effective at the time it is dispatched. In our example, Joe could revoke his offer by mailing a letter to Jim telling him that he, Joe, is revoking the offer or, in some cases, by leaving a message on his answering machine or by faxing him a note.

## Sources of Contract Law

Contract law has developed over the years from decisions made by judges hearing contract controversies in court. That law is called the common law, and it is based historically on the common law of England. When the English settled in the United States, they brought with them the law of their homeland and used it as the basis for settling disputes. Over time the English common law has been integrated into much of the statutory law of the United States. Only one state—

Louisiana—does not follow the principles of English common law as it has been adapted by the American judicial system.

Each state has adopted the federal Uniform Commercial Code (UCC) in whole or with some modifications. The UCC was written by legal specialists and has been modified several times. It is not law in and of itself but was compiled by scholars as a hypothetical ideal set of rules governing contracts. Each state has adopted laws based on the UCC, often adding to or subtracting from the UCC as a whole. As a result, the basic principles of contract law are the same from state to state, but each state may have special rules governing some contract matters. The areas of contract law covered by the UCC include sales of goods and services, leases, banking transactions, investment securities, and transactions between manufacturers of goods and retailers who buy those goods to sell to the public.

## CONTRACTS THAT MUST BE IN WRITING

The **Statute of Frauds** was initially described in a law in England in 1677 and has been incorporated into our current UCC (Sec. 2-201). As its name implies, the Statute of Frauds was designed to prevent fraud and perjury in contract transactions. It requires that certain agreements be in writing in order for them to be enforceable by a court if one party to an agreement fails to live up to his promises. Those agreements that must be in writing include:

1. A contract to purchase goods for five hundred dollars or more
2. A contract to lease property for more than one year
3. An agreement to buy or sell real property
4. An agreement that cannot be fully performed within one year from the date it is made
5. An agreement that cannot be performed during the lifetime of one of the parties, such as a will
6. An agreement to pay someone with money that is secured by real estate
7. An agreement to pay a debt that someone else owes

## REQUIRED ELEMENTS OF A WRITTEN CONTRACT

To meet the requirements of the Statute of Frauds, a written contract does not have to be complex or contain any special words. It must, however, (1) state the names of the parties, (2) describe the goods being sold, and (3) state how much money is being paid. The writing also needs to be signed by the persons making the promises. A court may refuse to enforce an agreement that does not include these basic elements. However, the court will usually try to fill in the missing terms if it determines that the parties intended to form a binding contract.

The court will enforce an agreement that would otherwise require a writing if the agreement is for a specially made item such as a custom-made wedding dress or if the buyer has already paid for the goods or if the seller has already delivered the goods to the buyer. In each of these examples the court will usually find that there is sufficient evidence of an agreement between the parties on the basis of their behavior—that is, paying money to a seller or giving goods to a buyer.

## CONTRACTS WITH MINORS AND MENTALLY INCOMPETENT PERSONS

Some persons cannot legally enter into a contract. These include minors (in most states a minor is anyone under the age of eighteen years) and mentally incompetent persons.

If a minor contracts to buy a car and changes his mind, he can disaffirm the contract (but he will have to return the car to the seller). However, if the minor continues to make payments on the car and does not disaffirm the contract before or upon reaching adulthood, he will not be able to get out of the contract later. There are some exceptions when a minor will not be legally able to invalidate a contract. Thus, when a minor agrees to support his or her minor child, when he or she enters into an employment agreement not to divulge trade secrets or when he or she is a party to any contract that has been approved by the court (for example, when a child actor contracts to star in a movie), he or she cannot disaffirm that contract.

It is important that the seller in a transaction make a sincere effort to determine if the buyer is a minor. If the buyer lies about his age and gives the seller false documents indicating he is older than he is, the courts usually require that the minor buyer return the goods to the seller. The minor can be charged with fraud under criminal and civil statutes and, in some states, may lose his driver's license until he reaches the age of twenty-one.

Mentally incompetent persons cannot contract because it is presumed that they are unable to understand what they are agreeing to do and cannot, therefore, form the intent that is required in a valid contract. Included in the category of mentally incompetent persons are the insane, the mentally ill, the mentally retarded, senile persons, and, in some states, persons who are intoxicated to the extent that they cannot understand what they are agreeing to. Contracts made by mentally incompetent persons are not automatically void but are voidable by the guardians of the incompetent persons or by the intoxicated persons when they become sober. If someone's mental incompetence or intoxication is not apparent to the other party to the contract at the time the agreement is made, the contract may be considered valid by a court of law. However, if it can be shown that the other party to the agreement took advantage of the mentally incompetent party, even though his infirmity may have been less severe than would qualify as mentally incompetent, the contract may be voidable. The nonmentally incompetent party cannot void the contract and may be bound by the contract if the guardian of the mentally incompetent party ratifies the contract.

## THE IMPORTANCE OF READING AND UNDERSTANDING THE CONTRACT

Some contracts, such as a purchase agreement and loan documents for buying a car or house, are long and difficult to understand. If a buyer does not understand what he is agreeing to when he signs a contract, he may be bound by the terms of the contract if the court determines that his negligence in failing to read the contract caused the misunderstanding.

If, however, the buyer reads and signs a contract that contains contradictory promises made by the seller, the buyer may be able to have the contract voided on the bases of misrepresentation. For example, Marie signs an agreement to purchase a refrigerator, and the written agreement states that there is no warranty. However, the salesperson tells her he will repair—for free—anything that goes wrong within six months. If the refrigerator stops working and the seller refuses to repair it as he orally promised, Marie can ask the court to void the purchase agreement and to force the seller to take back the refrigerator and return the money she paid the seller.

## CONTRACTS THAT MAY BE CANCELED OR RESCINDED

The purpose of a written contract is to ensure that both parties understand and agree to the same thing. This is sometimes called a *meeting of the minds*. The types of agreements that are covered by the Statute of Frauds include matters that involve a substantial amount of money, that involve the sale of a unique item such as real estate with a third party, or that cannot be completed in less than one year. In each of these cases there is a high risk that one of the parties could be injured by a substantial loss of money, that three people will not understand precisely the same thing, or that the parties will remember the agreement differently because of the long passage of time.

By requiring that certain agreements be written, the law tries to ensure that misunderstandings and the harm that could result from them are minimized. Since a written agreement is intended to protect both parties, neither party can arbitrarily back out of an agreement at will. However, there are times when one party can rescind a contract. These include:

**1. When the property that is the subject of the agreement is destroyed.** If Jim agrees to pay Joe four hundred dollars to paint his house and the house is destroyed by fire before Joe starts painting it, Jim will not be obligated to pay Joe the four hundred dollars he agreed to. However, if Joe has already purchased the paint for Jim's house and cannot return it because it is a special color, Jim may have to purchase the paint from Joe at Joe's cost. If Joe painted half of Jim's house before the fire, the court usually requires Jim to pay Joe half the amount of the contract. While this might seem unfair, the law's view of this situation is that because Jim was in a position to insure the house, he should bear the risk to the extent that Joe should be paid for the work that he actually performed. However, Jim should not be required to pay Joe for work that he did not perform since the fire made his performance impossible.

**2. When it is legally impossible to perform the acts required by the agreement.** Jim stipulates in his contract with Joe that Joe is to use Brand X paint only. Joe learns that the Brand X factory workers are on strike, and there is no Brand X paint available. Joe may rescind the contract on the basis of the impossibility of performance unless Jim is willing to modify the agreement to state that Joe can use Brand Y paint instead.

**3. When it is a door-to-door sales contract.** A contract for goods or services between a door-to-door salesperson and a consumer can be canceled anytime within three days of the time it is signed by the buyer. The buyer must notify the seller of the cancellation, and the seller must promptly return any deposit or other money that the buyer paid to the seller at the time the agreement was signed.

**4. When the contract requires commitment of an illegal act.** An agreement to commit an illegal act, such as purchasing illegal drugs, is unenforceable.

**5. When the agreement is made under duress.** If Joe coerces Jim into agreeing to let Joe paint Jim's house by threatening to harm Jim physically or to damage his property, the court would probably hold that Joe cannot enforce the contract against Jim because Joe used threats of violence to force Jim to accept the contract. Acts of duress violate the essential element of good faith and contradict the requirement that there be a meeting of the minds.

**6. When the law specifically allows a cancellation window of time.** Besides the example given above of the door-to-door salesperson, there are numerous other contracts that may be canceled if the cancellation is given within a specified period of time after the agreement has been signed. Usually such a cancellation must be in writing. Some examples of contracts that often may be canceled in most states are these: (1) a contract for the services of an immigration consultant, within seventy-two hours of execution; (2) a contract for services of a nonmedical weight-loss clinic; (3) a contract with a dance studio for dance lessons; and (4) a contract with a health or exercise club.

## IT IS IMPORTANT TO READ AND UNDERSTAND EVERY CLAUSE IN A CONTRACT BEFORE SIGNING IT

Contract agreements are often long, boring, and difficult to understand. They contain words and phrases that are unfamiliar to the general public and are often written by attorneys who use technical words understood only by other attorneys. The law, however, is harsh when a party fails to read and understand a contract before signing it. If an agreement contains words or terms that are unclear, it is very important to ask someone who does understand the contract to explain it fully before it is signed. When a party signs a document, the court presumes that he understood what he was signing and agreed to live up to the promises stated in the document. The law allows a party to an agreement to consult with an attorney before signing any contract.

A buyer who does not speak or read English and negotiates for goods or services in Spanish may, in some states, require that the dealer provide him with a Spanish translation of any documents he signs (see multistate compendium on Spanish translation on page 72).

Most businesses that use written agreements on a regular basis have prepared standard forms. Usually a standard form is drafted by an attorney to protect the interests of the business, and it contains a lot of language that is wordy, tedious, and confusing to the average consumer. It is very important, however, that a person take time to read any agreement and understand what he is agreeing to before he signs it. For instance, if Jose borrows money to buy a car, he may be surprised to find that the agreement he signed with the bank allows the bank to purchase an insurance policy and charge him for the premiums if he does not maintain the amount and type of insurance that the contract requires.

## ACCEPTING A CHECK ENDORSED AS PAYMENT IN FULL

Sometimes a debtor will issue a check to the creditor for less than the amount stipulated in the contract and may write "Payment in Full" on the back of the check above the space where the check is endorsed. If the debtor has, in good faith, disputed the amount he owes and issues the check to the creditor for the amount he thinks he actually owes, some courts will hold that the words *Payment in Full* will discharge the full amount of the debt. Other courts have held that the creditor may protect himself by writing "Under Protest" or "Not Payment in Full" on the check before cashing it, thereby reserving the right to collect the balance owed according to the terms of the contract.

The UCC (sec. 1-207) favors the position that the creditor may retain his rights to full payment under the contract by writing "Under Protest" or "Not Payment in Full" on the check before cashing it. However, some courts believe that the use of such language on checks is a reasonable means of resolving disputes and will not enforce language inserted by the creditor if the debtor has issued the check as payment in full. Any writing or endorsement on a check that attempts to discharge a debt or preserve the creditor's rights must be in large, noticeable letters. Words written in fine print will not be enforced.

When a party receives a check as settlement for an insurance claim, the insurance company will often have words imprinted on the back of the check above the endorsement line. Frequently the words state that the endorser accepts the check as payment in full and waives any further action against the insurance company. Language that purports to create a waiver of basic legal rights is known as *exculpatory language,* and courts in most states will not enforce exculpatory clauses in many situations.

Courts tend to favor the consumer over the merchant when enforcing endorsement addenda. A basic element of a contract is that the item or service that is the subject of the agreement be bargained for. When one party unilaterally writes "Under Protest" or "Payment in Full" on a check, the courts have often invalidated any binding requirement on the part of the consumer since the amended agreement lacks the bargained-for element. This position is consistent with the court's purpose of protecting the relatively powerless consumer against the merchant, who usually has more resources to protect himself than the consumer does.

One should be aware that the law in these cases is not absolute nor consistent, and both creditors and debtors should act with caution when confronted with such a situation.

## DISCHARGE OF CONTRACTUAL DEBTS

A contractual obligation may be discharged by fulfilling the terms of the contract, by accord and satisfaction settlement agreement, by bankruptcy, or by the running of the statute of limitations.

## RELEASE

A release is usually part of a negotiated settlement and is often related to personal injury claims. In executing a release, one party agrees to release another party from all claims arising out of a certain incident. Courts often allow an injured party to void a release if he learns that his injuries are much more serious than he thought they were when he signed the release.

## SUBSTANTIAL PERFORMANCE

If Bob hires Andy to paint his barn and Andy quits after he has painted two coats on the barn but has only put one coat of paint on the trim, the question might arise whether Andy substantially performed his obligations under the contract. If language in the contract specifically states that Andy must paint two coats on all surfaces of the barn, including the trim, Bob may tell the court that Andy did not comply with the express conditions of the agreement, and as a result Bob should not have to pay Andy for the work he did do. If the agreement did not specifically state the number of coats of paint, the court would probably find that Andy had substantially performed his obligations.

This concept is important because a finding of substantial performance is the legal basis for requiring Bob to pay Andy, even though Bob may not think that Andy did as good or thorough a job as Bob had expected when they made their agreement. The principle behind the doctrine of substantial performance is one of fairness. In our example, it would be unfair for Bob to withhold payment from Andy, who essentially did what he had agreed to do. In this case the court would probably require Bob to pay Andy the amount agreed to in the contract, minus the amount Bob would have to spend to hire another painter to paint another coat on the trim.

## CONTRACT BREACH

When either party to a contract fails to perform his or her obligations, as stated in the agreement, he is said to have breached, or broken, the agreement. A breach can be total or partial.

Joe agrees to paint Jim's car for one thousand dollars, beginning on May 1 and completing the job by May 15. If he never shows up to begin the job, he has committed a total breach of the contract. Joe's total breach means that Jim is excused from having to fulfill his obligations under the agreement.

If Joe begins painting Jim's car on May 1 but does not finish the job until May 25, he has partially breached the agreement, but Jim is still required to fulfill his obligation to pay Joe as stated in the contract. However, Jim can sue Joe for damages for failing to complete the paint job within the time stipulated in the agreement. In that case the court might award Jim damages equal to the cost Jim incurred in renting a car to get to work for the ten additional days that Joe took to complete the car.

# LIQUIDATED DAMAGES

A contract may contain a clause which states that the parties agree in advance to the payment of a specified amount if one party breaches the agreement. Liquidated damages clauses are frequently found in real estate purchase agreements. The purpose of liquidated damages clauses is to ensure performance by the buyer and to limit the amount the seller may collect if the buyer breaches the agreement. The amount of liquidated damages stipulated in the contract must be reasonable and must fairly reflect the actual loss that the seller will suffer if the buyer breaches the agreement.

Liquidated damages are used when it is difficult to establish the actual dollar amount of damage caused by the breach and when there are no other adequate remedies for the seller if the buyer defaults. A clause that requires unreasonably high liquidated damages is void since the court views excessive damages as a penalty.

# WARRANTY

A warranty is a promise by a seller of goods that those goods will meet certain standards. The primary types of warranty that we need to be concerned with are express warranty, warranty of merchantability, and warranty of fitness for a particular purpose. (See the chapter on landlord and tenant law for a discussion of the implied warranty of habitability, page 121.)

## EXPRESS WARRANTY

Any explicit statement made by the seller regarding particular goods is an express warranty. If the seller states unequivocally that the white paint he sells will completely cover a black wall in one coat, he is making an express warranty. If the buyer purchases the paint in the amount the seller or manufacturer recommends, based on the square footage the buyer needs to cover, and the paint does not cover the black wall, the seller has breached his express warranty.

## IMPLIED WARRANTY OF MERCHANTABILITY

The UCC considers the implied warranty of merchantability to be one of the most important warranties (UCC sec. 2-314). The UCC states, "A warranty that goods shall be merchantable is implied in a contract for their sale if the seller is a merchant with respect to goods of that kind." Food or drink that is sold to be consumed on the premises, such as in a restaurant, or to be consumed in another place, such as food sold by a grocery market, is also covered by the implied warranty of merchantability. Goods sold by a merchant who regularly deals in that type of goods must be fit for the ordinary purposes for which such goods are used. They must be of a quality that is acceptable within the trade or industry of which they are a part and must conform, at a minimum, to the acceptable standards of that industry. Restaurant food found to contain hair or insect parts is an example of goods that breach the implied warranty of merchantability.

Any promises made on the container or packaging of goods must also be satisfied in order for the goods to conform to the requirements of the UCC. If the laundry soap one purchases states on the package that the soap will remove dried grape juice stains, the manufacturer may be found to have breached the implied warranty of merchantability if the product fails to do as promised.

## WARRANTY OF FITNESS FOR A PARTICULAR PURPOSE

When a seller, at the time he sells the product, knows the intentions of the buyer and also knows the buyer is relying on the seller's judgment and experience to select a suitable product, the seller may be held liable if the product fails to perform as promised.

Jane explains to the salesperson in a local store that she needs a machine capable of running continuously fifteen hours a day to make crushed ice. She explains that she has a business that sells flavored ice at a swap meet on weekends. The seller tells Jane that a household blender would be adequate for her needs. Being new to the business, Jane buys the blender. The first day of business the blender works for three hours and then burns out from overuse. When she tries to return the blender to the seller, he tells her that she should have read the instructions which say the machine is just for home use. The seller will be liable for his promise to Jane because he knew what she intended to use the machine for and that she was relying on his recommendation and expertise.

In this case he will be liable for the cost of the blender and for the profits that Jane lost by not having the use of the blender for the remaining swap meet. He may also be liable for other costs that Jane incurred when she relied on the salesperson's recommendation, such as the costs of the booth at the swap meet and hiring someone to help her run the business.

## PUFFING IS NOT A WARRANTY

Puffing is not the same as a warranty or guarantee and does not create liability on the part of the seller as long as it is understood by the buyer as being clearly limited to the seller's opinion of the product. If the paint salesman states that the paint he sells is "the best value around," he is puffing. He is stating a subjective opinion that cannot be readily proved or disproved. One buyer may believe that the "best value" is the least expensive paint, while another buyer may think that the "best value" is the most expensive paint because it dries the fastest. However, when puffing becomes specific and objectively measurable, it is no longer puffing but an expressed warranty.

## DISCLAIMER OF WARRANTY

Sellers often attempt to reduce their liability by issuing verbal or written disclaimers regarding the quality or usefulness of their products. The UCC limits the extent to which a seller or manufacturer may limit such liability. *To be valid, any disclaimer must be conspicuous, be in writing, and acknowledged by the buyer, and it must not violate the industry standards of good faith and fair dealing.* Used goods may sometimes be sold with a disclaimer of warranty which states that the goods are sold in "as is" condition. However, the courts have often refused to limit liability of the seller of used goods when he knew or should have known that the goods were defective or unsafe. The most commonly encountered case in which a seller may be held liable even though the goods are sold "as is" occurs in the sale of used vehicles and real estate.

## REMEDIES FOR BREACH OF CONTRACT

Whenever one party breaches a contract, the other party often suffers some sort of injury or loss as a result of the breach. That loss may be economic and therefore measurable in terms of money, or it may be noneconomic in nature. In contract matters, damages are usually awarded to the injured party to compensate her for the losses she suffered because of the breach. The usual remedy for breach of contract is money damages.

In some situations money damages are not adequate to compensate the injured party. The court may order *equitable relief* to compensate the injured party. The two most common forms of equitable relief are specific performance and injunctions.

*Specific performance* is often applied to cases in which one party to a contract for the sale and purchase of a piece of real estate breaches the contract. Since each parcel of real estate is unique and cannot be exactly replaced by another parcel, the courts will often force the breaching seller to complete the sale and transfer the property to the other party because there is no other way to prevent serious injury to the buyer.

*Injunctions* are used to prevent someone from doing something. A classic example is that of a former employee who breaches an employment contract that states he agrees not to go to work for a competitor for six months after he leaves his former job. If the employee breaches the employment agreement by immediately accepting employment with a competitor, the court may issue an injunction prohibiting him from working for that competitor until the six-month period stipulated in the contract has elapsed.

Because violation of a court order for specific performance or an injunction subjects the violator to a contempt of court action, the court requires that any contract upon which specific performance or an injunction is sought contain clear and definite language demonstrating that the party has breached a contract.

In the majority of cases involving breach of contract, monetary damages will adequately compensate the party who was injured. Monetary damages are classified as (1) general damages, (2) special or consequential damages, and (3) punitive damages. General and consequential damages are commonly awarded in breach of contract matters. Only rarely are punitive damages awarded in contract matters, although they are common in tort cases involving injury to one party caused by the gross negligence or intentional misconduct of the other party.

General damages include expectation damages and reliance damages, although usually only one or the other will be awarded in a given case. Expectation damages are the most common in contract disputes. The purpose of expectation damages is to put the injured party in the position he would have been in if the contract had been performed. In awarding expectation damages, the court will require that the defendant pay the plaintiff for any expenses she has incurred in performing her part of the contract plus the profit she would have made if the defendant had not breached the agreement. The example cited earlier about the ice crusher that burned out after three hours of use during a weekend swap meet illustrates expectation damages. In that case the court awarded the swap meet vendor monetary damages equal to the cost of the blender plus the cost of the booth at the swap meet, the cost of hiring an employee, and the profit she would have made if the blender had continued to operate properly.

There may be times in contract disputes when reliance damages must be used because expectation damages are not suitable. The most common case occurs when one party breaches an agreement, yet the injured party is unable to calculate what his lost profits might have been. In such a case the court will award reliance damages so that the injured party is compensated for any expenses he had incurred in anticipation of full performance by the breaching party.

Say Rosa signs a contract with Jorge in which she promises to let Jorge be the exclusive dealer in his state to sell the boots made in a factory Rosa owns. After they sign their contract, Jorge rents a warehouse and three retail stores and buys a truck to transport boots from the warehouse to the stores. He also buys business licenses and runs ads announcing the opening of the stores. On the day that Jorge is to receive his initial shipment of boots, Rosa calls and tells him that she has decided to let her brother have the exclusive dealership instead of Jorge.

Jorge has no way of calculating what his lost profits might have been because he has never been in the boot business and he has never had a statewide dealership. He does know, however, how much he has spent getting ready to open his business on the basis of the contractual promises made by Rosa. When he sues Rosa for breach of contract, the court awards him reliance damages equal to the money he has paid out for rent for the stores and warehouse, for purchase of the truck, and for advertising. While Jorge will be required to mitigate his damages by attempting to find someone to rent the stores and warehouse as well as to buy his truck, the court could award damages equal to the entire value of the leases on all four properties if Jorge can prove that he has made a reasonable effort to find new tenants but has been unable to do so because the properties are unique or the real estate market is depressed.

## DUTY TO MITIGATE DAMAGES

In a breach of contract action the injured party is under a duty to take steps to limit the damage done to him by the circumstances of the breach. When a tenant breaches a lease contract by vacating the unit before the expiration of the lease, the law states that the tenant may be held liable for all payments due under the term of the lease. However, the landlord has a duty to make reasonable efforts to find a new tenant for the empty unit. When the unit is leased or rented to a new tenant, the liability of the tenant who breached the lease will be limited to the actual time he occupied the unit, the actual time the unit was vacant before being rerented, and the costs the landlord incurred in renting the unit to a new tenant. If the landlord fails to make reasonable efforts to locate a new tenant, the tenant who breached the lease will be able to offer as a defense to the court the fact that the landlord breached his duty to mitigate damages. If the court finds that the former tenant has a well-founded claim, it will probably limit his liability to the time the unit would have been vacant if the landlord had actively sought a new tenant after the first tenant had breached the contract. The court might look at how long it has taken other landlords with similar properties to find new tenants and use that information as the basis for determining the monetary damages owed by the first tenant for breach of the lease. If there were no duty to mitigate damages on the part of the landlord, the tenant would be liable for the lease payments up until the time the lease would have expired under the terms of the contract.

## RESTITUTION

Restitution may be awarded to the plaintiff in a breach of contract action for the purpose of preventing unjust enrichment to the defendant. Restitution is calculated on the value of the benefit to the defendant of the goods and services provided by the plaintiff. Because restitution may be based on subjective value, the award may bear little relation to the contract price. Restitution is available as a remedy only when the plaintiff has not fully performed according to the terms of the contract.

For example, Hector contracts with Sam to paint Sam's old Mustang a deep red and to replace the black interior with white velour. Sam agrees to pay Hector $750 for the work and materials. After Hector has finished painting the car but before he starts on the interior, Sam stops by the shop with a friend of his. Sam's friend spots the Mustang and falls in love with the spectacular bodywork and red paint that Hector has applied. He offers Sam $8,000 for it just as it is but tells Sam he won't buy it if the interior is changed. Sam knows the car, even with the new paint job, is worth only $2,750 to anyone else, so he demands that Hector stop working on the car, takes his friend's money, and refuses to pay Hector anything because Sam says Hector did not complete the work he agreed to in the contract. Hector obviously is entitled to restitution.

## NOMINAL DAMAGES

In some breach of contract matters there is no provable harm that has been done, but the defendant is found guilty of breach of contract. In that case the court may award nominal damages, which are a small sum not related to any degree of harm suffered.

## TORT REMEDIES FOR BREACH OF CONTRACT

In a contract dispute the parties may bring an action for breach of contract and ask the court to award compensatory damages (expectation or reliance damages) or noncompensatory damages (nominal or punitive damages). However, there may be one or several claims under tort and criminal law that can be brought against the defendant related to the breach of contract. If threats of force were involved in the breach, there may be a basis for charging the defendant with tortuous or criminal assault. Fraud, misrepresentation, duress, battery, false imprisonment, and tortious breach of the covenant of good faith and fair dealing are just some of the common charges that may be associated with a breach of contract action. Criminal penalties such as fines and imprisonment could be levied for commission of criminal acts, and additional fines and punitive damages could be awarded the plaintiff if the defendant is found to have committed torts associated with the breach of contract matter.

Anyone who has been involved in a serious breach of contract matter should seek the advice of an attorney before proceeding. There may be numerous issues related to the breach of contract that an attorney can advise about.

## ASSIGNMENT OF RIGHTS AND DELEGATION OF DUTIES

An assignment occurs when one party to a contract transfers his rights under the contract to a third person. Assignments are "gratuitous" and do not, therefore, require any consideration.

A delegation occurs when one party to a contract delegates or transfers his duties or obligations under the contract to a third party.

In business relations, an assignment and a delegation are often coupled together in the same agreement or transaction. The law generally favors allowing assignments and delegations, and antiassignment clauses in some contracts have been declared void by the courts. However, some types of contract cannot be assigned because they would put the other party to the contract at a greater risk of potential injury.

Let's say Elizabeth contracts with the Royal Painting Contractors to paint her castle. Having spent a lot of time and energy searching for painters who are skilled in restoration of castle walls, she hires the Royal Painting Contractors after learning that it has a superior reputation and comes highly recommended by other castle owners who have used the firm. On the day the painters are to begin work, a crew that Elizabeth has never seen or talked to appear at her castle door. Their truck, parked near the moat, has the name Painters Etc. written on the side. When Elizabeth questions the woman who introduces herself as the crew leader, Elizabeth is told that the Royal Painting Contractors has delegated its duty to paint the castle and assigned its right to payment to Painters Etc. The crew leader, responding to Elizabeth's questions, says that they have never painted a castle before but that "painting is painting."

The contract between Elizabeth and the Royal Painting Contractors cannot be assigned without her permission. Because the nature of the services she has contracted for is specialized and she would be put at greater risk than she had agreed to, Royal Painting Contractors may not delegate its duties to Painters Etc.

Other contracts that may not be assigned are personal service contracts. A contract to have a particular hairstylist cut one's hair or an agreement to have a particular artist paint a picture of one's children is a personal service contract and cannot be delegated to someone else without the agreement of the second party.

# 5

# Consumer Law

Consumer law is designed to protect the public from dishonest salespersons and defective merchandise. Over the past twenty-five years tougher consumer laws have made it more difficult for manufacturers and merchants to sell or trade merchandise that is of lesser quality than claimed by advertisement or demonstration.

## FEDERAL AND STATE LAWS REGULATE CONSUMER TRANSACTIONS

There are both federal and state laws that regulate the quality of retail merchandise and the conditions under which merchandise can be sold, and both federal and state governments have agencies to which the consumer can turn for assistance.

Under federal law a consumer product is any tangible personal property that is distributed in commerce and is normally used for personal, family, or household purposes (15 USC 2301). The federal rules governing consumer protection are contained in Title 15, Section 2302 of the United States Code.

In Texas the Consumer Protection Agency is listed under the attorney general's office, which is found in the government section of the phone book. Any person who has been unable to resolve his or her complaint with a merchant directly should contact the local consumer complaint office. The majority of states have similar agencies and procedures.

## INVESTIGATING THE CONSUMER COMPLAINT

Upon receipt of any complaint, the Department of Consumer Affairs in the various states may notify the person against whom the complaint is made and may request appropriate relief for the consumer. Any valid complaint will be transmitted to the local, state, or federal agency whose authority provides the most effective means to secure relief. When it is appropriate, the consumer will be advised of the action taken on the complaint and of any other remedies that are available to secure relief.

## IMPLIED AND EXPRESS WARRANTIES

Most consumer products sold in the United States carry a consumer warranty, either implied or expressed. An *implied warranty* means the consumer goods meet each of the following:

1. They pass without objection in the trade under the contract description.
2. They are fit for the ordinary purposes for which such goods are used.
3. They are adequately contained, packaged, and labeled.
4. They conform to the promises or affirmations of fact made on the container or label.

The retail seller is implying that the goods will meet the particular needs of the buyer. Under state laws the implied warranty must have a specified duration following the sale of goods to the consumer.

An *express warranty* is a written statement that says the manufacturer, distributor, or retailer will undertake to preserve or maintain the utility of performance of the product or to provide compensation if the product fails to perform.

Both implied and express warranties are enforceable by law.

## REMEDIES FOR DEFECTIVE GOODS

Consumer law is there for the consumer's protection. If a consumer asks a retailer to assist him with defective merchandise and the retailer fails to do so, or if the consumer is asked to sign a contract that he does not understand, then the consumer has the right to seek redress. Any person who thinks he may have a complaint against a seller of defective goods should contact the Department of Consumer Affairs in his state or consult with an attorney.

If a buyer purchases goods covered by an express or implied warranty and then discovers that those goods are defective, usually he is entitled either to recover the purchase price (less any wear) or to have the goods replaced or repaired. The California Civil Code contains a detailed explanation of buyers' rights and illustrates the general principles and factors involved in warranty cases in almost all states.

California law is very specific. If the manufacturer of consumer goods does not honor the express warranty and fails to provide service and repair facilities, the consumer may return the product to the retailer, who must then do one of the following:

1. Service or repair the goods to conform to the warranty
2. Direct the consumer to a reasonably close independent repair or service facility
3. Replace the goods with goods that are identical or reasonably equivalent to the warranted goods
4. Refund to the consumer the original purchase price minus the amount attributable to use by the consumer before he discovered the defect

If it is not possible to take the defective product to the retailer, the consumer may notify the retailer, who then must service or repair the goods at the buyer's residence, pick up the goods, or arrange for someone else to pick up the goods and transport them to the retailer's place of business. The cost of such transportation is the responsibility of the retailer.

## GOODS NOT COVERED BY WARRANTY

Not all goods carry warranties. Some items such as those sold at auction are sold "as is" or "with all faults." This means the seller has disclaimed all implied warranties in the product, and the buyer has no recourse against the seller if the product or item is defective or fails to perform as expected. This is legal in some cases, and the consumer should be sure to ask about any warranties before making a purchase.

## INSTALLMENT CREDIT PURCHASES AND COSIGNERS

There are certain items that consumers choose to buy on a time payment plan. This is called consumer credit buying and usually requires the signing of a promise-to-pay contract. For various reasons some buyers do not have acceptable credit ratings (financial histories) and need cosigners to guarantee the loans.

Any prospective cosigner should be aware that most states have laws requiring a creditor to give any borrower a notice, written in both English and Spanish or other appropriate language, explaining his obligations as a cosigner. A cosigner is usually obliged to take over the payments if the buyer fails to meet the demands of the contract as agreed. A prospective cosigner should be given this notice before or at the time he signs. It is very important that the cosigner read the document carefully and make sure he understands his obligations. All parties have the right to consult with an attorney before signing any document. Everyone should always ask to be given a copy of anything he signs.

## CREDIT DISABILITY COVERAGE

Anyone who purchases an item, such as a car or household appliance, on a time payment plan may find that the contract includes a provision for credit disability coverage. This means that if the purchaser becomes so ill or so severely injured that he is certified disabled by a doctor, the finance company (the creditor) will continue to make the payments on the merchandise until he is no longer disabled. A purchaser who wants credit disability coverage will usually have to pay a small additional fee for this protection.

## INTEREST RATES

Interest rates are the amount of interest paid, usually expressed as a percentage of the amount of the underlying debt. States such as California and New York have maximum legal rates that can be charged on consumer loans. In Arizona, Illinois, Florida, New Mexico, and Texas, parties may agree to any interest rate amount. Thus, in New York the maximum legal interest rate that can be charged on a consumer transaction is 6 percent, and parties may not agree to anything higher than that. If the amount exceeds the legal rate, it is considered unconscionable and is punishable under the state's usury law. Most states have usury laws that punish the lender. In New York the borrower may recover any amount in excess of the legal rate. If the lender is a bank or a savings and loan, then the interest is forfeited, and the borrower may recover twice the interest paid.

## LEMON LAWS

"Lemon" laws, or new car warranty laws, are laws that protect consumers of new cars. A car is a lemon when it has so many defects it cannot be fixed. However, before a car can be construed as a lemon, the manufacturer must be given a chance to cure the defect within a specified period. The period is usually the time of the express warranty, one year or twelve thousand miles (mileage may vary with states), whichever comes first. If the car cannot be fixed, meaning that the defect substantially impairs the use and value of the car, the consumer is entitled to compensation of either a new car or a cash refund. Only Florida and New York expressly give the consumer the option to choose the remedy.

## Table 5-1: Spanish-Language Translation Required

### ARIZONA

Yes. In consumer loan transactions, disclosures prescribed under the consumer credit protection laws shall be provided in English and Spanish at the borrower's request. All promissory notes shall disclose that the borrower may request the Spanish language.

### CALIFORNIA

Yes. Any person in trade or business who negotiates primarily in Spanish, orally or in writing, in the course of entering into a contract or agreement, loan, extension of credit, or lease, shall submit Spanish-language translations and disclosures.

### FLORIDA

No statutory provision.

### ILLINOIS

No statutory provision.

### NEW MEXICO

No statutory provision.

### NEW YORK

No statutory provision.

### TEXAS

Yes. If the negotiations that preceded the execution of the executory contract are conducted primarily in Spanish, the seller shall provide a copy in Spanish of all written documents relating to the transaction.

## CIVIL RIGHTS

Civil rights laws are becoming increasingly necessary and controversial. Civil rights laws guarantee nondiscriminatory treatment and equality under the law. However, there are still groups of individuals whose rights are being infringed upon by the government and private individuals.

Civil rights are personal rights that are protected by the federal Constitution and the Bill of Rights. They include the right to own property, the right to vote, freedom of speech and association, and freedom from discrimination based on sex, age, religion, race, and national origin (sometimes called alienage).

There is a difference between national origin and race. When someone is being discriminated against because of his place of origin, it is discrimination based on national origin. An example of national origin would be Hispanics. *Hispanics* are defined as all persons designating themselves to be of Mexican, Puerto Rican, Cuban, Latin American, or Spanish descent (*Ulloa v. Philadelphia* [1982] 95 F.R.D. 109).

There are federal and state civil rights laws. These laws were enacted to protect people from any interference when they exercise their rights, such as the right to be free from discrimination based on national origin. If a landlord discriminates against anyone for being Hispanic, his civil rights have been violated, and he can sue under the civil rights laws. Any interference with civil rights laws may be deemed criminal or actionable in civil court.

Federal civil rights derive from the federal Constitution and various federal statutes. Since the Civil War many statutes have been enacted in the civil rights area. The most comprehensive is the Civil Rights Act of 1964, which covers discrimination in public places and facilities, in public schools, in federally assisted programs, and by employers (42 U.S.C.S. §1981). Federal laws are enforceable by the U.S. Justice Department and punishable by fines and injunctions (an injunction stops or prevents the discrimination).

As long as a cause of action is based on a federal statute, a private individual may bring a lawsuit under federal civil rights laws, and he does not have to exhaust any state remedies before making such a claim. (42 U.S.C.S. §1983). For example, if an employer discriminates against a person because he is Hispanic, that person may bring an action against the employer under 42 U.S.C. 2000(e).

State civil rights laws are usually defined in state constitutions and state statutes. State laws may give administrative agencies the power to hear civil rights cases. In Arizona it is the Department of Fair Employment and Housing; in Florida, Illinois, New Mexico, New York, and Texas it is the Department of Human Rights. These agencies are specifically designed to prevent violations and to enforce civil rights laws.

These administrative agencies also provide procedures and remedies in civil rights actions. These procedures and remedies may differ from those brought in a private cause of action. For example, the administrative agency may limit the amount of money one may recover.

State laws differ regarding whether one has to file a complaint with the administrative agency first or one can file a private cause of action initially. In Florida a person has the option of filing one or the other, whereas in Texas there is no administrative action, so only a private cause of action is available. If confronted with a civil rights violation, one should examine all options, meaning the person should look into both the administrative agency and the private cause of action to determine which is the best for his individual case.

If someone believes his civil rights have been violated, he should consult an attorney who specializes in civil rights cases. This should be done immediately in order to comply with any time limits imposed by law. If the violator is a government employee—for example, in police abuse and brutality cases—the time allowed to file a claim may be very short. If a claim is not filed within the time limit, he will lose his right to compensation and other remedies.

# 6

# Government
# Benefit Programs

The federal, state, and local governments sponsor a wide variety of programs that provide assistance for education, health and welfare, business, housing, and employment matters. There are numerous programs available, and eligibility criteria vary with each program.

Anyone who has a problem with a federal agency or federal benefits can contact one of his U.S. senators or his representative for assistance. State senators and representatives provide similar assistance for state-related matters. Help from elected officials is provided free of charge by pleasant, knowledgeable, and very efficient staff members.

Local libraries are tremendous resources for anyone seeking help with a particular problem, and the research librarians at most local libraries can be a valuable help.

## SMALL BUSINESS ADMINISTRATION

The Small Business Administration (SBA) provides counseling and financial assistance to independent small-business owners. Low interest loans for business start-ups are available through local banks. The SBA has offices in all major cities.

## MINORITY BUSINESS DEVELOPMENT AGENCY

The Minority Business Development Agency is sponsored by the U.S. Commerce Department and helps individuals and organizations with finances, marketing, development, and expansion. This program is especially designed to assist the minority business owner.

## SOCIAL SECURITY

The Social Security system was created by the Social Security Act of 1935. It provides retirement benefits, death benefits to the surviving dependents of insured workers who have died, payments to qualified people who are disabled, medical insurance benefits, and a program for assisting the aged, the disabled, and the blind who are not able to support themselves.

The Social Security system is funded by employers and employees who contribute amounts equal to approximately 7.5 percent of the employee's salary. People who are self-employed must pay the entire Social Security assessment.

### RETIREMENT BENEFITS

Social Security retirement benefits are not usually subject to income taxes. Under a complicated and constantly changing formula, up to one-half of Social Security retirement benefits can be taxed if the adjusted gross income plus one-half of the retirement benefits plus other earnings (interest) exceeds twenty-five thousand dollars for an individual, or thirty-two thousand dollars for a married couple who file a joint return. Retirement benefits were not intended to be enough to enable people to rely on as their only income. They were designed to supplement savings and private pension plans.

To qualify for retirement benefits, a worker must have earned enough work credits and be old enough. Work credits are applied for each quarter in which the minimum amount is earned from covered employment. Currently a worker must have at least forty quarters (ten years) of credit to retire. The amount of retirement benefits depends on how much the worker paid into the Social Security system (through deductions from salary) throughout his working years and the age at which he retires.

The standard retirement age is presently sixty-five but will increase to sixty-seven in 2000. A worker can retire at age sixty-two, but his benefits are permanently reduced by 20 percent. Retirement benefits are increased beyond 100 percent if retirement is delayed beyond sixty-five with the maximum benefits at age seventy. Benefits can be reduced if the worker who has retired at sixty-five earns more than the maximum limit in any year. Unmarried minor children, spouses over age sixty-two or spouses caring for a child under sixteen or a disabled child may also be eligible for benefits when the primary worker retires.

## SOCIAL SECURITY DISABILITY BENEFITS

Workers who become disabled and cannot earn a living may be able to qualify for Social Security disability benefits. Like retirement benefits, disability benefits require the worker to have earned a minimum number of credits. A worker who is disabled before age twenty-four must have at least six quarters of credit during the three years prior to the disability. A complicated sliding scale is used for those who become disabled between twenty-four and forty-two. Workers over forty-two must have twenty quarters of credit during the previous fifteen years and meet the required total quarters requirement, which increases by two quarters every two years with a maximum of forty quarters (ten years) required at age sixty-two. Qualifying disabilities include physical or mental disabilities that are certified by a doctor.

The disability can result from any cause but must be total and long-term. This means that the worker cannot perform gainful activity and that the condition will last at least twelve months or will result in death.

The Social Security Administration has a list of qualifying disabilities. If the disabling condition is not on the list, the worker must prove that his condition makes it impossible to earn a living. The number of disability benefits is based on a complicated formula and can be explained in detail at no cost by a representative of the Social Security office.

## DEATH BENEFITS FOR DEPENDENTS

The surviving spouse of a qualified worker may be able to receive death benefits. To qualify, the spouse must be raising minor or disabled children, be at least sixty-two years old, or be at least fifty years old and disabled. Certain former spouses (divorced) may qualify for survivors' benefits if the marriages lasted at least ten years and the applicants are at least sixty-two years old.

Dependent children of a qualified deceased worker may be entitled to survivors' benefits if they are unmarried and under eighteen years old or if they became disabled before they were twenty-two years old. More than one dependent can receive survivors' benefits as long as they qualify. Dependent parents of qualified deceased workers may also be entitled to receive death benefits. In every case, the surviving claimant must have been dependent on the deceased worker at the time of death.

The Social Security regulations state that before any dependents can receive survivors' benefits, the deceased worker must have been eligible for or receiving retirement or disability benefits. The dollar amount of the monthly death benefits is based on complicated and constantly changing formulas. Accurate and timely information can be obtained at no charge from the Social Security Administration. The amount is based on the earnings of the deceased worker and the age and circumstances of the survivor. Survivors' benefits are not usually reduced on the basis of other income from private pensions, but they may be reduced by certain pensions for government service. Survivors' benefit payments may also be reduced if the income from employment exceeds certain limits.

## SUPPLEMENTAL SECURITY INCOME

Supplemental Security Income (SSI) has often been referred to as a form of welfare. It is paid from general funds and not from Social Security taxes. Eligibility is based on financial need (low income), and the recipient must be at least sixty-five years old or blind, disabled, or retarded. Many people believe that they must sell their houses to qualify for SSI. This is not true. A home, certain vehicles, and specific personal property are excluded from the assets limitation for benefits.

The laws regulating all of the different benefits of the Social Security system are constantly changing. Always check with the Social Security office or with an attorney who handles Social Security cases in order to find out if you are eligible for any of the benefits at the time you apply.

## FINANCIAL ASSISTANCE FOR COLLEGE AND UNIVERSITY STUDENTS

There are several government-sponsored programs available to assist someone who wants to attend a college or university. Some of the programs available follow.

The **College Work-Study Program** provides part-time employment to students who need financial help to meet the costs of postsecondary education. To qualify, students must maintain satisfactory grades, have financial need, not owe on other grants or loans, and meet citizen and residency requirements.

**Federal Stafford Program** loans are available to students who need aid to pursue studies at colleges or universities. Eligibility criteria require that the student prove a need for assistance and maintain satisfactory grades.

**Nellie Excel** is available to students attending postsecondary educational institutions. This program provides loans for tuition and books.

**Pell grants** and certain other grants are available to students who meet the requirements. These grants are in reality gifts from the federal government as they do not have to be repaid.

## FAMILY PLANNING

The U.S. Department of Health and Human Services sponsors projects that provide education, counseling, medical, and social services to assist individuals with family planning. County health services can also provide information on the availability and location of other programs.

## FOOD STAMP PROGRAM

The U.S. Department of Agriculture sponsors the food stamp program for low-income families. Participating families receive coupons that they may exchange for food at authorized grocery stores. A family's monthly coupon allotment is based on household size and income. This program is also available to elderly and handicapped persons. The local social services department has information and eligibility criteria available.

## HOUSING

The federal Department of Housing and Urban Development (HUD) has programs available to assist low-income persons with the purchase of a home, with mortgage needs, with subsidized housing for low-income families and the elderly, and with rehabilitation of housing that is old or in disrepair. Insurance for some types of housing is also available through HUD programs. Contact the local HUD office for more information.

## PUBLIC DEFENDERS

In any criminal prosecution a person accused of a crime but unable to afford to pay for an attorney to represent him is entitled to be represented by counsel under Article VI of the U.S. Constitution. Both the federal and state court systems have public defender offices, and anyone who needs this service may ask the court to appoint an attorney to represent him.

## PUBLIC HEALTH SERVICE

The federal government provides numerous public health services, but most public health services are administered through state or county health departments. The five federal health agencies are Alcohol, Drug Abuse, and Mental Health; the Food and Drug Administration; Health Resources and Services; the National Institutes of Health; and the Centers for Disease Control. The white pages of local telephone directories list the telephone numbers of these agencies.

## UNEMPLOYMENT INSURANCE

Unemployed workers who have been laid off or fired without good cause may be eligible for financial assistance through state unemployment insurance programs. The white pages of the local telephone directory in most states list the administrative office under the State Employment Development Department, Unemployment Insurance Claims.

## WELFARE ASSISTANCE

Welfare assistance is a federally funded program administered by the states. It provides needy families with children with financial assistance to meet such basic living expenses as food, shelter, and clothing. County social services offices administer this program.

## WIC PROGRAM

WIC stands for "women, infants, and children" and is a special supplemental food program for women, infants, and children up to five years of age who are identified as low-income and who suffer from inadequate nutrition and health care. Local social services agencies have information on the WIC program.

## ELECTED OFFICIALS' DUTIES

Typical services that a state senator provides to his or her constituents are:

1. Analysis of legislation
2. Information on ballot propositions
3. Legislator's voting records
4. Consumer protection information
5. Legislative publications
6. Information on tours of the capital

7. Information on homeowner, senior citizen, disabled, and tax relief programs
8. Assistance with the state tax board, department of motor vehicles, employment development department, and medical plans

Typical services that a state assemblyman provides to his or her constituents are:

1. Taxpayer assistance
2. Assistance with state government forms
3. Assistance with state tax board, department of motor vehicles, Medicaid
4. Cutting through bureaucratic red tape
5. Handling of consumer complaints
6. Assistance with unemployment and disabilities insurance

Typical services that a member of Congress provides to his or her constituents are:

1. Local representation, serving as ambassador and advocate in Congress for views and needs of constituents
2. Constituents' service: assisting in obtaining federal benefits and solving problems by acting as a middleman between the citizen and the federal government
3. Oversight and investigation of the executive branch
4. Education of constituents on government activities

### Table 6-1: Voting Ballots and Election Materials in a Language Other Than English

The federal Voting Rights Act states that no state or political subdivision shall provide voting materials only in the English language if the state or political subdivision has census data proving that 5 percent of its citizens speak a single language.

**Arizona**   Follows federal voting act.

**California**   Ballot measures and instructions shall be given in English and Spanish.

**Florida**   The supervisor of elections may request, sixty days prior to an election, that a statewide ballot be translated into the language of a minority group.

**Illinois**   Follows federal voting act.

### Table 6-1: Voting Ballots and Election Materials in a Language Other Than English (cont.)

| | |
|---|---|
| **New Mexico** | Voting instructions, notices, forms, and proclamations shall also be in Spanish. |
| **New York** | Follows federal voting act. |
| **Texas** | Both English and Spanish materials shall be provided where 5 percent of the voting population in the voting precinct is Spanish-speaking according to the most recent federal census. |

# 7

# Professional Ethics

## DEFINITION OF ETHICS

*Ethics* is defined as a system of moral principles and rules of conduct of an individual person or group such as the members of a class of professionals. While ethics is an important matter in all dealings between individuals, the subject is of particular importance in a relationship between an individual and someone who considers himself an expert and in whom the public is asked to place a high level of trust.

Attorneys, doctors, religious leaders, psychologists, and social workers, among others, are professionals in whom the public places great trust. The public turns to them for help when they are sick or in emotional pain. One of the reasons that these professionals are expected to live by a higher code of ethics is that an individual is often in a state of confusion and concern when he seeks their services. Someone who is confused or burdened with grief is often in vulnerable state of mind; thus the rules of ethics governing professionals are intended to protect him while he is in this state.

## RIGHT TO DIE

There is much controversy over right to die laws, also referred to as "mercy killing," "euthanasia," "living wills," "durable power of attorney," and "assisted suicide." These laws are designed to protect someone who becomes incompetent or incapacitated.

The United States Supreme Court in *Cruzan v. Director of Missouri Health Department* (1990), 110 S.Ct. 2841, held that a competent person has a constitutionally protected liberty interest in refusing unwanted medical treatment.

However, this right is not absolute when the person is incompetent. Under the due process clause of the U.S. Constitution a state may require that an incompetent person's wishes for the withdrawal of life-sustaining medical treatment be proved through clear and convincing evidence because a state has a legitimate interest in protecting and preserving human life. A state may also decline to make judgments about the quality of life that the particular person may enjoy and may simply assert that the preservation of life by the state be weighed against the constitutionally protected interest of the person.

A *living will* is a legal instrument that is usually drawn up by a competent person. It states that person's wishes in the event that life support and life-sustaining treatments are needed should he become incompetent or incapacitated because of an illness or accident.

A *durable power of attorney* is an instrument similar to a living will in that it gives another person the authority to authorize life support or life-sustaining treatment. The person who has power of attorney makes these decisions, and his decision has the same legal effect as though the patient had made it himself.

## IMMIGRATION CONSULTANTS

To protect consumers against harm, some states including California and Illinois require that immigration consultants be licensed by the state. Common regulations require the immigration consultant to use a state-approved contract that lists the services he will provide and the fees and expenses being charged. The contract must also contain a clause which states that the contract may be canceled by the client at any time, in writing. If the client cancels the contract within seventy-two hours of the time he or she signed it, the immigration consultant is required to refund all monies paid, and the client is not liable for any further fees or expenses. After the seventy-two-hour time limit, the client will be required to pay the full amount of the contract if the immigration consultant does what he has agreed to. If the consultant only partially performs the duties he has agreed to, the client is required to pay only for the reasonable value of the services he receives.

Moreover, documents submitted in support of an application for nonimmigrant, immigrant, or naturalization status may not be kept by the immigration consultant for any purpose, including to secure payment of compensation or costs.

Moreover, in Illinois an immigration consultant who is not a licensed attorney and who advertises such services in another language must advertise in both English and the other language, "I am not an attorney licensed to practice law and may not give legal advice or accept fees for legal advice." Furthermore, the literal translation of the word *licensed* into a language other than English is prohibited. This specifically refers to the word *licenciado,* which means "licensed" and in some countries means or is used as "attorney."

When the immigration consultant and the client complete and sign the contract, a copy must be provided to each client party. The immigration consultant is required to provide the client with a copy of the contract in English and in his language if he does not read and understand English. The immigration consultant cannot charge the client an extra fee for providing a translated copy of the contract. The translation should appear on the reverse side of the English contract.

Immigration consultants are regulated in Arizona, California, Illinois, and New Mexico. An immigration consultant for the most part is defined as any person who renders services, including the completion of forms and applications, to a client if the services are related to the client's desire to affect or change his legal status in an immigration or naturalization matter. An immigration or naturalization matter includes any law, action, filing, or proceeding related to a person's immigration or citizenship status in the United States.

Private individuals who provide immigration services have a substantial impact on their clients' ability to remain in the United States, to reside as residents, and to work. Therefore, the attorneys general of the various states enforce laws to promote honesty and integrity for the service that immigration consultants provide. To achieve such goals, the law limits who can perform such services.

A person seeking immigration and naturalization services in **Arizona** may seek representation from:

1. Licensed attorneys
2. Law students who are enrolled in an accredited law school or law school graduates who are not yet admitted to the bar
3. Reputable individuals of good moral character
4. Persons who represent an organization accredited by the Board of Immigration Appeals and have been accredited by the Immigration Board
5. Accredited officials of the U.S. government, to which an alien owes allegiance, if the official appears solely in his official capacity

A person seeking immigration and naturalization services in **California** may seek representation from:

1. Licensed attorneys
2. Persons authorized by federal law to represent persons before the Board of Immigration Appeals or the Immigration and Naturalization Service
3. The U.S. Immigration and Naturalization Service

A person seeking immigration and naturalization services in **Illinois** may seek representation from:

1. Licensed attorneys
2. Legal interns
3. A not-for-profit organization recognized by the Board of Immigration Appeals
4. Any organization that employs or desires to employ an alien or nonimmigrant alien and whose employees or agents provide assistance in immigration matters to aliens or nonimmigrant alien employees or potential employees but without compensation from those individuals

A person seeking immigration and naturalization services in **New Mexico** may seek representation from:

1. Licensed attorneys
2. Law students enrolled in the final year at an accredited law school or law school graduates who have not yet passed the bar
3. Reputable individuals of good moral character
4. Persons who represent an organization accredited by the Board of Immigration Appeals and has been accredited by the Immigration Board
5. Accredited officials in the U.S. government, to which an alien owes allegiance, if the official appears solely in his official capacity and with the alien's consent

For the most part, immigration consultants are prohibited from making any guarantees or misleading statements or promises to a client while providing services, and they cannot make any guarantees or promises unless these are in writing and unless they have some factual basis for making such promises. It is unlawful for an immigration consultant to make a statement that he can or will obtain special favors from, or has special influence with, the U.S. Immigration and Naturalization Service.

In California it is illegal to charge a referral fee, and this prohibition must be conspicuously displayed in the immigration consultant's office.

It is unlawful for anyone, other than persons authorized to practice law or authorized under federal law, to represent persons in certain immigration matters or to provide any service constituting the unlawful practice of immigration and naturalization law or otherwise to violate immigration and naturalization law practice. Such a violation in Arizona, California, Illinois, and New Mexico is a misdemeanor.

## NOTARY PUBLIC

It is important to discuss here the difference between a *notary public* in the United States and a *notario público* in Latin American countries.

In the United States a notary public can be anyone who is reasonably trustworthy and is able to pass a simple test. It is common for secretaries, bank clerks, and private postal employees to be commissioned as notaries public in the United States. Their role is to certify that a person signing an important document has adequately proved his or her identity to the notary public. An important document, such as a deed to transfer real estate, may need to be notarized by a notary public before the county recorder will allow it to be recorded in the official government records. Someone wishing to have a document notarized or acknowledged seeks out a notary public, who usually requires that the party signing the document prove his identity with a driver's license with his or her picture on it or with a current passport with a picture. The notary public keeps a book in which he or she records the name, address, and identification used by each person for whom he or she is certifying a signature. The party executing the document must sign the notary public's record book next to his name, and his signature must match the one he places on the document.

While "notary public" in English translates to *notario público* in Spanish, the differences between the two are enormous. In Mexico, for instance, in most jurisdictions someone who is designated a *notario público* must be an attorney and pass a highly rigorous series of examinations before he or she can be so called. Only a very few select individuals ever become *notarios públicos*. When they do, however, they become quasi-governmental officials. The *notario público* is authorized by law to resolve legal disputes and to arbitrate judicial matters. Furthermore, in California, Florida, Illinois, and Texas a notary public who advertises in a language other than English must disclose the fact that he is not an attorney and cannot give legal advice.

Because of the differences between a notary public and a *notario público,* the law in many states like California, Florida, and Illinois prohibits a notary public from using the Spanish term. Even if the majority of his business is conducted in Spanish, a notary public in those states can use only the designation *notary public,* never *notario público.* Furthermore, in most states the law limits the amount a notary public can charge to notarize a document.

Notaries public in Arizona, Illinois, New Mexico, and New York are appointed by the secretary of state, whereas in Florida and Texas they are appointed by the governor. In Arizona, Florida, Illinois, and New Mexico, notaries serve four-year terms, and in Texas they serve two-year terms.

For the most part notaries public administer oaths, take and certify acknowledgments of written documents, take and certify depositions, and make declarations and protests.

# 8

# Bankruptcy

Using credit to purchase goods and services has been common throughout recent history. At the time America's Founding Fathers came to settle the new land, there was a widespread practice in Europe of placing persons who could not pay their debts in debtor's prison. The writers of the U.S. Constitution sought to ensure that persons in debt would be able to resolve their credit problems without being imprisoned, so they provided for bankruptcy in the U.S. Constitution (Art. I, Sec. 8[4]): "The Congress shall have the power to . . . establish uniform laws on the subject of Bankruptcy throughout the United States."

## CREDIT AND DEBT

In early commercial transactions one party would give goods or services to another, contingent upon the promise by the receiving party to pay for the goods or services at a future time. For example, a farmer provided feed for a cow while the cow farmer promised to give the feed farmer milk or meat when the cow produced milk or was slaughtered.

When the practice of exchanging land for goods and services became common in Europe, the concept of credit was extended to allow former slaves of the nobility to purchase land for their families. From those beginnings we have evolved into a society that depends on credit in most aspects of our lives. We purchase homes and vehicles on credit, pay for our education on credit, and often purchase goods and services on credit.

The credit industry has become a major economic force in American business. Businesses that issue credit cards typically charge a fee to the retailer, who accepts the card for payment, and also charge the cardholder interest if the amount owed to the credit company is not paid in full within a certain number of days after the bill is sent to the cardholder. Because the interest charged by credit card companies is usually quite high—often 18 to 20 percent per year—the companies are interested in finding customers who have stable jobs and have demonstrated that they are responsible and will make the monthly payments when they are due.

Oftentimes this arrangement works to the advantage of both the credit card issuer and the consumer. The business owner pays the credit card issuer a small fee, and the credit card issuer bears the risk associated with giving credit to the consumer. The consumer has the opportunity to purchase goods and services at his convenience, such as when something is on sale, and to pay for the goods when he is paid by his employer, and the credit card issuer makes money as described above.

## DEFAULTING ON CREDIT OBLIGATIONS

When a person cannot pay his credit obligations, he is considered in default. This may come about because of loss of a job, an illness, or an accident, or it may result from using credit irresponsibly.

When the problems that prevent the debtor from paying his credit obligations are temporary, such as during a short illness, it is usually best to contact the creditors and ask for more time to make payments. If circumstances are uncertain but the debtor thinks he will be able to pay off the debts, he may wish to seek the services of a credit and debt counseling agency. If the consumer owes more than he thinks he can reasonably repay, he should consult an attorney who specializes in bankruptcy for advice on seeking relief from all or part of his credit obligations.

## CREDIT COUNSELING AGENCIES

If the debtor has contacted those to whom he owes money and been unable to make alternative arrangements to pay the money he owes, he can seek the services of a credit and debt counseling agency. He should be aware that such organizations charge fees for their services.

If a debtor seeks advice from a credit counseling agency, it is very important to ensure that the company is legitimate and is properly licensed. One national organization that is recommended by some state legal associations is Consumer Credit Counselors, a nonprofit organization that is sponsored by banks and department stores. Even if the debtor has been unable to come to an agreement with his creditors, a professional credit counseling agency may be able to arrange a satisfactory payment plan.

## BANKRUPTCY

A debtor who has been unable to make arrangements with his creditors to repay his debts should seek the advice of an attorney who specializes in bankruptcy. A list of bankruptcy attorneys may be obtained from the attorney referral service of the local bar association.

Bankruptcy is a federal matter; thus bankruptcy actions are filed in a special federal court. However, state laws may affect the exemptions that the debtor can claim.

There are three basic classifications, called chapters, of bankruptcy protection available to the individual:

**Chapter 13** is called a debt repayment plan and requires that the debtor owe less than $350,000 in secured debts, such as a mortgage and car loan, and have less than $100,000 in other debts, such as credit card debts and medical bills.

**Chapter 11** is also a debt repayment plan but is for those having more than $350,000 in secured debt or more than $100,000 in other debts.

**Chapter 7** is what is commonly referred to as straight bankruptcy. Under Chapter 7 a debtor who is unable to repay his debt may have the entire amount he owes, with some exceptions, discharged by the bankruptcy court.

While the debtor can file for a Chapter 13 or Chapter 7 bankruptcy, the court has the power to decide which one is more appropriate.

## ADVANTAGES OF FILING FOR BANKRUPTCY

Once a person has filed a petition for bankruptcy with the court, his creditors will be notified. From that time on the creditors will be required to follow the directives issued by the court. If the petitioner is represented by an attorney, his creditors will be advised of this, and they will be legally required to contact the petitioner only through his attorney. The creditors cannot call the petitioner repeatedly at home or contact him or his employer at work. If the petitioner has been sued and a monetary judgment has been issued against him, the marshal will not be able to seize and sell his assets to satisfy the judgment except as directed by the bankruptcy court judge.

## PROPERTY EXEMPTIONS

When a debtor files a petition for bankruptcy, he is required to complete a schedule of exempt property as part of his declaration of assets. Exempt property is not taken from the petitioner. In a Chapter 11 or Chapter 13 bankruptcy, he is often allowed to keep most of his property that is not security for a particular debt. In a Chapter 7 bankruptcy action, however, the court trustee is authorized to sell any property that is not exempt and to use the proceeds of the sale to pay creditors.

Usually a petitioner in bankruptcy may choose either of two ways of determining what property is exempt. The first exemption method is the same as that used to exempt property from being seized to satisfy a judgment for money. In California, for example, under state law those exemptions include up to $50,000 in equity in one's home if the petitioner is single ($75,000 if the petitioner is the head of the household and $100,000 if the petitioner is sixty-five or older, or disabled, or fifty-five or older and living on a low income); up to $1,900 equity in vehicles; up to $5,000 in tools or other items needed for work; up to $5,000 worth of jewelry, heirlooms, and works of art; life insurance policies on which he can borrow up to $8,000; up to $2,000 in a bank account into which his Social Security checks have been directly deposited; household furnishings and clothing that he and his family need; a cemetery plot; all or part of retirement, disability, and health insurance; workers' compensation; and welfare, unemployment, union, and other benefits that are necessary to support his family. This exemption option is usually preferred by those petitioners who have equity in a home.

The second exemption option in California allows the petitioner to keep up to $15,000 in equity in his home or burial plot. If he does not own either, he may apply the $15,000 to other property that would otherwise be nonexempt. He is also allowed an $800 floating exemption that can be applied to nonexempt property; $2,400 in equity in vehicles; any items worth up to $400 that fall into the categories of household furnishings and goods, clothing, appliances, books, animals, crops, and musical instruments; $1,000 in jewelry; $1,500 worth of books and tools that are needed to earn a living; a life insurance policy; and Social Security and veterans' benefits, unemployment insurance money, and pension and profit-sharing plans. (See multistate chart for homestead exemptions on page 96.)

## SECURED DEBTS VS. UNSECURED DEBTS

An *unsecured debt* is one in which there is no written contract pledging property as collateral against the debt. An example of an unsecured debt is a credit card purchase, a medical bill, or any loan in which a person has not offered property as security for the repayment of that loan.

A *secured debt* is one that allows the lender to retake the secured property if the loan is not paid according to the terms of the contract. A security agreement must be in writing and signed by the borrower. A credit agreement to purchase a home or an auto is usually secured with the property. Other items such as major appliances may be secured debts if the contract specifically allows the lender to reclaim the property if the debt is not paid.

If a debt is secured, the debtor must either surrender the property to the lender or agree to continue to pay for it until it is paid off. If a creditor repossesses secured property and sells it to pay off the loan, he may sue the debtor for the difference if the sale price is not enough to pay off the balance due.

## DEBTS THAT CANNOT BE DISCHARGED IN A BANKRUPTCY

When the federal bankruptcy court discharges the debts of a bankruptcy petitioner, it issues a legally binding ruling that says the debtor or petitioner is no longer required to pay the debt. While the purpose of bankruptcy is to give the petitioner a chance at a fresh start, there are some debts that cannot be discharged, including:

1. Secured debts
2. Debts to creditors that were not listed in the bankruptcy petition
3. Income taxes and penalties (in most cases)
4. Student loans
5. Child and spousal support
6. Any judgment owed as a result of being sued for drunken driving
7. Any debts incurred through fraud or lying to a creditor
8. Debts incurred just before filing a bankruptcy petition

If a creditor proves that the debtor lied about his assets or that he is hiding property to avoid having it seized to pay his debts, the court will refuse to discharge the debts and may dismiss the case. If that happens, the creditor can then sue the debtor and attach his nonexempt assets to pay the judgment ordered by the court.

## BANKRUPTCY PETITIONS BY HUSBAND AND WIFE

A husband or wife can file a separate bankruptcy petition. However, the non-petitioning spouse may be held liable for some or all of the debt of the petitioning spouse if the debt incurred by the bankruptcy petitioner is for such necessities as food, shelter, and clothing. One spouse cannot transfer all the assets of the couple to the other spouse to avoid having the assets seized to pay for his or her debts. Such a transaction would be considered fraud and would cause the court to dismiss the bankruptcy petition.

## CHAPTER 13 DEBT REPAYMENT

Chapter 13 is designed to allow the debtor to pay off part or all of his debt over three to five years. Regular payments are made to a trustee—an employee of the bankruptcy court—who then distributes the money to the various creditors. At the end of the time stipulated by the court, if the debtor has made all the payments as agreed, the bankruptcy judge issues an order stating that the debtor does not have to pay any additional money to the creditors. To take advantage of the Chapter 13 debt repayment plan, the debtor must owe less than $350,000 in secured debts, such as a mortgage and car loan, and have less than $100,000 in other debts, such as most credit card debts and medical bills. He must also have a regular source of income such as a job or income from a trust account. If the petitioner does not have a regular source of income, he will be found ineligible for Chapter 13 and will be required to file under Chapter 7.

## CHAPTER 7 BANKRUPTCY

If an accident, illness, or loss of employment has caused the petitioner to file for protection under the bankruptcy laws, it may be in his best interest to file a Chapter 7 bankruptcy to discharge all his debts without requiring him to make payments. Because nonexempt assets can be seized and sold to satisfy the debts in a Chapter 7 bankruptcy, it is important to seek competent legal advice before filing.

## BANKRUPTCY AS A LAST RESORT

Bankruptcy is a serious step and should be considered only after all other means of solving one's credit problems have been exhausted. When the bankruptcy petition is filed, credit reporting agencies such as TRW and Equifax will report the bankruptcy on the petitioner's credit record. Usually information about a bankruptcy remains on a credit file for ten years. While some creditors may be willing to extend credit to someone after a bankruptcy, the debtor usually pays a higher interest rate than the average borrower and is probably denied a home mortgage by most major lenders. If he has filed a bankruptcy petition because of an accident or illness, some creditors may take those circumstances into consideration if he asks for credit.

Bankruptcy cannot be filed more than once every six years.

## Meeting with a Bankruptcy Attorney

For an attorney to advise a debtor on bankruptcy, he must first review the debtor's financial records. It is important to keep good records and ensure that the documents given to the attorney are complete and accurate. There may be legal ways in which a debtor can convert nonexempt assets into exempt assets before filing the bankruptcy petition, but he needs to rely on his attorney's advice. The courts are ever-watchful for indications of fraudulent transfer of assets prior to the filing of bankruptcy petitions, and a petitioner who lies or "forgets" to list assets may have his petition dismissed and may be prosecuted for fraud.

In preparing to meet with a bankruptcy attorney, the debtor should compile a list of all his creditors and their addresses, account numbers, how much is owed, what payments have been made, and any phone conversations or letters that have been written to them regarding the financial situation. Phone calls should be noted on a piece of paper and should include the date and time of each call, to whom the debtor spoke, and what each party said. If a debtor writes letters to the lender, he should keep a photocopy of each letter. If a creditor objects to a petition, the debtor may be helped by being able to show the court that he tried to work out a payment schedule before he filed for bankruptcy.

When the debtor meets with his attorney, he needs to take along copies of his pay stubs, any contracts relating to his employment, bank books and statements, his mortgage agreement and payment history or his rental agreement, any contracts for secured debts, such as a car, and any letters he has received from his creditors; in addition, he must make a list of all his assets. Once the list is complete, his attorney will be able to determine which assets are exempt and which may be seized and sold by the bankruptcy trustee to pay the creditors.

## Filing and Attorney's Fees

Filing fees are set by statute and vary depending on the chapter of the Bankruptcy Code that the petitioner is filing under. The current filing charge for a Chapter 7 petition is $175, and for a Chapter 13 petition, $150. In addition to the filing fees, the attorney will charge a fee for completing the petition, notifying the creditors, appearing at the bankruptcy hearings, and dealing with the creditors if they call. Depending on the complexity of the client's financial situation, the attorney may charge between $500 and $5,000 for her or his services. Usually the petitioner is required to pay the attorney's fee before the bankruptcy petition is filed. If he is unable to pay the fee, he should seek legal assistance through legal aid or a legal services organization that charges its clients on a sliding scale according to ability to pay.

## Voluntary vs. Involuntary Bankruptcy

Whenever a person files a bankruptcy petition as the debtor, the act is called a *voluntary petition*. However, a creditor can also initiate a bankruptcy against a debtor. If the creditor files a bankruptcy petition, it is called an *involuntary petition*. Whether the debtor files a voluntary petition or is forced into bankruptcy through an involuntary petition, the requirements and procedures are essentially the same. If a debtor is notified that a creditor has filed an involuntary petition against him, it is essential that he immediately seek legal advice from a bankruptcy attorney.

## The Bankruptcy Process, Hearings, and Discharge

Bankruptcy is a federal matter, and each state has at least one special federal bankruptcy court. The attorney files the petition in the court that serves the area in which the debtor lives. After the petition is filed, a hearing is set. The debtor and his attorney appear at the hearing to answer any questions the bankruptcy judge or the creditors may have. At the initial hearing a trustee is assigned to each case. The trustee's job is to investigate the validity of the information the debtor has provided in his petition and to protect the interests of the creditors. If a debtor files a Chapter 11 or 13 petition, payments are made to the trustee, who pays the creditors as directed by the court. As an officer of the court the trustee has certain rights and powers, and it is important that the debtor cooperate with the trustee. A debtor who is unsure about how to respond to the trustee's demand for information should discuss the matter with his attorney.

The creditors are notified of the time and place of the hearing, and they have a right to attend it. However, creditors usually do not attend bankruptcy hearings unless there is a large amount of money involved or they are objecting to the petition on the basis of fraud.

When a debtor has filed a Chapter 11 or 13 petition, the judge directs him to pay a certain amount each payday or month to the trustee. At the hearing the judge decides how long the debtor will be required to make payments—usually three years—but the bankruptcy judge has the discretion to extend the payment period up to five years. At the end of the stipulated time, if the debtor has made all the payments as directed by the court, the judge issues a discharge order. Even if the debtor has not fully paid off all the creditors but has paid the amount ordered by the court, the discharge cancels any remaining obligations that he may have. If the judge determines that the debtor does not have enough money left after paying for essential living expenses, he may order that a Chapter 13 petition be changed to a Chapter 7 bankruptcy.

When a debtor files a Chapter 7 bankruptcy petition, the judge directs the trustee to seize and sell his nonexempt assets and pay the proceeds to the creditors. If the debtor has no assets that can be sold, the court allows the creditors time to file any objections they may have—usually six months. If no objections are filed by creditors or the trustee, the court discharges the debts in the bankruptcy petition at the end of the waiting period. If objections are filed, the court holds a hearing to listen to the objections and rules on them. After the objections have been satisfied, an order discharging the debts and approving the bankruptcy is entered. Once the discharge is ordered by the court, the petitioner is no longer required to pay those debts that have been discharged. If the judge determines that the petitioner has the ability to pay some or all of his debts, the court may change the petition from a Chapter 7 to a Chapter 11 or 13 bankruptcy.

The discharge is ordered at a second hearing. The bankruptcy attorney will advise the debtor if he is required to attend that hearing.

### Table 8–1: Homestead Exemption

Maximum amount protected under the homestead exemption:

| | |
|---|---|
| **Arizona** | $100,000 |
| **California** | $75,000 if head of household is under 65 years; $100,000 if one spouse is 65 years or older or disabled and cannot be substantially employed, or if 55 years or older and gross income is less than $15,000 and the sale is involuntary, or if the debtor is 55 years or older and is married; all others $50,000. |
| **Florida** | $10,000 if owner is over 65 years; $9,500 if owner is disabled and been a permanent resident for the last five years before the claim; $5,000 for everyone else. |
| **Illinois** | $7,500 |
| **New Mexico** | $30,000 |
| **New York** | $10,000 |
| **Texas** | The homestead is protected from forced sale or payment of all debts except for property taxes due, work and material used in constructing or making improvements on the property, and mortgage loans. |

# 9

# Wills, Trusts, and Probate

## WILLS

A will is a document that provides for the disposition of property, both real and personal, upon death. Every person of sound mind and over the age of majority may dispose of his or her separate property, real and personal, by a will. Each state has its own laws regarding wills, probate, and trusts, and any person executing a will or trust should ensure that its form complies with his or her state laws.

## BENEFITS OF HAVING A WILL

There are several benefits to having a will. The most important is knowing that the maker's property will be left, upon his death, to the persons named in the will. Furthermore, a well-prepared will makes it easier for the heirs and beneficiaries to settle the matters of the estate.

## TYPES OF WILLS

There are different types of wills, but modern law requires that a will be written to be valid. A handwritten will is called a *holographic will.* To be valid, a holographic will must be completely handwritten in legible form. The person preparing the will must explain clearly what he or she wants to leave and to whom. The instructions must be clear so that friends, family, and a probate judge will be able to understand easily the wishes of the person who wrote the will. The will must be dated and signed by the person making it. A holographic will does not need to be notarized or witnessed, but it is wise to have it witnessed by someone who will not inherit anything under it.

A **form will** that allows the maker simply to fill in the blanks is valid in most states, provided the maker is either a parent or a married person whose estate is not large. There are two accepted form wills, the standard will and the will with trust. Using either of the approved form wills, a parent may leave his estate to his children or spouse and may leave money to one other person or charity. A married person may distribute his estate according to the same limits. On both forms, the maker of the will can name a guardian for minor children and an executor of his estate. A will with trust allows the maker to put his or her estate into a trust fund to support and care for his or her children until they reach the age of twenty-one years.

## ATTORNEY-PREPARED WILLS

The laws governing wills, trusts, and probate are complex and subject to numerous other regulations such as those promulgated by the Internal Revenue Code. Estate planning is a complex subject, and there are both attorneys and accountants who devote their practices exclusively to this specialty.

Anyone who has even a modest estate should consult with an attorney before writing his will to ensure that the will is properly written and expresses his true intentions. An attorney who specializes in estate planning can advise a client of the tax consequences of structuring a will or trust in a manner that will be most advantageous to the individual and his heirs.

Two witnesses who will not inherit under the will must watch the maker sign the will and then sign their names as witnesses. A will prepared by an attorney will be typed or printed.

## SEPARATE WILLS FOR SPOUSES

Each spouse must have a separate will even if the majority of the property owned by two married persons is community property. Since it is impossible to know which spouse will die first, a will must assume that the maker will be the first to die and should include provisions for distribution of the estate if both spouses die within thirty days of each other.

## CHANGING A WILL

A will can be changed and should be updated whenever the maker has any significant changes in his estate or family situation or after the death or incapacity of the person named executor.

To make minor changes in a will, the maker may execute a document called a *codicil,* a legal document that is attached to the original will. The maker of a will should never cross out or change the original will. A codicil must be written and witnessed in the same manner as an original will. Different witnesses from those who witnessed the maker's signing of the original will may witness the signing of the codicil.

The person making and signing his will is called the testator. If the testator wishes to make major changes to his will, an attorney may advise him to revoke the previous will and execute a new one. To be revoked, an old will must be replaced by the writing contained in a new will or be completely destroyed by the person who made it.

A person who makes a will and later becomes incompetent may not change the terms of the most recent will written before he was declared incompetent. Upon regaining competency, he may then change the will.

## NOTIFYING OTHERS OF THE WILL

The only person who must know about the existence of a will is the attorney who prepares it. However, a maker should notify the person named executor that he has been designated to handle the maker's estate when he dies.

To ensure that any wishes regarding one's burial or cremation are carried out by his heirs, anyone who makes a will should inform a family member or close friend whom he trusts about the will's existence and its location.

## IF THERE IS NO WILL

Whenever a person dies without a valid will, the laws of the state determine who gets any property owned by the deceased. When a person dies without a will, he is said to have died *intestate.* Since someone who dies intestate has not prepared a will or named an executor, the court names an administrator to settle the estate.

An administrator is responsible for preparing a list of the deceased's assets and for locating any heirs who may have an interest in his estate. The administrator files any tax returns that are required, pays any taxes or other debts from the assets of the deceased's estate, and distributes the remaining assets according to the laws of the state for *intestate succession* and under the supervision of the probate court. An administrator is entitled to payment for the services he renders according to a fee schedule established by the court.

## PROBATE LAW

*Probate law* deals with the transfer of property from a decedent (one who has died) to his heirs or beneficiaries. The probate process includes testing and proving the validity of the decedent's will, paying the expenses of the estate, and distributing the assets of the estate according to the instructions contained in the will.

When a person has made a will before his death, he is said to have died *testate.* The decedent should have named an executor in the will to handle his affairs. The duties of the executor are similar to those of an administrator of an intestate estate.

## TRUSTS

A *trust* is an instrument that creates a fiduciary relationship—one of trust—in which a person or institution holds and administers the property of another person for the benefit of a third party or parties, called *beneficiaries.* In a trust the person who administers the property is called the *trustee,* and the person who contracts with the trustee to manage the property is called the *trustor.*

## THE LIVING TRUST

Some people elect to transfer the property of their estates to trusts while they are still living. To enable someone to transfer property yet retain control of the assets, the law provides for an instrument called a *living trust.* The person whose assets are placed in the trust may have control over the assets during his lifetime, with a provision whereby the administration of the trust transfers upon his death to a successor trustee named in the trust document. A person who has a living trust should also have a will that is incorporated into the trust document.

## GUARDIANSHIP

When a trust is created for the benefit of a minor child or an incompetent person, it is called a *guardianship.* The guardian may be an individual or an institution, such as a bank, appointed by the court to protect the interests of a minor or an incompetent beneficiary.

## TOTTEN TRUST

A *totten trust* is created when a bank savings account is established for the benefit of a minor, and the individual who establishes the account remains on the account as trustor. The minor in a totten trust is the trust beneficiary, and the bank is the trustee.

## PROPERTY NOT INCLUDED IN A WILL

Any property not specifically provided for in a will must pass to the heirs of the deceased under the laws of succession. Succession is the transfer of property to those heirs who have a legal right to inherit the property, either real or personal, of a deceased person. In most states a legally adopted child is treated, for succession purposes, the same as a natural child, and a child is entitled to inherit property from either parent even if the parents were never married.

Anyone considering a trust should consult an attorney who specializes in trusts and estate planning.

# 10

# Employee and Employer Rights in the Workplace

There are vast opportunities for employment in the United States in a wide variety of fields, and everyone with a legal right to work in the United States is entitled to seek any job that appeals to him. The employer, however, has the right to test an applicant's skill and qualifications for a job. In most jobs the employer can require an applicant's consent to talk with former employers and get character references about such matters as the applicant's dependability, honesty, integrity, and work habits, and if the applicant refuses to authorize him to investigate the items on his application, the employer may refuse to hire him. Employers may also require that prospective employees submit to tests for drug and alcohol use and to physical exams performed at the employers' expense to determine if they are physically fit to do the job.

An employer must provide each employee with a description of the duties of his job, and the work the employee is asked to perform must be substantially the same as the job description. Once someone has been hired, he has an obligation to fulfill the duties of his job. Labor laws in the various states generally cover the same basic areas. Labor codes usually state that an employee shall substantially comply with all the directions of his employer concerning the service in which he is engaged, except where such obedience is impossible or unlawful or would impose new and unreasonable burdens upon the employee.

## WORK HOUR RESTRICTIONS

In most states a day's work consists of eight hours of labor unless the employee and employer expressly agree by contract to different terms. Employees in any occupation are usually entitled to one day's rest every seven days. However, an employee and employer may agree by contract to any work schedule. In many states, if an employee is paid by the hour, the employer must pay the employee at one and one-half times his regular hourly rate for any time worked over eight hours in any twenty-four-hour period and for any time worked over forty hours in any seven-day week.

### *Table 10-1: Legal Workday and Final Paycheck Requirement*

The legal workday is the number of hours an employee must work on each work-day in order to earn his or her regular paycheck. Time worked in excess of the legal workday is to be as overtime, usually time and a half. The majority of the states have established a limit on the number of hours an employee has to work to collect his or her regular paycheck—usually forty hours; additional hours are to be compensated at a higher rate.

#### ARIZONA

| | |
|---|---|
| Legal workday | Eight hours. |
| Time limit for employers to disburse a final paycheck | If fired, within three days; otherwise next pay period. |

#### CALIFORNIA

| | |
|---|---|
| Legal workday | Eight hours. |
| Final paycheck due | Immediately or within seventy-two hours. |

#### FLORIDA

| | |
|---|---|
| Legal workday | Eight hours. |
| Final paycheck due | Next pay period. |

#### ILLINOIS

| | |
|---|---|
| Legal workday | Eight hours. |
| Final paycheck due | Next pay period. |

### Table 10-1: Legal Workday and Final Paycheck Requirement (cont.)

#### New Mexico

| | |
|---|---|
| Legal workday | Eight hours. |
| Final paycheck due | If fired, within five days; otherwise next pay period. |

#### New York

| | |
|---|---|
| Legal workday | Eight hours. |
| Final paycheck due | Next pay period. |

#### Texas

| | |
|---|---|
| Legal workday | Eight hours. |
| Final paycheck due | If fired, within six days; otherwise next pay period. |

## Jury Duty

Workers sometimes fear they will lose their jobs if they are asked to appear in court as witnesses or to serve on jury duty, but most states have laws that protect employees in these cases. In most states no employer may discharge or in any manner discriminate against an employee who takes time off work to serve on a jury or appear in court, as long as the employee gives the employer reasonable notice before his absence. Any person served with a summons issued by a court is required to appear when and where the summons says, and failure to do so could lead to his being arrested and jailed.

In Arizona, New Mexico, New York, and Texas an employer may not threaten to terminate employment because the employee has jury duty. In California, Florida, and Illinois any employee who is discharged, threatened with discharge, demoted, suspended, or in any other way discriminated against because he takes time off to appear in court or serve on a jury is entitled to reinstatement and reimbursement for lost wages and work benefits.

## Wage Discrimination and Minimum Wage Requirements

All employees are entitled to equal pay for equal work without regard to sex, race, or nationality. It is unlawful for an employer to pay an individual a wage less than that paid to a person of the opposite sex who works in the same establishment and performs equal work on jobs requiring equal skills, efforts, and responsibilities under similar working conditions. A wage scale based on seniority, merit, quality or quantity of production, or another bona fide factor other than sex is legal and may result in different persons' being paid different wages for performing substantially the same work.

Wage protection measures are administered and enforced by the federal Division of Labor Standards, a division of the Department of Labor. An employee who is paid less than the wage to which he is entitled may file a civil action against the employer for wages due him plus legal costs associated with his lawsuit. All employers must comply with the federal minimum wage laws. In those states that have more stringent laws, the employer must also comply with the state laws.

The law limits the amount an employee can collect in a wage discrimination lawsuit. Since there are often both state and federal laws governing the same issues, the employee may collect damages only under one system. If he recovers under the federal system and then recovers again under the state system, he must return to the employer the lesser of the two awards.

A civil action to recover wages must begin within the specified period after the cause of the action occurs. In the case of a willful violation on the part of the employer, the employee usually has a longer statute of limitations period.

## DISCHARGE BECAUSE OF WAGE GARNISHMENT

If a judgment issued by a court against an employee results in the employee's wages being garnished, the employer may not use that fact to discharge the employee. Federal law has similar protection for employees whose wages have been garnished and further protects employees from being discharged because of bankruptcy.

## MINIMUM WAGE REQUIREMENTS

The federal Department of Labor publishes minimum standard wage scales that are adjusted periodically for inflation. An employee who is paid less than the minimum wage or is not paid the legal minimum for overtime work is entitled to recover the unpaid balance plus legal costs. An employee cannot agree to work for less than the minimum wage, and if the employee is paid by the hour, in many states the employer must pay him one and one-half times his hourly wage for any time worked in excess of eight hours in any twenty-four-hour period.

Each state has a department that is responsible for ensuring that employees are properly paid. In carrying out their responsibilities, these departments are required to review each employer's records to ensure that he is in compliance with the minimum wage requirements. Complaints regarding failure of an employer to pay minimum wage should be addressed to the federal Division of Labor Standards Enforcement or to the state industrial welfare agencies. The Labor Department will investigate any complaints and initiate action to enforce payment as required by law.

## FINAL CHECK PAYMENT

If an employee quits his job, his wages are usually due and payable under state laws no later than seventy-two hours after he quits. If he has given the required previous notice of his intentions to quit, that employee is entitled to his wages at the time of quitting.

An employee who is not employed for a specified term is called an *at will employee.* Any at will employee who is dismissed by his employer or quits is entitled to compensation for services rendered up to the time of such dismissal. If an employer discharges an employee, the wages earned and unpaid at the time of discharge are usually due and payable immediately. When a group of employees is laid off because of the end of seasonal employment, their wages are due no later than seventy-two hours after their termination. If an employee requests that his wages be mailed to him and provides the employer with an address, the law requires the employer to mail the wages as directed.

## PAYMENT FOR VACATION TIME

When an employment contract provides for paid vacations and an employee is terminated without having taken his vested vacation time, that vacation time shall be paid to him as wages at his final pay rate. An employment contract that calls for forfeiture of vacation time upon termination, however, is legal.

## REPORTING UNLAWFUL EMPLOYMENT PRACTICES

State and federal governments have provisions that prohibit unfair employment practices. Title 29 of the U.S. Code and state fair employment practices acts are examples of fair employment laws.

## EMPLOYMENT DISCRIMINATION BASED ON PHYSICAL OR MENTAL HANDICAP

Federal and state laws prohibit an employer from discriminating against handicapped employees. The federal Rehabilitation Act of 1973 requires employers who do business with the U.S. government to take affirmative action to ensure that handicapped persons have equal employment opportunities. An employer, however, may refuse to hire an applicant who cannot safely perform the work for which he has applied.

## DISCRIMINATION BASED ON MEDICAL CONDITIONS

Most states make it unlawful for an employer to refuse to hire an applicant, to refuse to promote an employee, or to discharge an employee because of that person's medical condition unless it endangers the health and safety of the employee or others or prevents the employee from performing his duties.

## DISCRIMINATION BASED ON HIV/AIDS

The spread of acquired immune deficiency syndrome (AIDS) is of great concern. Research indicates that AIDS is not spread through the casual contact of the normal business relationship. Since it is currently considered a medical condition, people with AIDS or who are HIV-positive are protected under the Rehabilitation Act and the Americans with Disabilities Act. Discrimination against people with AIDS is prohibited since AIDS is considered a physical handicap. In some cases in which an AIDS carrier could endanger the health of others, the courts have determined that an employer could refuse to hire or retain that employee. In one case a surgeon was denied employment because of the potential danger of his transmitting the AIDS virus to a patient.

Several states have laws restricting the use of AIDS tests in employment screening. Since this is an emerging legal issue, anyone involved with an AIDS testing controversy should contact an attorney for advice.

## SEXUAL HARASSMENT

Sexual harassment is a prominent issue in the workplace and in society. *Sexual harassment* is defined as any unwelcome sexual advances, requests for sex, or physical or verbal conduct of a sexual nature. Because of the damage that can be done, sexual harassment is an especially important issue in the work environment, and the law requires the employer to bear a special responsibility for ensuring that the work environment is free of sexual harassment. If the employer fails to act to eliminate sexual harassment in his business, he can be held liable for damages along with the perpetrator of the sexually harassing acts.

If a supervisor or employer lets an employee know, directly or indirectly, that her employment or promotion is dependent on the employee's engaging in sex with her superior, he is engaging in a clear case of sexual harassment. However, sexual harassment is often far more subtle. Practices that may have been acceptable in the past and may be allowed today in other cultures are not permitted under the law in this country.

It is illegal to refer to the physical anatomy of another person in sexual language. Telling sexually offensive jokes or stories or showing sexually explicit cartoons or pictures is illegal. Even referring to a woman as "babe" and "doll" may lead to a sexual harassment action if the perpetrator has been told that the woman finds such names offensive and he fails to cease his sexually harassing behavior.

The purpose of sexual harassment legislation, as it pertains to the workplace, is to create an environment where men and women can work and earn livings free of intimidation, sexual offensiveness, and hostility. Today men and women work side by side in virtually every occupation. Women work as assemblers in factories and as doctors while men are nurses and schoolteachers. Women serve on ships alongside men and as coworkers on spaceflights, and they are frequently the primary or only sources of financial support for families.

The law encourages a zero-tolerance policy regarding sexual harassment in the workplace. In order to create a productive workplace environment, it is essential that coworkers show tolerance, if not respect, for their coworkers without regard to their sex.

The prevailing philosophy today is that the individual's sovereignty is based upon her ability to do a particular job and that retention and promotion should be based upon performance. The law recognizes that every person, regardless of sex, has a basic right to work in an environment free from fear and from the violation of her physical person and dignity.

The role of the employer in preventing sexual harassment in the workplace is very important. The law charges him with the responsibility of implementing an effective policy that prohibits sexual harassment in his workplace. To ensure compliance, the employer must provide training for all employees to make them aware of what constitutes sexual harassment and of the action the company will take against any employee found to be sexually harassing another. The remedies may include discharge or demotion. The employer must have a system for investigating sexual harassment complaints, and it must be designed to protect the complainant. All claims must be taken seriously and treated promptly, and an effective remedy must be used to stop any proved sexual harassment. An employee who claims she has been the victim of sexual harassment cannot be fired, demoted, or otherwise penalized for filing the claim. If a sexual harassment matter is not promptly resolved, the victimized employee may file a civil action against the offending employee, his supervisors, and the employer who failed to stop the offensive behavior.

A sexual harassment claim is a civil matter, but the penalties for the employer can be severe. If an employee is fired because she filed a sexual harassment complaint, she may be awarded civil damages, including back pay and pay for any promotions that she might have reasonably expected before being fired. Since it often takes years for such a case to be heard in court, the employer may have to pay the fired employee for months or years during which she did no work. He may also be required by the court to pay exemplary damages for embarrassment and emotional distress related to his failure to ensure that the workplace was not a hostile or offensive environment.

No employer may at any time inflict sexual harassment on any employee. Employees are protected from this abuse under both federal and state laws, and employers can be held liable for harassment. Any explicit request for sexual favors or sexual conduct that creates a hostile and stressful working environment for an employee constitutes sexual harassment.

Employees have the right to report any harassment and to have the claim investigated by their employers. An employee should be prepared to offer valid evidence to support her claim. It is advisable to try to have another party witness the harassing acts and to keep a written diary in which the date, time, place, and persons involved in each act are recorded.

## SEX DISCRIMINATION

Sex discrimination is prohibited under Title VII of the federal Civil Rights Act of 1964, which applies to employers with fifteen or more employees in each of twenty or more calendar weeks in the current or preceding calendar year. Under 42 U.S.C.S. §2000(e), "It shall be unlawful employment practice for an employer to fail or refuse to hire or discharge any individual, or otherwise to discriminate against any individual with respect to his compensation, terms, conditions, or privileges of employment because of such individual's race, color, religion, sex, or national origin."

The Equal Employment Opportunity Commission (EEOC) has imposed gender-neutral guidelines for employers to follow. Individual states and municipalities also have laws prohibiting sex discrimination.

Sex discrimination occurs when an employer discriminates against an employee or prospective employee because of sex. Traditionally it has been women who have been discriminated against in the work force. An employer may not make employment decisions based on female stereotypes or assumptions. These stereotypes might include the idea that women are capable of performing only secretarial or clerical duties, that women are emotionally unstable, or that women have higher turnover and absentee rates because of pregnancy.

Under the EEOC and state law, an employer must give equal opportunities to men and women. This means that they must have sexually neutral employment advertising and testing procedures, and they must not use sex as a basis for hiring, firing, or promoting. Women must be afforded the same fringe benefits such as medical, insurance, and retirement benefits, profit sharing, sick and personal days, and seniority as those offered men.

It is not unlawful employment practice for an employer to apply different standards of compensation or different terms, conditions, or privileges of employment in carrying out a seniority or merit system in good faith as long as the system is not based on discrimination because of race, religion, sex, or national origin (42 U.S.C.S. §2000[h]).

An employer may practice discrimination based on sex when there is a good faith *bona fide occupational qualification* (BFOQ). In practice BFOQs usually are not upheld because the employer must have a factual basis that one sex cannot perform the job. If it is upheld, an employee can argue that the BFOQ is really a pretext for sex discrimination. Among the jobs that have *not* been considered BFOQ are vice president of international operations, truck driver, bus driver, male customer tour guide, child development supervisor, and flight attendant.

## PREGNANCY AS A BFOQ

An employer may, however, discriminate against pregnancy if it can be shown that not being pregnant is a bona fide occupational qualification. Furthermore, a pregnant woman may be placed on mandatory leave under BFOQ if her physician and employer reasonably believe she is unable to perform her job because of the pregnancy. For example, a flight attendant in the later part of her pregnancy may be required to take leave because her job entails securing the safety of passengers, and being pregnant in that position may hinder her ability to fulfill her duties.

Under the PDA an employer may not prohibit a pregnant woman from working in an environment that may expose a fetus to hazardous material. These conditions are not considered bona fide occupational qualifications. It is up to the female employee to decide whether or not to work under such conditions because everyone is entitled to equal opportunity in the workplace despite safety concerns.

## MARITAL STATUS DISCRIMINATION

Any type of marital status discrimination is illegal no matter whom it benefits. Typically, marital status discrimination occurs when a married female is treated differently from a married man. However, married men may also be discriminated against. Marital status discrimination is prohibited as sex discrimination under Title VII of the Civil Rights Act of 1964 and enforced by the EEOC. For example, an airline that hires only unmarried female flight attendants and requires those attendants to retire when they marry is violating the law if it hires male flight attendants regardless of their marital status.

## ABORTION

Abortion laws are very controversial and are constantly changing. *Abortion* is the term used for the termination of a pregnancy before the fetus can survive on its own.

The most famous abortion case is *Roe v. Wade* (1973), 410 U.S. 113, in which the Supreme Court held that a woman has the right to have an abortion and that states cannot impose criminal penalties for having or causing an abortion, if it is done before the fetus is viable. There is no real definition for viability; it is determined on an individual basis by the woman's physician. It is unconstitutional for a state to define viability. The Supreme Court also declared that a fetus is not a person and is not entitled to Fourteenth Amendment rights.

Even though the Supreme Court has held that a woman has the right to have an abortion, individual states may place limitations on abortions because a state has an interest in providing safety to the woman and protecting a potential human life. A state may

1. Regulate an abortion once the fetus is viable
2. Require informed consent
3. Require a mandatory twenty-four-hour waiting period
4. Not be required to provide funding for abortions
5. Require a physician to have certain privileges at a hospital
6. Regulate abortion facilities as long as the regulation does not interfere with the right to obtain an abortion

A state must be careful about putting certain restrictions on women. It may not

1. Prohibit abortions within the first trimester
2. Regulate an abortion in the second trimester unless it is to protect the mother's health

3. Place residency requirements on women having abortions
4. Prevent a doctor from performing a legal abortion
5. Require a physician to have certain qualifications (but it may require certain hospital privileges)

## WORKPLACE SECURITY

Random violent acts in the workplace have become a serious concern for employees and employers. Some of the violent acts are perpetrated by disgruntled former employees who want to retaliate against their former bosses for firing them. Other acts of violence result from persons who use the workplace to settle personal or marital disputes.

It is important that every employee know his company's plan for dealing with violent acts in the workplace. An employee who knows or suspects that a former employee is planning a violent attack on a coworker should immediately notify management of his concerns. An employee who has been threatened by a lover or spouse and fears that he may try to harm her at work should also notify her supervisor and any available security staff.

An employer is not required to protect the employee from all unforeseeable risks, but he is required to provide adequate security to ensure that each employee can perform her job without the fear of random violent attack. The employee who makes her employer aware of potentially violent situations can protect both herself and her coworkers.

Any employee who has obtained an injunction or restraining order against someone should make her employer aware of the situation. In granting a restraining order, the court has determined that the person who is protected is in danger. The police department that serves the workplace should have a copy of the restraining order or injunction on file so that it can act quickly if necessary.

In California the Ralph Civil Rights Act (CC §51.7) and the Bane Civil Rights Act (CC §52.1) prohibit acts of violence, threats of violence, or interference with one's constitutional or statutory rights by threats of violence.

## FAMILY LEAVE LAWS

The federal family leave laws are part of the Family and Medical Leave Act (FMLA). On the state level, family rights acts (FRA) address the same general concerns as the federal law and the state pregnancy disability acts.

Pregnancy of female employees is now classified as a disability in most states, and employers are required to provide unpaid leave for pregnant workers. If a pregnant worker has been granted family leave, when she returns she has the right to a similar position, same benefits, salary, and other work conditions as she was entitled to before (U.S.C.A. §2614).

The federal and the state laws mandate that employers provide pregnant employees twelve weeks of leave in a twelve-month period. The federal program allows the leave for a serious health condition of the worker or for care of a parent, spouse, or child who is ill or for the birth or care of a newly adopted or foster care child. States follow the federal guidelines and state pregnancy disability provisions, which allow up to an additional four months of unpaid leave for disability related to pregnancy, childbirth, or associated medical problems. While the federal rules apply only to the employers of fifty or more employees, the more restrictive state pregnancy disability rules can require any employer with as few as five full-time or part-time employees to comply with the law. Under the federal FMLA the employer must provide the same benefits during the leave period as if the employee were working. However, the employer is not usually required to provide health benefit coverage during the four months of pregnancy disability if that is taken in addition to the twelve weeks of leave under FMLA or FRA.

## PREGNANCY DISCRIMINATION

Under the Pregnancy Discrimination Law, all employees should be treated equally. The law forbids discrimination based on sex or gender. "This includes discrimination based on pregnancy, labor or related medical conditions; women affected by such pregnancies, labors or related medical conditions should be treated equally in all that relates to employment, including the receipt of benefits under the programs of supplementary benefits. This does not include romance or sexual attraction among employees and employers (*Cairo v. O.H.* [1989] 7100 F. Supp. 1069). A violation of this section occurs when there is discrimination between pregnant and nonpregnant women. An employer cannot deny employment or lay off a worker for being pregnant. The employer cannot establish arbitrary rules that require women to leave their work or take time off. A pregnant worker has the right to work during her pregnancy. A pregnant worker does not have to take leave of absence for maternity and is entitled to her job after giving birth. Even though it is not mentioned explicitly in Title VII of the PDA, employers must give a pregnant woman time off for pregnancy and other family-related situations as long as she is treated equally in relation to other employees. Employers are forbidden to determine a specified amount of time for rests for pregnancy if other disabilities are not similarly restricted. A woman is entitled to the same job when she returns to work. Employees are not obligated to offer male employees the same free time. Employers must provide wives of male employees the same medical benefits for pregnancy-related conditions they offer female employees.

Under most state pregnancy disability laws, an employer with five or more employees must allow an employee to take up to four months' leave for pregnancy- and childbirth-related needs. If the employer allows more than four months' leave for other types of disability, he must allow the same amount for pregnancy disability. The four-month pregnancy leave does not have to be taken all at once.

When a woman returns to work after a pregnancy-related disability leave, she is entitled to the job she had before she began the leave. If the job she previously held is not available because of a business necessity, she must be offered a job similar to her previous position in terms of pay, location, content, and promotional opportunities.

If the employer hires a temporary replacement for the pregnancy-disabled employee, he must permit the employee to return to her previous position even if he thinks the temporary employee is more competent.

An employer with fifteen or more employees is required to provide health insurance coverage for pregnancy on the same terms as it is provided for other conditions.

A woman can request the use of her accumulated vacation and sick leave during the disability period, but the employer cannot force her to do so. If she so requests, the employer must allow the disabled employee to use the leave permitted by law for pregnancy disability and to reserve her accrued sick and vacation leave for future use.

The employee is required to give the employer reasonable notice of her intention to take pregnancy disability leave, but the law allows her to modify her plans on the basis of her changing medical condition.

## WORKERS' COMPENSATION

Workers' compensation benefits are available to most people who have work-related injuries. All the states have workers' compensation laws, which regulate the types, amounts, and duration of benefits as well as the requirements, conditions, and limitations that determine eligibility and other related matters.

While state laws often vary with respect to minor aspects of a workers' compensation program, the basic concept and overall methods of providing benefits are similar. Essentially, workers' compensation is a no-fault system that provides medical and financial benefits to qualified injured workers regardless of who caused the work injuries. The benefit to the worker is that he does not have to prove that the accident or injury was caused by his employer or that he did not cause or contribute to the accident. Unfortunately, injured workers cannot receive compensation for pain and suffering (general damages), which is often the largest part of a compensation award for injuries.

## COVERAGE

In most states all "employees" are covered by workers' compensation with a few exceptions, such as domestic or agricultural workers. Partners or owners of a company are usually not covered since they are not considered employees in most states. Workers who are independent contractors by definition are also not employees and therefore are not entitled to workers' compensation benefits. Whether a person is an employee or an independent contractor can be a very significant and controversial issue since thousands and even hundreds of thousands of dollars in benefits can be at stake.

The greater the amount of control exercised over the worker, the greater the probability that the worker will be considered an employee. Facts that tend to indicate that the worker is an independent contractor are that he has his own tools, that he is already trained and able to perform the services with little or no supervision, and that he is paid by the job rather than by the hour. If the worker is providing services that help the employer perform the usual tasks of the business, the worker will usually be considered an employee. Contracts that state that the worker is an independent contractor have little or no effect, and the determination will always depend on the circumstances of the relationship as stated above. In most states volunteers are not covered unless they received some form of payment such as meals or gas money.

## INJURIES

Under the early workers' compensation laws, only injuries that resulted from accidents were covered. Over the years the laws have changed to include other types of injuries and even certain occupational illnesses.

The most commonly covered injury is the ***specific injury,*** which can be identified at a particular time and place. For example, you slip and fall at work while moving some boxes and break your leg. The covered injury can also result from an automobile accident while you are driving or riding as a passenger as part of your job.

***Continuing trauma*** injuries are those that result over time and involve a particular part of the body. A bricklayer can develop a back injury after years of lifting heavy loads, or a cashier can develop an injury to his wrist after years of moving groceries and operating a cash register.

In today's fast-paced work sites workers can develop high levels of stress that can cause heart attacks or emotional and even psychological damage. Some states include these as covered workers' compensation injuries although strict procedures are used to determine if they resulted from employment or from life in general.

More recently most states have accepted certain occupational illnesses as qualified work-related injuries. This could include a doctor or dentist who is infected with the HIV virus while treating a patient and a janitor who develops a skin disease from contact with cleaning chemicals.

## COURSE AND SCOPE OF EMPLOYMENT

The accident, injury, or illness must arise out of and occur within the course and scope of employment. If a worker is attacked and harmed at work by an angry lover, his injury will not usually be considered work-related since being at work was not its cause. But even an off-duty hotel manager who tries to break up a fight at the hotel, in most states, will be considered harmed in the course of employment. This results from the fact that if he had not worked there, he would probably not have gotten involved. Workers involved and injured in horseplay are usually considered not in the course of employment, but a few states have included it as a reality of human conduct.

Injuries that occur while a worker is traveling to and from work are usually not regarded as occurring in the course of employment. The result may be different when the employee has no fixed place to work or when he is promoting the business of his employer. Many states disqualify workers who are injured as a result of their own willful misconduct. Workers who willfully disobey safety rules or were intoxicated at the time of the injury are usually disqualified as well, as are workers who commit suicide.

Many states have separate systems for compensating injured workers who work for the state and local governments, and the federal government has its own system for its employees.

Employers who are aware of unsafe working conditions and fail to correct them can be fined if an injury occurs. For example, in California employers are required to pay an additional amount equal to 50 percent of the workers' compensation benefits.

Workers' compensation laws also make it illegal for an employer to retaliate against an employee for filing a workers' compensation claim. An employer who retaliates by firing an employee can be forced to reinstate the employee and pay him back pay and lost benefits, plus pay penalties up to ten thousand dollars.

The benefits paid to injured workers are usually provided by workers' compensation insurance, which is paid for by the employer. There are substantial penalties and fines imposed on employers who fail to provide the insurance since it is mandatory. To protect injured workers, a state fund exists for the payment of benefits to workers whose employers are not insured. There are usually no waiting periods before an injured worker can qualify to receive benefits although the first benefit check may take longer to process and deliver to the worker than subsequent checks.

## BENEFITS PROVIDED

### MEDICAL EXPENSES

Workers' compensation insurance will pay all medical expenses that are necessary and proper for services provided to an injured worker. This includes the cost of ambulance, hospital, laboratory tests, X rays, nursing care, specialized physicians and assistants, appliances, and any other related products, items, materials, and services.

The choice of a primary physician is a major issue for the injured worker, who wants a doctor who will act solely in his interest without the risk that necessary treatment will be withheld in order to save money. The insurance company, on the other hand, wants to choose the doctor in order to ensure that medical services are held to an absolute minimum. Some states allow the employee to choose his own doctor, and a few even allow him to get a second opinion. Other states require the worker to go to the employer's doctor at least for a specified period, usually thirty days, before he goes to a doctor of his own choosing. Still other states allow the worker to choose from a list of "approved" doctors. Medical treatment must be provided for as long as it is required, even for life, if necessary. Workers are reimbursed for transportation expenses while traveling to medical providers; usually this is in the form of reimbursement on a per mile basis. Injured workers must be sure to keep logs and to write down each mile they travel to receive medical services.

### TEMPORARY DISABILITY PAYMENTS

While an injured worker is certified by a doctor as unable to work as the result of a work-related injury, he is entitled to receive temporary disability payments. The amount varies from state to state but usually is paid at between 60 and 80 percent of the worker's gross weekly salary up to the legal maximum. These payments continue until the worker is able to return to work or his condition has stabilized permanently.

## Permanent Disability Payments

If the injury results in any permanent disability, the worker can receive a permanent disability benefit payment. The amount of this benefit is set by law and is paid after the worker has been found to be in a permanently stable condition or after he has completed a vocational rehabilitation program. The extent of the disability is rated, and each percentage point of disability increases the value of the benefit. Employers are required to provide modified work duties or to assist in finding the worker a different job if the injury makes it impossible to do his present job. The worker must request these benefits in order to receive them.

## Death Benefits

Death benefits are paid to the dependents of someone who dies as a result of work-related injuries. The amount paid is usually limited to the amount that the injured person would have received if he had lived and been totally and permanently disabled. Dependents, in most states, must be relatives and have been dependent on the deceased worker at the time of death.

Many states terminate the death benefits' monthly payment to a surviving spouse who remarries. This can sometimes be avoided in states that allow payment of a lump sum for death benefits. Usually people who live together while not married do not quality for death benefits; however, a few states do allow payment if the parties lived together for a specified period (one or two years), were living together at the time of death, and had a child together. Workers' compensation benefits also include payment of burial expenses.

## Dispute Resolution

If the injured worker and the workers' compensation insurance company cannot agree on any one or more of the important issues, the worker can insist on a trial conducted by a workers' compensation board or industrial relations board. Trials in these cases are very informal. There is no jury, and evidence is presented without regard to the formal rules of evidence used in court. Cases are processed and decided in administrative hearings by commissioners who are not judges. While injured workers are not required to have attorneys represent them, it is almost always a good idea since the insurance company certainly will. It is very common to find that the insurance company attempts to reduce or deny benefits to an injured worker by alleging that he was not an employee at the time of the injury, that he was not injured, that the medical treatment was not necessary or was excessive. It also routinely alleges that the injury occurred while the employee was not in the course of employment or that the injury was the result of improper willful misconduct. Insurance companies can, and all too often do, require injured workers to submit to one or more *independent medical examinations*. These IMEs are actually conducted by doctors selected and paid by the insurance companies. An assertive worker's attorney can often limit the number of these exams and help ensure that the reports made are fair and accurate.

Attorneys can also help workers prove when allegations are not true. Attorneys are paid contingency (conditional) fees, meaning that they get paid only if they are successful in obtaining benefits for the workers. Fees are approved by the hearing officer and are based on the amount and quality of the attorney's services, and often the result is also considered. Attorney's fees usually range from 10 to 15 percent of the amount awarded to the worker for permanent disability. Attorneys can also help force insurance companies to make decisions regarding eligibility and payment of benefits more quickly.

One of the frequent complaints of injured workers is that insurance companies take too long to make decisions and to pay benefits. Without an attorney to hold them accountable and to take them before the board if necessary, insurance companies often ignore workers. In many states attorneys can request the hearing officer to set a special *expedited hearing* to expose unfair delays by insurance companies and to obtain an order for prompt payment of benefits to the injured workers.

A worker should always notify a supervisor immediately after being injured or suffering a job-related illness. The laws of all the states require prompt notice to the employer (usually within ten to thirty days). Also, all states have established statutes of limitations for the filing of a formal application for benefits with the appropriate agency, usually the workers compensation board or industrial relations board.

## THIRD-PARTY CLAIMS

If a worker is injured by someone who is not his employer or a coworker, he may also have a claim for damages based on negligence law. This can happen when the injured worker was driving on the job and is involved in an accident. Negligence claims are also available when the worker is injured by a defective machine or product or by the negligent act of a person working for a different employer such as a different contractor at a construction site.

Third-party claims can be very beneficial to an injured worker since they can result in very large sums of money that are not available under workers' compensation laws. For example, a third-party claim enables the claimant to receive money for *pain and suffering* that can sometimes be in the millions of dollars. Both the claimant and his or her spouse can also each receive substantial amounts for *loss of consortium,* meaning the loss of the enjoyment of their marital relationship and services because of the injury.

Future medical expenses are available both in a workers' compensation claim and in third-party cases, but in third-party cases claimants can receive very significant amounts for the loss of future earnings. Also, in third-party cases, claimants can receive payment for loss of earnings during periods of disability resulting from the accident. In third-party cases the claimant should always note that there is a separate statute of limitations for the claim, and if the negligent party is a government entity such as a school district, transit district, or police department, the time limit to file a claim can be very short (as short as one hundred days or even less). In some cases, if an injured worker receives a large third-party settlement, he must reimburse the workers' compensation insurance company for money it has paid. Very often the reimbursed amount can be reduced substantially in the worker's favor.

An injured worker in the United States may be able to receive many different types of benefits, but the system can be confusing and bureaucratic. Extreme delays and insufficient payment of benefits are often the norm, and employers, insurance companies, and even those that provide medical services often act in ways that are adverse to the worker. Injured workers should always seek the assistance of attorneys who are highly specialized in the area of workers' compensation law.

# 11

# Landlord–Tenant Law

Several different bodies of law define the rights and responsibilities of tenants and property owners. State housing law, real estate law, contract law, state tort law, state and local building code requirements, state health and safety codes, local zoning regulations, and, in some cases, local code enforcement regulations have an impact on the legal relationships between landlords and tenants.

In the United States today there is a lack of affordable housing especially in urban areas. Because of the high cost of buying a home, most low- and moderate-income families are renters. To protect the renter and to encourage rental property owners to invest in apartments, the states have developed a system of laws that define the rights and responsibilities of both landlords and the tenants, based on the belief that every U.S. resident should be able to live in a decent, sanitary, and safe home.

## RENTING AND LEASING

Both a rental agreement and a lease are contractual agreements in which the landlord (or lessor) agrees to give the renter (or tenant or lessee) exclusive rights to possess a house or an apartment unit and the renter (or lessee) agrees to pay rent and to abide by other requirements of the contract.

A lease is a contract for a fixed period of time—for example, one or five years—and it automatically terminates on a predetermined date. A lease is advantageous to a tenant because it may establish a monthly rent amount and stipulate that the rent cannot be increased during the lease term. Another advantage is that the landlord cannot terminate the agreement unless the tenant has violated a provision of the contract. A disadvantage to the tenant is that he may be legally obligated to pay for the entire term of the lease even if he moves from the unit before the lease expires. If the lease is for one year or more, it must be in writing to satisfy the requirements of the Statute of Frauds.

The primary difference between a rental agreement and a lease is that a rental agreement is usually a month-to-month tenancy, although it may also be a week-to-week tenancy or a tenancy for any other specified period of time. Under a rental agreement, rent is paid for a period of time (one month or one week) in advance, and either the landlord or the tenant may terminate the agreement by giving the other party thirty days' advance written notice, as long as the reasons for terminating the agreement do not violate the law. A rental agreement should be in writing and should be signed and dated by the tenant or tenants and the landlord or landlords. However, an oral agreement may be enforced by the court if the terms of the agreement can be adequately proved by other means.

## RENTAL DOCUMENTS

The local board of realtors or apartment owners association has forms that are written to comply with state and local laws and that may be completed and signed by the tenant and the landlord. Printed rental and lease forms are also available at stationery stores. Usually, however, the landlord supplies a form for the tenant's signature. Lease and rental forms are not standard and may vary substantially. It is therefore very important that a prospective tenant read the entire agreement carefully and know what he is agreeing to before he signs the document.

While some clauses in an agreement may be void because they are illegal, the other provisions will be binding. Violation of those provisions could result in the tenant and his family's being evicted from their home and ordered by the court to pay additional money to the landlord in the form of damages.

Some of the restrictions that are common in a rental or lease agreement include a prohibition against having a pet on the premises, a restriction against subletting the unit, a limitation on the number of persons who may live in the unit, and a mandate that all occupants abide by the common area rules.

## MAINTENANCE RESPONSIBILITIES OF THE LANDLORD

California law provides an excellent example of the way most states regulate landlords. In California the landlord cannot rent a house or apartment unit that does not meet the following standards:

1. The exterior of the unit must provide adequate protection from the weather and water, and there must be no broken windows or doors.
2. The plumbing and electrical systems must be in good working order and must include a kitchen sink, a toilet, a shower or bathtub, and electrical lighting.
3. There must be hot and cold running water, and the plumbing must be connected to an approved sewage disposal system.
4. There must be an adequate heating system.
5. Garbage receptacles must be provided by the landlord and maintained in good condition.
6. Floors, stairways, and railings must be in good repair.
7. The common areas must be kept clean and free from rodent and vermin infestation.

The primary purpose of the law is to ensure that the dwelling unit is safe enough to prevent endangering the health, property, safety, or welfare of the occupants or the public. An older building does not have to meet the most current building code requirement as long as the components that were approved at the time of construction have been maintained in good order.

Structural hazards such as buckling floors, leaking roofs, sagging ceilings or walls, a listing or bulging fireplace, deteriorated or crumbling or loose plaster, the accumulation of exterior weeds and debris that may create a health or fire hazard, junk stored on the premises, and stagnant water and dampness in habitable rooms are conditions that are considered unsafe and must be corrected and maintained by the property owner.

The owner is not required to provide the tenant with an aesthetically pleasing unit. He does not have to ensure that the unit is freshly painted or that it has new carpeting, but he must ensure that the unit is clean and safe when the tenant moves in.

## BREACH OF IMPLIED WARRANTY OF HABITABILITY

There is a common-law implied *warranty of habitability*. This means that the landlord promises that premises leased for living quarters will be maintained in a habitable state for the duration of the lease. Any clause in the lease or rental agreement by which the renter agrees to waive the responsibility of the landlord is void if the purpose of the waiver is to require the tenant to live in an uninhabitable unit. However, the landlord and tenant may agree that the tenant will improve, repair, or maintain all or part of the dwelling as part of the consideration for rental.

In some states the law allows the tenant and landlord to agree that the tenant will accept certain features of a substandard housing unit, but the exact items for which the landlord will not be held accountable must be specifically stated in a written contract.

The landlord is considered to have breached the warranty whenever he has been notified, by personal observation or letter or phone call, that there are uninhabitable conditions in the unit that are not caused by the tenants themselves. The fact that the tenant continues to live in the uninhabitable premises after learning of the defects does not relieve the landlord of his responsibility to correct the defects.

If the landlord breaches the warranty of habitability and then seeks to evict the tenant who has not paid his rent as agreed to under a lease or rental agreement, the tenant has a legal basis for stopping the eviction if he can prove to the court that the landlord has violated the law. This tenant right is based on the fact that the tenant's duty to pay rent is dependent on the landlord's complying with the implied warranty of habitability. If the tenant can prove that the landlord breached the warranty, the tenant may show that the nonpayment of rent was justified and that no additional rent is due and owing to the landlord. Under such circumstances, the landlord cannot evict the tenant because the landlord is not entitled to possession of the premises.

To ensure that the tenant has complied with the law, he must follow this procedure:

1. The tenant must notify the landlord of the defects.
2. If the landlord fails to remedy the defects within a reasonable time, the tenant may stop paying rent.
3. The landlord must then serve the tenant with a Three-Day Notice to pay the rent or quit the premises.
4. When the tenant remains in the unit, the landlord may sue to evict the tenant for nonpayment of the withheld rent.
5. The tenant can then serve and file an answer in which the facts constituting the breach of the implied warranty are alleged.

The issue of breach of the implied warranty of habitability may also be raised by the tenant in an independent action against the landlord for rent abatement or damages.

## TENANT RESPONSIBILITIES

The tenant is under a duty to keep his part of the premises as clean and sanitary as is reasonably possible. All trash and rubbish must be disposed of in a clean and sanitary manner, and the tenant must use and operate all electrical, gas, and plumbing fixtures properly and keep them as clean and sanitary as their condition permits. The tenant is also responsible for ensuring that neither he or any guest or family member destroys, defaces, or in any way damages any part of the unit or any appliance or other equipment in the unit. Furthermore, the law states that the tenant must use the various areas of the unit only for the purposes for which they were designed. The living room cannot be made into an extra permanent bedroom, and cooking must be done only in the kitchen.

The tenant is responsible for repairing any damage other than normal everyday wear and tear on the unit. Doors, walls, windows, screens, and appliances that are damaged through the abuse or neglect of the tenant, his family, or guests must be repaired at the tenant's expense. If the tenant fails to maintain the unit, the landlord may seek the court's assistance in evicting the tenant and may seek monetary damages to repair the damage done by the tenant. Furthermore, the tenant will not be allowed to bring an action against the landlord for failing to maintain the unit if the tenant has failed to keep the unit clean, sanitary, and undamaged. If the tenant vacates the unit, the landlord may be able to retain all or part of the tenant's security deposit to pay for repairs (see "Security Deposits" below).

The lease or rental agreement may contain other specific requirements that the tenant must comply with. It may limit the number of persons who may live in the unit and may restrict the tenant from keeping any pet while living in the unit.

## SUBLETTING

A common restriction in a rental agreement is one that prohibits subletting. This means that the tenant who signs the contract with the landlord cannot move out and let someone else move in and "take over" paying the rent without the landlord's approving the change. It also means that the original tenant cannot let someone else move in to share the rent if the other party is not on the original lease or does not have the permission of the landlord. A tenant who has signed a rental agreement that prohibits subletting will have violated the contract if he does any of the prohibited acts, and the landlord may be able to proceed to evict him for breach of the contract.

## SECURITY DEPOSITS

At the time a tenant and landlord agree to a rental or lease contract, the landlord often requires that the tenant pay a *security deposit.* This is money that is kept by the landlord while the tenant occupies the unit, and it may be used by the landlord to pay for any extraordinary damage the tenant may do, to compensate the landlord for any unpaid rent at the time the tenant vacates, to clean the unit upon termination of the tenancy, and to repair or replace personal property or furnishings that were damaged beyond ordinary wear and tear. A landlord may not keep any part of a security deposit as compensation for ordinary wear and tear.

Within a specific period (usually three weeks) after a tenant has vacated the unit, the landlord is required by law to provide the tenant with an itemized statement indicating the amount and reason for his not returning any part of the security deposit. Any funds due the tenant must be returned with the itemized statement within the specified period. The landlord is required to mail the statement and security deposit to the tenant or to deliver it in person.

If a landlord fails to return to the tenant the security deposit or any part of it as required by law, the tenant may file a small claims action and may obtain a judgment from the court for actual damages plus, in some states, damages for bad faith retention of the security deposit. In most states no lease or rental agreement may contain any provision for a nonrefundable deposit.

In California there are strict restrictions on security deposits. The amount charged by the landlord for a security deposit cannot exceed two months' rent for an unfurnished unit and three months' rent for a furnished unit.

## BENEFICIAL ENJOYMENT AND CONSTRUCTIVE EVICTION

When a tenant rents a dwelling unit, he is said to be given the right to *beneficial enjoyment* of the unit. This includes being able to live in a unit that is in good repair but also includes being able to live in the unit free of harassment by the landlord. If the landlord violates the law, he deprives the tenant of his beneficial enjoyment. This situation leads to what is termed a *constructive eviction*. For instance, if the tenant notifies the landlord that the heater is not operating properly and the landlord fails to have the heating unit repaired promptly, the tenant may consider the failure to act a constructive eviction. In such a case the tenant may vacate the unit and file a suit against the landlord for return of any rent he paid from the date that the landlord failed to repair the heater. Often such a claim is filed in small claims court.

However, if the tenant fails to notify the landlord of the problem and does not vacate the unit after a reasonable period of time, he may be deemed to have waived his right to claim a constructive eviction and will not be entitled the return of rent.

## GAS AND ELECTRIC SERVICE METERING

If the tenant is required to pay the gas or electric company directly for those utilities, the landlord is required by law to notify him if the meter serves any other unit or area. For instance, if the electric lights in the hallway of an apartment building are metered through a tenant's electric meter, he would have to be informed of that situation before he agrees to rent the unit.

## LANDLORD'S LIABILITY FOR NEGLIGENCE

A landlord is liable for any injury caused by his failure to exercise ordinary care or skill in the management of the property.

## VOID LEASE PROVISIONS

Certain lease provisions are void as a matter of law. They include any provision of a residential lease or rental agreement by which the renter agrees to modify or waive any of the following rights:

1. The rights or remedies that govern the security deposit paid by the tenant or that require that the landlord give him adequate notice prior to entering the rental
2. The right to assert a cause of action against the lessor that may arise in the future
3. The right to a notice or hearing required by law
4. The procedural rights in litigation in any action involving his rights and obligations as a tenant
5. The right to have the landlord exercise a duty of care to prevent personal injury and personal property damage

## WHEN THE LANDLORD MAY ENTER THE DWELLING UNIT

Typically a landlord may enter the dwelling unit only in the following cases:

1. In an emergency
2. To make necessary or agreed upon repairs, decorations, alterations, or improvements; supply necessary or agreed upon services; or exhibit the dwelling unit to prospective or actual purchasers, mortgagees, tenants, workers, or contractors
3. When the tenant has moved out of the premises
4. When authorized by a court order

Except in cases of emergency the landlord may not enter the unit except during normal business hours unless the tenant agrees to another arrangement.

*Twenty-four hours' advance notice is considered reasonable notice.*

It is against the law for the landlord to harass the tenant by entering his unit without authorization.

## TENANT'S RIGHT TO REPAIR OR VACATE

Most states have laws very similar to California's with respect to repairs. When the landlord fails to make repairs, the tenant may make the repairs himself if the cost does not exceed one month's rent. He may then deduct the cost of the repairs from the next month's rent. Before the tenant may take this action, he must notify the landlord of the needed repairs and give him a reasonable time to make them. Thirty days is considered a reasonable time, but less time may be appropriate if the circumstances dictate. For instance, if the heater does not work and it is very cold, the landlord's failure to make the repair promptly would permit the tenant to make the repair to protect his health and safety. The repairs must be of the kind that are the landlord's responsibility and not caused by the tenant. The tenant can do this only twice in any twelve-month period.

If the tenant wishes, he may vacate the unit, and the court will discharge him from any further obligations to pay rent or perform other obligations of the agreement.

## RETALIATORY EVICTION

If the tenant files a complaint against the landlord for failing to maintain the unit in tenantable condition, the landlord may not retaliate by seeking to evict the tenant, raise his rent, or decrease any services. If the landlord takes steps to evict the tenant, raise his rent, or withhold services within 180 days of the action by the tenant, the landlord will be liable for damages, including actual damages to the tenant such as the cost of moving or paying for substitute services and punitive damages plus reasonable attorney's fees.

In a court action for retaliatory eviction the tenant must prove that he did not owe any back rent at the time the landlord took action. Any waiver by a tenant of his rights in this regard shall be void.

## RIGHT TO TERMINATE ON THIRTY DAYS' NOTICE

A periodic rental agreement (usually month to month or week to week) is considered renewed at the end of the term unless one of the parties gives written notice to the other of his intention to terminate the agreement. The written notice must be given at least as long before the expiration as the term of the rental itself but no more than thirty days. A month-to-month agreement may be terminated by either of the parties by giving at least thirty days' written notice at any time, and the rent shall be due and payable to and including the date of termination.

The notice must be in writing and may be sent by certified or registered mail addressed to the other party. The tenant may also give such notice by sending a copy by certified or registered mail addressed to the agent of the landlord to whom the tenant has paid the rent for the month before the date of such notice or by delivering a copy to the agent personally.

## NOTICE REQUIRED FOR LANDLORD TO EXERCISE RIGHT OF REENTRY

Whenever the right of reentry is given to a landlord in any lease or otherwise, the reentry may be made at any time after he gives advance notice as required by state law. Moreover, an action for the possession of real property (for example, an action for eviction) may be carried out without giving a notice of reentry.

## TERMINATION OF UTILITY SERVICE AND OTHER WILLFUL ACTS

A landlord is prohibited from interrupting the utility service of any tenant with the intent of causing termination of the tenancy. This requirement applies to utilities provided by the landlord as well as those billed directly to the tenant by the utility provider.

It is unlawful for the landlord to prevent a tenant from gaining access to his house or apartment by changing the locks or making them inoperable. It is also unlawful for him to remove the doors or windows or remove any of the tenant's personal property from the dwelling unit without the prior *written* consent of the tenant or without a court order.

Any landlord who violates this provision is liable to the tenant for the actual damages suffered by the tenant such as the cost of staying in a motel for the time during which the breach occurred, plus a minimum penalty of $250 or up to $100 per day in some states. The tenant may also seek an injunction in a municipal or superior court against a landlord who has violated these provisions. The tenant may also file an action in small claims court to recover monetary damages but cannot seek an injunction in small claims court.

## LANDLORD'S LIABILITY TO THIRD PARTIES

The landlord owes a duty of care to his tenants and to visitors or social guests.

## UNLAWFUL DETAINER: THE EVICTION PROCESS

Eviction, or *unlawful detainer,* is the process of permanently removing a tenant from rented or leased premises and may be initiated by the landlord for failure to pay rent or for a violation of a lease or rental provision. While an eviction is often the result of a breach of contract on the part of the tenant, that is not always the case.

The eviction process requires both parties to follow certain explicit rules. If a person has been served with papers that begin an eviction process, it is very important that he not ignore them. There are legal ways for a tenant to protect his interests, but the time periods for filing a response or answer to an eviction are short. Failure to file within the prescribed period of time will result in the landlord's obtaining a default judgment and the marshal's ultimately being authorized to remove the tenant and his belongings physically from the unit.

The typical steps in an unlawful detainer action (eviction) in most states follow a definite process.

1. The landlord serves the tenant with a *three-day notice to pay (or perform) or quit.* "Perform" means the tenant must comply with nonpayment terms of the rental agreement.
2. If the tenant pays his rent as demanded, his status is restored, and no other action is taken.
3. If the tenant does not pay, the landlord files a *complaint for unlawful detainer* with the court. This action may be filed in the municipal or similar court that serves the area of the property in question.
4. After the complaint for unlawful detainer has been filed with the court, a copy of the complaint and a *summons* demanding that the tenant appear at a hearing must be served. The service is best made by a sheriff, marshal, or registered process server.
5. If the process server is unable to serve the tenant personally, most states provide that the server may leave a copy of the summons and the complaint with a person of suitable age at the place where the tenant lives, affix a copy of the complaint and summons conspicuously to the building or entry area, and mail a copy to the tenant at the address of the property, by registered mail.
6. The process server must file a *proof of service* with the court, stating that

the summons and complaint were properly served as well as the date, time, and details of service.

7. The tenant usually has five days, including Saturdays and Sundays but excluding court holidays, to file an answer with the court. If the tenant can show a good reason for needing additional time to file an answer, the court may allow additional time. The answer filed by the tenant may be in the form of a defense such as a statement that he paid his rent but that the landlord lost the check. Or it may be an affirmative defense. An *affirmative defense* would be the statement that the tenant should not be obligated to pay his rent because the landlord has failed to maintain the unit in habitable condition. Other defenses that the tenant may assert are that the landlord failed to serve a proper three-day notice to pay or quit or that the service was improper.

8. If the tenant files an *answer,* the court will set a date for a hearing.

9. If the tenant fails to file an answer or fails to attend the hearing scheduled after an answer has been filed, the landlord will ask the court to find in his favor and to enter a *default judgment.* The judge or clerk will immediately enter a judgment for restitution of the premises and issue a *writ of execution.* The landlord will also ask the court to issue a monetary judgment against the tenant, requiring him to pay any rent that is due, pay for any damages that he has caused, and pay for the attorney fees and court costs that the landlord incurred in bringing the unlawful detainer action.

10. The clerk of the court will then mail the decision of the court to the landlord and to the tenant at the property address. If the tenant fails to vacate the premises voluntarily after he has been notified of the writ of execution and judgment, the landlord may contact the marshal to remove the tenant and his belongings physically from the rental unit.

11. Even after the tenant has been removed from the premises, the landlord may pursue collection of the monetary judgment issued by the court.

If a tenant who has a month-to-month rental agreement has not violated conditions of his rental agreement and has paid his rent as stipulated, the landlord may begin the eviction by delivering to the tenant, by certified or registered mail, a thirty-day notice to quit. Since the tenant is not being given a chance to cure a default, such as paying overdue rent, the landlord is not required to give the tenant a three-day notice in this case.

In certain circumstances, the law affords special protection to the families of military personnel. Under the Soldiers' and Sailors' Civil Relief Act (50 USC App. §510 et seq.), active military personnel and their families may be given additional time to pay delinquent rent. In such cases the federal Military and Veterans Code §399.5 supersedes state law and must be followed by the court.

Unlawful detainer is a serious matter, and it is important that anyone who is served with a complaint for unlawful detainer and summons respond. There may be legal ways to stop an eviction of the tenant, but failure to respond to the complaint and summons usually results in the tenant's being evicted and having a judgment issued against him, one that may affect his credit record for ten or more years.

# 12

# Family Law
## Marriage, Divorce, Child Custody, Domestic Violence, Adoption, and Parental Responsibility

The Tenth Amendment to the U.S. Constitution allows each state to make its own laws regarding marriage, divorce, child custody, and other matters related to family relationships. The full faith and credit clause of the Constitution requires each state to recognize and honor the laws, judgments, and decrees of the other states. A man and woman who are legally married in New York are considered legally married in each of the other states, and an adoption granted by one state will be recognized by the other states.

The nature, extent, and continued validity of this principle have been tested by the state of Hawaii, which has become the first state to allow homosexuals to marry. As a result, the federal government may take steps to enable individual states to avoid giving full faith and credit (recognition) to Hawaiian homosexual marriages. If this is upheld by the Supreme Court, it will be a drastic change in the application of the requirement that the states respect the laws and judgment of the other states.

However, there are also federal laws that are designed to protect children who may be involved in child custody disagreements and to help custodial parents who are owed family support by absent parents. Prior to the enactment of federal laws mandating cooperation among the states in enforcing divorce, child custody, and family support decrees, one party to an action would often move to a state where the judgment of the court would not be enforced. Today each state must enforce the court orders of every other state regarding child custody and support.

## The Family Law Attorney

Family law can be complicated and usually involves the preparation of complex legal documents. To ensure that a family law matter is handled properly, the parties should discuss their situations with an attorney who specializes in family law.

## Marriage

### Legal Definition of Marriage

Each state establishes its own laws governing marriage, divorce, spousal and child support, child custody, and other matters of family law. Most states define *marriage* as "a personal relation arising out of a civil contract between a man and a woman, to which the consent of the parties is necessary." However, consent alone does not constitute marriage; it must be followed by the issuance of a license and solemnization as authorized by law.

### Minimum Age to Marry

Each state determines the minimum age of consent to marry for a male or female. A male or female under that age may marry if the written consent of one or both parents or legal guardians is filed with the clerk of the court issuing the marriage license.

If an underage minor has no parent capable of consenting, the superior court may grant permission for that minor to marry by ordering a consent for issuance of a marriage license.

In most states the court reserves the right to order premarital counseling concerning social, economic, and personal responsibilities prior to granting a marriage license. (Please see multistate chart for legal age to marry on page 141.)

### Foreign and Out-of-State Marriages

Certain minimum standard requirements must be met in order for a foreign marriage to be upheld. U.S. residents considering a quickie marriages in foreign countries should be aware that their marriages may not be valid in the United States. For example, for a Mexican marriage to be valid for U.S. citizens, the couple must have married in full compliance with Mexican law.

## Premarital Agreements

A premarital agreement is a contract between prospective spouses made in contemplation of marriage. It becomes effective when the marriage takes place.

Premarital agreements are governed by law under the Uniform Premarital Agreement Act. A premarital agreement that complies with the UPAA is legally binding and legally defines the property rights of a husband and wife.

A premarital agreement may be recorded with the county recorder in the county in which it is executed, but failure to record the document does not make it invalid.

A minor may make a valid premarital agreement if he or she is emancipated or is legally able to marry. Parental consent and the consent of the superior court are conditions that would permit a minor to execute a legally binding premarital agreement.

Premarital agreements executed before January 1, 1986, may be subject to different rules. Anyone who has questions about such an agreement should consult with a family law specialist.

A premarital agreement must be in writing and signed by both parties. No consideration is required for a valid premarital agreement (please see the chapter "Contracts," page 51, for a discussion of consideration).

A premarital agreement may define the authority of a party to sell, lease, or encumber property; other personal rights and obligations; how the separate and community properties of the parties will be held during the marriage; and how the property will be disposed of in the event of a divorce or death of one of the parties. A premarital agreement may *not* waive any legal rights to the support of any minor children of the marriage, however.

After a marriage has taken place, the premarital agreement may be modified or revoked if both parties agree to such changes in writing.

## Requirements for a Valid Premarital Agreement

To be valid, the parties to a premarital agreement must have executed the agreement voluntarily. A premarital agreement that the court determines is unconscionable because one party did not adequately disclose his or her property or financial obligations to the other party before the agreement was executed will not be enforceable.

## Premarital Agreements and Annulment

When a nullity declaring a marriage to be void is issued by the court, a premarital agreement will be enforced only to the extent that the court determines is necessary for fairness.

## DIVORCE, ANNULMENT, AND LEGAL SEPARATION

### DISSOLUTION OR DIVORCE

The legal term for *divorce* is *dissolution.* Dissolution is a matter for the superior court in most states. When a judgment of dissolution of marriage becomes final, it restores the parties to the state of unmarried persons.

The court has the authority to decide the status of the marriage, the custody of any minor children to the marriage, the division of property, support of the children and spouses, and payment of legal costs and attorney's fees.

### GROUNDS FOR DISSOLUTION OR LEGAL SEPARATION

A divorce or legal separation may be based on irreconcilable differences or on the incurable insanity of one of the parties. *Irreconcilable differences* are defined as reasons that have caused such an irremediable breakdown of the marriage that the marriage should not be continued.

A petition for divorce based on *incurable insanity* requires that a competent doctor testify that the insane party was insane at the time the petition was filed and that the insanity is not curable. The court may require the sane party to support the insane party.

### RESIDENCE REQUIREMENTS FOR FILING A DIVORCE

The law requires that one of the parties must have been a resident of the state for a prescribed period of time (usually six months) and a resident of the county in which the petition is being filed for a specified period immediately prior to filing a divorce petition. If a divorce petition is filed and the residency requirements have not been met, the parties may file an amended petition after the time required to meet the residency requirements has elapsed.

### THE COURT HEARING

After the petition and summons have been served on the defendant and a proof of service has been filed with the clerk of the court, the defendant has a specific amount of time to file an answer with the court. If an answer is filed, the court will hold a hearing at which temporary support may be ordered for the spouse and minor children along with the temporary division of property, such as allowing the spouse and children to remain in the family home until the court can investigate the financial condition of each spouse and determine the equitable division of property and spousal and child support.

If the court determines that irreconcilable differences exist, it will enter a judgment of dissolution. In most states the judgment does not become final until six months after the summons and petition were served on the defendant or the date the respondent appears in court, whichever occurs first. The date on which the judgment becomes final is specified on the document issued by the court. If circumstances merit, the court may extend the six-month period.

If the court determines that there is a chance that the parties may be able to resolve their differences, it may extend the dissolution proceedings. If the parties are unable to reconcile, either one may ask the court to grant a judgment of dissolution after the prescribed waiting period expires.

## SEVERANCE OF THE ISSUES AND BIFURCATION

In a petition for divorce in which there are complex property or financial issues, the parties may ask the court to grant a judgment of dissolution while it continues to resolve matters pertaining to the division of property and spousal and child support. In such cases the judge will issue temporary orders for support and property. Upon receiving the judgment on the dissolution, the parties will be allowed to regain their status as unmarried persons but will remain under the jurisdiction of the court for the unresolved financial issues.

## PAYMENT OF ATTORNEY'S FEES

The court orders the parties to pay attorney's fees on the basis of the ability of each party to pay and the needs of each party. The court is interested in ensuring that all parties to an action have access to legal representation. To this end it orders the party better able to pay to pay the fees for the opposing party's legal representation. Community real property owned by the parties may be encumbered to pay attorney's fees when the parties have no other assets with which to secure the services of attorneys.

## LEGAL SEPARATION

The grounds for legal separation are the same as those for dissolution. However, a party may file a petition for legal separation without having met the residency requirements for dissolution. The petition for legal separation contains the same information as the petition for dissolution, and it may be converted to a dissolution when one party has met the residency requirements.

## RESTORATION OF WIFE'S FORMER NAME

In a dissolution the wife may ask the court to restore her previous or maiden name, and the law requires that the court grant the request except where such an action would constitute fraud.

## ANNULMENT AND VOIDABLE MARRIAGES

Under some circumstances the court may be asked to declare a marriage null. Some of the bases upon which a marriage may be considered null are:

1. The party filing the petition, or upon whose behalf the petition is filed, was incapable of consenting to the marriage at the time it took place.
2. The husband or wife of the other party was living and married to the other party at the time the marriage took place.
3. The husband or wife of the other party was presumed dead at the time the marriage took place but was subsequently found to be alive.
4. Either party was of unsound mind at the time the marriage took place.
5. The consent of either party to the marriage was obtained by fraud or force.
6. Either party was physically incapable of entering into the marriage state, an incapacity that continues and appears to be incurable.

A party claiming any of the conditions for nullity must act within the time limits specified by law. If a party does not object to the marriage after learning of the conditions that would make the marriage voidable and continues to live with the spouse as husband and wife, the court may determine that the party has ratified the marriage, and it may refuse to grant a judgment of nullity.

## THE PUTATIVE SPOUSE

If the court determines that a marriage is void or voidable and that either or both parties thought the marriage was valid, it will declare the party seeking a judgment of nullity to be a putative spouse. A putative spouse is considered by the court to have acted in good faith and is therefore entitled to the same rights under the law as if the marriage had been valid. Division of community property, child support and custody, and spousal support will be determined by the court in the same manner as in a dissolution.

## VOID MARRIAGES

Incestuous marriages—that is, marriages between parents and children, brothers and sisters (full or half), uncles and nieces, or aunts and nephews—are void by law. Since they are void, they are not recognized by law, and the parties to void marriages do not have any of the legal rights and responsibilities associated with marriage.

## CHILD CUSTODY

In a divorce in which the parties have minor children, the court will decide how the parents will care for the children and who will have the rights and responsibilities for making decisions about the children's health, education, and welfare. Custody may be physical, legal, or both physical and legal, and it may be joint or sole.

### JOINT CUSTODY

When both parents are present and capable of properly caring for the children, the court often grants them joint custody. Under this arrangement, both parents have joint physical and joint legal custody. In a situation where only one parent is able to care physically for a child, the court may grant one parent physical custody and both parents joint legal custody. In this arrangement the child lives with one parent, but the other parent shares in the right to make decisions regarding the child's health, welfare, and education.

In granting joint legal custody, the court specifies the circumstances under which the consent of both parents is required and the consequences of failing to comply with the requirement. Those situations not specified by the court may be decided by either parent.

### SOLE CUSTODY

When one parent is absent or there is an issue of child abuse or habitual alcohol or drug use, the court may award the other parent sole legal custody. A parent with sole legal custody has the right and responsibility of making decisions related to the child's health, welfare, and education.

More often the court gives the responsible parent sole physical custody. In that case the child resides with the responsible parent and is under his or her supervision, but the court retains the right to order visitation rights for the noncustodial parent.

### RIGHTS TO CUSTODY

Both the mother and the father of a minor child are equally entitled to custody of the child. If one parent is dead or is unable or refuses to take custody of a child, the other parent is entitled to custody.

## FACTORS IN DETERMINING WHO WILL HAVE CUSTODY

In determining which parent will have custody of a child, the court will evaluate the best interests of the child. In so doing, the court considers the following:

The health, safety, and welfare of the child

Any history of abuse by one parent against the child or against the other parent

The nature and amount of contact with both parents

Allegations of abuse must be verified and substantiated by the court, and in most states the law permits the court to fine anyone who falsely accuses a party of abuse or neglect during a child custody proceeding.

## VISITATION RIGHTS

Unless it is shown that visitation would be detrimental to the child, the court will grant visitation rights to a parent or any other person who has an interest in the welfare of a child such as a grandparent, an uncle, or a former stepparent. In cases where the visitation may endanger the child, the court may grant the visitation only under supervision by a third party. In cases where domestic violence has been alleged, the court issues detailed orders on when and how the child is to be transferred to the other parent so as to protect the safety of all the parties. If one parent is staying in a shelter for victims of domestic violence, the court's order must protect the confidentiality of the location of the shelter.

## GRANDPARENTS' VISITATION RIGHTS

Grandparents may be granted visitation rights by the court if such visitation is in the best interests of the child. However, if the child's parents agree that the best interests of the child would not be served by visits with the grandparents, the court will give careful consideration to the parents' opinion. If, however, the court finds that there is a bond between a child and a grandparent, the court will balance the interests of the parties in favor of the child's best interests.

## APPOINTMENT OF AN ATTORNEY TO REPRESENT A CHILD

The court may appoint an attorney to represent the interests of a child in a custody or visitation matter if it determines that the child's interests may be compromised without counsel. The court may order that the parties to the custody or visitation petition pay the fees of the child's attorney.

## *Table 12-1: Marriage—Legal Age*

### ARIZONA

| | |
|---|---|
| With parental consent | Sixteen years old |
| Without parental consent | Sixteen years old |
| With court authorization | Under sixteen years old |

### CALIFORNIA

| | |
|---|---|
| With parental consent | No age limit |
| Without parental consent | Eighteen years old |
| With court authorization | Under eighteen years old |

### FLORIDA

| | |
|---|---|
| With parental consent | Sixteen years old |
| Without parental consent | Eighteen years old |
| With court authorization | Under eighteen years old |

### ILLINOIS

| | |
|---|---|
| With parental consent | Sixteen years old |
| Without parental consent | Eighteen years old |
| With court authorization | Under sixteen years old |

### NEW MEXICO

| | |
|---|---|
| With parental consent | Fourteen years old |
| Without parental consent | Eighteen years old |
| With court authorization | Under eighteen years old |

### NEW YORK

| | |
|---|---|
| With parental consent | Fourteen years old |
| Without parental consent | Eighteen years old |
| With court authorization | Under sixteen years old |

*Table 12-1: Marriage—Legal Age (cont.)*

### Texas

| | |
|---|---|
| With parental consent | Fourteen years old |
| Without parental consent | Eighteen years old |
| With court authorization | Under sixteen years old |

## Child Support

### Declaration of Paternity by Unmarried Fathers

When an unmarried woman gives birth, the medical personnel responsible for completing the birth certificate must ask her and any man who has been identified as the father to complete a declaration of paternity. The completed declaration is filed with the birth certificate. The declaration creates a legal obligation on the part of the man to support the child and may be used to establish child custody or support. A man who signs a declaration of paternity and later learns that he may not be the child's biological father or a man who thinks he might be the child's father may petition the court to order that blood or genetic tests be done to determine paternity. Any challenge to the declaration of paternity must be made within the time limits specified under state law.

### Reasons for Establishing Paternity

Establishing paternity is important for several reasons. The law requires that a father support his child if he is financially able to. There are also several other issues in which paternity is important. A father has the same rights to custody of a child as the birth mother as well as rights associated with consent to adoption. Moreover, by the court's establishing the legal relationship between the father and child, the child will have rights of inheritance and the right to claim certain other benefits such as Social Security benefits, which might be available to a child whose father died when the child was young.

### Determining the Amount of Child Support

Each parent is legally responsible for the support of his or her children, and each state has its own laws governing child support. In general, the following factors are considered in determining the amount of support each parent will be required to pay:

The financial abilities of each parent, including income and assets

The parents' standard of living prior to the divorce

The needs of the child, including any special medical or developmental needs

The particular circumstances of each case

The parent who has physical custody of the child the greater amount of time will usually receive payments from the other parent unless the court determines that the absent parent is unable to support the children.

## CHILD SUPPORT DELINQUENCY REPORTING LAW

California and other states require that delinquent child support obligations be reported to the consumer credit reporting agencies by the state Department of Social Services. Whenever a child support payment is more than thirty days late, the parent who is to receive the payment may file a notice of delinquency with the court. If the delinquent amount remains unpaid for thirty days after the delinquent party has been served with a notice by the court, the outstanding balance will incur a penalty of 6 percent per month for each month it remains unpaid. The maximum penalty that can accrue is 72 percent. A parent who has failed to pay support because of illness, unemployment, or other emergency conditions may ask the court not to impose the penalty.

## UNIFORM RECIPROCAL ENFORCEMENT OF SUPPORT ACT

If the state court was legally able to make the order for support, the support order will be valid and binding even if the parties move to other states. Failure to pay court-ordered child support may subject the delinquent parent to both civil and criminal sanctions.

## CRIMINAL ENFORCEMENT OF CHILD SUPPORT OBLIGATIONS

A parent who is ordered by the court to pay child support and leaves the state to avoid paying that support may be extradited from the other state under the same laws as those governing extradition of criminals in other matters.

## STEPPARENT RESPONSIBILITY TO SUPPORT CHILDREN

Stepparents are not usually held financially or legally responsible for the support of their stepchildren. However, if a stepparent adopts a stepchild, he may be held liable for support.

## EARNINGS ASSIGNMENT ORDER (GARNISHMENT OF WAGES) TO PAY SUPPORT

A support order issued by the court may contain an earnings assignment order. This allows the parent receiving child support to require the employer of the paying parent to deduct child support payments from the employee's pay and to make those payments to the court if the supporting parent is in arrears. Once the employer has been notified, he must begin withholding child support from the employee's pay. The employer may charge the employee a fee for processing each payment withheld. The earnings assignment order issued by the court applies to any future employer of the parent responsible for payment of child support. If the employee is able to prove to the court that he will make the child support payments as ordered, he may ask the court to terminate the wage assignment order. An employer who fails to comply with the court order to withhold child support from an employee's wages is liable for payment to the parent receiving it and may be charged with contempt of court.

## DISTRIBUTION OF DEBTS AND ASSETS IN A DIVORCE

The manner of asset distribution and debt allocation at the time of a divorce is governed by the laws of the state where the petition is filed and the laws of the state where the assets are located. California and eight other states are community property states. The rest of the states are *common-law* jurisdictions. Under the community property system, one-half of the earnings of each spouse is considered owned by the other spouse, whereas in a common-law jurisdiction, each spouse owns whatever he or she earns.

### DEBTS INCURRED BEFORE MARRIAGE

Debts incurred by either spouse before the date of the marriage are the responsibility of the spouse who incurred them; the other spouse will not be held liable for them.

### DEBTS INCURRED DURING MARRIAGE

A married person is liable for the debts of his or her spouse during the marriage if those debts were incurred to provide the necessaries of life. This responsibility may also apply when the spouses are living apart.

## DEBTS INCURRED AFTER SEPARATION
## BUT BEFORE JUDGMENT FOR DIVORCE

Debts that are incurred after separation but before a judgment for divorce is entered and are for the necessaries of life of a spouse or children will be the responsibility of the spouses according to the parties' respective needs and abilities to pay. Debts incurred for nonnecessaries are usually the responsibility of the person who incurred the debt.

Necessaries in the most basic form include food, clothing, medical care, and suitable shelter. However, the court will determine necessaries based upon the lifestyle of the parties prior to separation and will extend its definition to include those items suitable to the social position of the individual. For many, a car is considered a necessary as are a telephone and possibly even cable TV service.

## SEPARATE PROPERTY

The property owned by a spouse before the marriage is considered his or her separate property and does not become part of the community estate.

## COMMUNITY PROPERTY

In a community property state all the earnings of both spouses form the community estate. Each spouse owns half of the other spouse's earnings.

In community property states, assets acquired during the marriage are given a financial value by the court, and each party is entitled to one-half of the community property. The law states that the court shall divide the community estate of the parties equally.

Where the economic circumstances warrant, the court may award any asset to one party on any conditions it deems proper to effect a substantially equal division of property. It may also award, from a party's share, any sum it determines to have been deliberately misappropriated by one party to the exclusion of the other party.

Each party is entitled to keep his or her separate property. This includes any assets each party brought into the marriage and any assets that were given to each party specifically and individually during the marriage or that one party inherited at any time.

The court will ask to see a record of the parties' assets, both community and separate, and will divide the community property between the two spouses. If they cannot reach an agreement about how the community property is to be distributed, the court may order that assets be sold and the capital divided between them. It is advisable to make an effort to work out an agreeable distribution of assets before filing for divorce. The court will make every effort to abide by the agreements of the parties.

## SPOUSAL SUPPORT OR ALIMONY

### DUTY TO SUPPORT ONE'S SPOUSE

The law recognizes that each spouse has a duty to support the other spouse.

### A MARRIAGE OF LONG DURATION

A marriage of a specified duration, usually ten years or more, is considered by the courts in most states to be a marriage of long duration. This designation is an important factor in establishing spousal support since the court retains the right to modify, terminate, or extend spousal support when the marriage is considered of long duration. In some cases the court may classify a marriage of less than the specified duration as one of long duration if the principles of justice and equity so require.

### FACTORS CONSIDERED IN ESTABLISHING SPOUSAL SUPPORT

In the event of a dissolution of the marriage, the court considers the following factors in determining if one spouse should receive support from the other and for how long:

The earning capacity of each spouse and the standard of living established during the marriage

The marketable skills of the party less able to support himself or herself and the job market for those skills

The time and expense required for the nonworking or underemployed party to get training or retraining to develop marketable skills

The extent to which the nonworking or underemployed party's present or future working capacity is impaired by periods of unemployment during the marriage so that the party could devote his or her full efforts to domestic duties

The extent to which a party contributed to the education or career advancement of the other party

The working party's ability to pay based on earning capacity, assets, and standard of living

The needs of each party based on the standard of living established during the marriage

The obligations and assets, including separate property, of each party

The duration of the marriage

The ability of the nonworking or underemployed party to work full-time without unduly interfering with the needs of dependent children in his or her custody

The ages and health of the parties

The tax consequences to each party

Any other factors that the court determines are just and equitable

## DOMESTIC VIOLENCE

### CHILD ABUSE, NEGLECT, AND ABANDONMENT

Children are frequently the victims of abuse and neglect. Recently laws have changed throughout the country to make it easier to report incidents of child abuse and to provide help for both the victim and the offending parents and caregivers.

All fifty states now have mandatory child abuse reporting laws. These require people who suspect the abuse of a minor to report it to a child protective agency. The reports should be made to any police or sheriff's department or county welfare agency. The incident will be investigated, and if necessary, the child will be placed in safe custody away from the alleged abusers until a full investigation can be completed.

The courts make every effort to get the parent or parents into a counseling session where they can get professional help. Abuse is often the result of financial or emotional stress, job dissatisfaction, loss of employment, or other factors that a counselor may help the family resolve. If a resolution is not possible, the child may be assigned to a foster home. As with custody cases, the court always considers the child's best interests and makes its ruling accordingly.

A person who is under stress and believes that he may not be able to control his actions should contact the county welfare agency for assistance. There are many programs available to assist families such as Aid to Families with Dependent Children (AFDC), a program cosponsored by the federal government and administered through county welfare agencies, able to supply financial aid (see Chapter 5, "Consumer Law," for additional government benefit programs).

### SPOUSAL ABUSE

Almost one-third of all police calls in the United States involve domestic violence, especially wife beatings. Abuse is not limited to legally married women. Live-in girlfriends are also frequently victimized by abusive lovers. Tragically only a small percentage of women who have been abused file charges against their attackers. Doing nothing to protect oneself sends a message to the attacker that it is okay for him to continue abusing and disrupting the family.

The first step is to protect oneself. Authorities advise a potential victim to leave the house or place of abuse and call the police. If the person is unable to get away and must use deadly force to protect herself, the police must be called immediately. It is critical that a person involved in a confrontation not run away or make any attempt to alter or destroy possible evidence.

Everyone is entitled by law to protect himself from death or great bodily harm, but self-defense is a messy and complicated issue. Many times the police have difficulty sorting through all the facts and evidence to determine a case of self-defense.

When the police arrive, they will analyze the situation and make a decision on whether to let the parties go or to file criminal charges with the district attorney's office. If they determine that a party's action was indeed self-defense, he may be released from further investigation. If the facts do not clearly indicate self-defense, the police will probably file charges. If the district attorney decides that self-defense is questionable, the person will be brought before a judge for a probable cause hearing. At that hearing the judge will determine if there is sufficient evidence to suggest that a crime was committed and is worth prosecuting.

Depending on the findings of the court, the judge will either release the party or send the case to the trial court where the accused person will stand trial. At this trial a jury will hear and review evidence to determine his guilt or innocence.

Each state creates its own laws governing self-defense. In California the justifiable homicide law reads, in part, as follows:

Homicide is also justifiable when committed by any person in any of the following cases:

When resisting any attempt to murder any person or to commit a felony or to do some great bodily injury upon any person;

When committed in defense of habitation, property, or person, against one who manifestly intends or endeavors by violence or surprise to commit a felony, or against one who manifestly intends and endeavors in a violent, riotous or tumultuous manner to enter the habitation of another for the purpose of offering violence to any person therein.

The laws defining and explaining self-defense are very complicated and often hard to understand. The courts make every effort to protect victims who have resorted to deadly force to save their own lives, but it must also protect all persons from wrongful death and make a thorough investigation of all self-defense claims. Whenever possible, it is important to explore other avenues before resorting to deadly force.

## Abused Women's Shelters

If possible, a party involved in a domestic confrontation should stay overnight with a friend or go to an emergency relief shelter. Many cities and counties offer shelter programs through their departments of social services. The telephone number for this agency can be found in the white pages of the telephone directory under "City" or "County Government."

A word of warning about public shelters: In some states any record or file regarding a stay at a public shelter can be subpoenaed and used as evidence in a trial. A woman who tells a therapist or social worker anything that implicates her, such as "I made him mad" or "I know he did not mean it," may find that those statements may be used by the spouse's attorney to support his defense. It is important to seek shelter and refuge, but it is also important to be careful of what is said.

## Documenting Physical Abuse

Any party who has physical injuries should have someone take photographs of the injuries. In most cases photographs will be admissible court evidence to substantiate a complaint.

Many shelters will take photographs for an injured party. It is best to take photographs of both the visibly injured area and the victim's face (these are necessary for identification). The person being photographed should ask the photographer for the negatives as well as the prints.

## Filing Criminal Charges Against the Abuser

As soon as possible, the victim should contact an attorney. It is important that anyone who has been abused understand that seeking legal help will not make the situation worse. In the long run legal intervention will be beneficial to both spouses. An attorney can arrange for professional family counseling. In the meantime he can get a court order to protect a domestic violence victim and her children from abuse. If a spouse violates a restraining order and continues to attempt to harm someone who has previously been abused, he may be taken into custody.

There are legal remedies available to protect a person from abuse and domestic violence. It is the right and obligation of everyone to employ these remedies and to protect him and his family.

## ADOPTION

Adoption is a complicated legal and emotional matter and should not be considered without the advice of an attorney who specializes in family law.

Most adoptions fall into one of four categories:

Agency adoptions

Independent adoptions

Stepparent adoptions

Foreign adoptions

In addition to the standard adoptions, there are adoptions associated with surrogacy contracts.

### AGENCY ADOPTIONS

Adoption agencies must be licensed and are usually regulated by the departments of social services of the various states.

### CONSENT OF BIRTH PARENTS FOR ADOPTION

When a child is adopted in an independent adoption, the birth parents must consent to the adoption by signing an adoptive placement agreement. The consent form usually cannot be signed by either the birth parents or the prospective adoptive parents before the birth mother is discharged from the hospital; furthermore, the child may not be released to the adoptive parents until the agreement has been signed and witnessed by the birth parents and the adoptive parents. An adoption service agency must advise the birth parents of their rights ten days before the child is released to the adoptive parents and must offer counseling services to the birth parents. When the child is released to the adoptive parents, the adoption service agency must offer to interview the birth parents again within ten days. At that interview the service provider must again advise the birth parents of their rights and must obtain health and social histories of the birth parents.

In most states a birth parent who is a minor may sign a consent for the adoption of her child; the consent is not subject to revocation based on the birth parent's being a minor.

Once a birth parent has given her consent for adoption of the child, that consent can be withdrawn only by petitioning the court.

## Birth Parents' Rights to Revoke Adoption Placement

The birth parents usually have 120 days after placement to revoke their consent to the adoption and to request return of their child. This revocation and request must be in writing. If the birth parents revoke their consent to adoption of the child, the child must immediately be returned to them. Even if the prospective adoptive parents believe that the welfare of the child is in danger, they must return the child and then report their concern to the adoption agency or local child welfare agency.

## Birth Parents' Waiver of Right to Revoke Adoption Placement

Before the 120-day period has expired, the birth parents may execute a waiver of the right to revoke consent. The adoption service provider must interview the birth parents before a valid waiver is signed. The waiver makes the placement irrevocable. Once the waiver has been signed, the birth parents have no further legal rights or responsibilities for the child.

## Stepparent Adoption

A stepparent who wishes to adopt the child of his or her spouse may petition the court in the county where he or she resides. The county welfare department or a qualified court investigator will make an investigation of the stepparent and file a report and recommendation with the court. The stepparent will be liable for the costs of the adoption up to a stated maximum, but the fees may be waived when there is financial hardship.

The prospective adoptive parent or stepparent and the child must appear in court before the adoption can become final.

## Adoption of Adults and Married Minors

An adult or a married minor may be adopted by another adult. If the adult is married, he or she must obtain the consent of his or her spouse in order to be adopted. An adult wishing to adopt another adult or married minor must also have the consent of his or her spouse before the adoption will be approved. Consent of the parent or parents of the proposed adoptee is not required.

An adult who is adopted may take the family name of the adoptive parent.

## *Table 12-2: Multistate Compendium on Adoption*

### ARIZONA

| | |
|---|---|
| Adoptive parents | Any adult, married or not, may adopt. |
| Adopted person | Any minor child or legally admitted alien under age twenty-one may be adopted. |
| Residency | There is no minimum residency requirement. |
| Challenge period | Any legal challenge to the adoption must be made within one year of the adoption. |
| Consent requirement | Adopted person must consent if age twelve or over. |

### CALIFORNIA

| | |
|---|---|
| Adoptive parents | Any adult who is at least ten years older than the adopted person or is a family member or a relative may adopt. |
| Adopted person | Any unmarried minor child may be adopted. |
| Residency | There is no minimum residency requirement. |
| Challenge period | Challenges made on procedural grounds must be made within three years; all other challenges must be made within five years. |
| Consent requirement | Adopted person must consent if age twelve or over. |

### FLORIDA

| | |
|---|---|
| Adoptive parents | Any adult may adopt. Spouse must also adopt unless it is the natural parent or is excused. |
| Adopted person | Any person may be adopted. |
| Residency | There is no minimum residency requirement. |
| Challenge period | Any legal challenge must be made within one year. |
| Consent requirement | Adopted person must consent if age twelve or over. |

### ILLINOIS

| | |
|---|---|
| Adoptive parents | Any adult may adopt. If he is married, his spouse must also adopt if she is not the natural parent. |
| Adopted person | Any child as well as an adult who has lived in the house |

for at least two years or who is a relative of the adopting parent(s) may be adopted.

| | |
|---|---|
| Residency | Adopting parents must have lived in the state for at least six months unless they are relatives of the adopted person. Military personnel need have lived in the state for only ninety days. |
| Challenge period | Any legal challenge must be made within one year if the alleged natural father has not been given notice. |
| Consent requirement | Adopted person must consent if age fourteen or over. |

## NEW MEXICO

| | |
|---|---|
| Adoptive parents | Any adult may adopt. If the adult is married, the spouse must also adopt unless he or she is excused by the court. |
| Adopted person | Any person may be adopted. |
| Residency | The adopting parents must have lived in the state for at least 90 days if the child is less than one year old and 180 days if the child is over one year old. |
| Challenge period | Any legal challenge must be made within one year. |
| Consent requirement | Adopted person must consent if age ten or over. |

## NEW YORK

| | |
|---|---|
| Adoptive parents | Any married adult may adopt. Married couples may adopt if they are not separated. Minor spouses may adopt a child born in or out of wedlock. |
| Adopted person | Any person may be adopted. |
| Residency | Adopting parent(s) must have lived in the state for at least six months. |
| Challenge period | Any legal challenge must be made within forty-five days of the adoption. |
| Consent requirement | Adopted person must consent if age fourteen years or over. |

## TEXAS

| | |
|---|---|
| Adoptive parents | Any adult may adopt. If the adult is married, the spouse must also adopt. |

*Table 12-2: Multistate Compendium on Adoption (cont.)*

### TEXAS

| | |
|---|---|
| Adopted person | Any person may be adopted. |
| Residency | Adopting parent(s) must have lived in the state for at least six months. |
| Challenge period | Any legal challenge must be made within two years of the adoption. |
| Consent requirement | Adopted person must consent if age twelve years or over. |

## SURROGACY

Couples who desire a child but are unable to bear one are turning to surrogates more frequently. They enter into a contractual agreement whereby the surrogate mother agrees to provide the function of incubating the fertilized ovum during the gestational period in exchange for money. A central part of the contractual agreement is that the surrogate agrees to give up any parental rights to the child after it is born. In California the state supreme court has upheld the validity of such contracts and has ruled that they are not in violation of public policy (*Johnson v. Calvert* [1993] Cal 4th 84, 95–97). Surrogacy law is an emerging legal field. The laws governing surrogacy have been established by the courts on the basis of individual cases, using existing law regarding paternity, adoption, and contract law.

There are two kinds of surrogacy arrangement. They result from two types of fertility procedure:

1. *In vitro* fertilization involves the laboratory fertilization of a woman's egg and implantation in the uterus of another woman. In in vitro surrogacy, the child is biologically related to the mother and not to the surrogate. In California no adoption is required to confirm this type of surrogacy, and the issue of parentage has been decided under the federal Uniform Parentage Act.

2. Fertilization of the donor egg of the surrogate with the sperm of the intended father results in the second type of surrogacy contract. The surrogate is the biological mother of the child but agrees to give up parental rights to the child. In order to establish the legal relationship between the intended parents and the child, the intended mother must legally adopt the child through the stepparent adoption process. Because the father is the biological father of the child, he may not need to be a party to the adoption in order

to establish parental rights, but some legal scholars recommend that he be included in the adoption process because of the legal issues surrounding paternity and the requirement that the surrogate acknowledge the father's paternity in order for his parental rights to be firmly established.

## WHEN THE SURROGATE CHANGES HER MIND

Much of the current law regarding surrogacy agreements has been established in cases in which the surrogate has refused to comply with the terms of the contract and has asked the court to give her custody of the child after it is born. The cases which have been heard in court regarding surrogate withdrawal of consent to adoption have usually been resolved in favor of the intended parents, on the basis of the best interests of the child. However, a serious legal issue has been raised: should the natural parent's consent—in this case that of the surrogate—or the intentions of the parties as defined in the contract agreement prevail? In surrogacy contracts involving *in vitro* fertilization, where the child is biologically related to the intended mother, the courts have upheld the contractual agreement. Those cases where the surrogate is the biological mother obviously present more serious considerations with their attendant emotional issues.

## SEEKING LEGAL ADVICE REGARDING SURROGACY

It is critical that any party who intends to enter a surrogacy agreement, whether as donor surrogate or as intended parent, seek the counsel of a specialist in surrogacy matters. This is especially important because this burgeoning legal field is changing daily as the courts establish new precedents with each case.

### *Table 12-3: Multistate Compendium on Legal Abortion*

#### ARIZONA

| | |
|---|---|
| Legal abortion | Abortion is legal in order to save mother's life. |
| Penalty for illegal abortion | Two to five years in state prison. |
| Consent requirement | Parental consent is required if the person is an unmarried minor. No parental consent required if the abortion is necessary to save minor's life. Court may authorize abortion without parental consent. |
| License requirement | There are no special licensing requirements. |

## *Table 12-3: Multistate Compendium on Legal Abortion (cont.)*

### CALIFORNIA

| | |
|---|---|
| Legal abortion | Abortion is legal if done to save mother's life, or to protect her health, or if she was the victim of rape or incest. |
| Penalty for illegal abortion | Sentencing to state prison. |
| Consent requirement | Written consent of parent is required for minors. Juvenile court can authorize abortion for minors without parental consent. |
| License requirement | The doctor must be certified and the hospital or clinic approved by the state medical board. |

### FLORIDA

| | |
|---|---|
| Legal abortion | Abortions are lawful in the last trimester if done to protect the mother's health or to save her life. |
| Penalty for illegal abortion | Misdemeanor, including a six-hundred-dollar fine and up to sixty days in jail. |
| Consent requirement | Parental consent is required if the mother is an unmarried minor, unless the minor obtains a court order. |
| License requirement | The medical facilities must be licensed. |

### ILLINOIS

| | |
|---|---|
| Legal abortion | Legal if performed before the baby is viable. Abortion is legal after the baby is viable if it is done to protect the health or save the life of the mother. |
| Penalty for illegal abortion | Class 2 felony. |
| Consent requirement | Parental consent is required if the person is an unmarried minor. Doctor may perform an abortion if medically required in his/her judgment. Judge may authorize abortion by court order. The minor must give consent forty-eight hours before the abortion. |
| License requirement | Doctor must be licensed to perform abortion. |

## New Mexico

| | |
|---|---|
| Legal abortion | Legal if done to protect mother's health or save her life or if she is the victim of rape or incest. |
| Penalty for illegal abortion | Felony. Can result in a state prison term. |
| Consent requirement | If the mother is a minor, both the minor and the parent(s) must request the abortion. |
| License requirement | Doctor must be licensed and the medical facility must be certified. |

## New York

| | |
|---|---|
| Legal abortion | Legal if performed within the first twenty-four weeks or if necessary to save the life of the mother. |
| Penalty for illegal abortion | Felony. Can result in a state prison term. |
| Consent requirement | The mother must consent. |
| License requirement | Duly licensed physician. |

## Texas

| | |
|---|---|
| Legal abortion | Legal if performed within the first twenty-four weeks if the doctor reasonably believes it is necessary to save the life of the mother. |
| Penalty for illegal abortion | Administrative as well as civil and criminal liability. |
| Consent requirement | The mother must express her consent to the abortion. |
| License requirement | The doctor and the medical facilities must be licensed unless procedure was done to protect the health or save life of the mother. |

## Table 12-4: Vicarious Liability of Parents

### ARIZONA

Parents or guardian are liable for the malicious, willful acts of minors, including theft and shoplifting.

### CALIFORNIA

Any willful misconduct of a minor that results in injury or death or damage to property of another shall be imputed to the parent or guardian.

### FLORIDA

Parents are liable for the willful and malicious acts of their minors.

### ILLINOIS

Any willful misconduct of a minor that results in injury or death or damage to property of another shall be imputed to the parents or guardian.

### NEW MEXICO

No statutory provision.

### NEW YORK

Any willful misconduct of a minor shall be imputed to the parent or guardian.

### TEXAS

Parents are liable for property damages proximately caused by negligent conduct of the child. Parents can be held negligent for failure to exercise their duties. They are also liable for the malicious and willful conduct of minors twelve to eighteen years of age.

## MEETING WITH A FAMILY LAW ATTORNEY

In choosing a family law attorney, it is important that the parties seek someone knowledgeable and experienced in the type of problem that needs attention. While some family law attorneys handle several types of family law matters, others focus primarily on dissolution, adoption, or surrogacy. During the initial meeting with a prospective attorney, the client should ask what percentage of the attorney's practice is devoted to the specialty for which he is seeking advice. As social customs change, the law often changes to meet new situations, and it is important that the attorney be involved in the legal specialty enough that he is aware of any changes in the law and new case law established by the courts.

When the client meets with the attorney for the first interview, he should take with him any documents applicable to the matter for which he is seeking help. These may include birth certificates of all the parties, including spouses and children; marriage certificates; orders to pay child support from previous marriages; certificates of adoption; pay stubs for any party who may need to prove financial need or ability to support others; documents showing any property owned, along with the property's value and outstanding loans on the property; any lease agreements, bank account statements, or retirement plans that the parties may participate in; Social Security numbers of all the parties; addresses and telephone numbers of the parties; and the name and phone number of any attorney who may be representing an opposing party. The party filing a complaint or response will also be asked to provide a physical description of the other party so that anyone serving court documents will be able to verify that the proper person was served.

# 13

# Motor Vehicles

## PROCEDURE TO TRANSFER TITLE

### DOCUMENTS REQUIRED FOR PRIVATE SALE

In order to transfer the title of a vehicle from one owner to another, the seller must sign the certificate of ownership and deliver it to the buyer. The buyer must sign and write his address on the document and then deliver or mail the endorsed certificate of ownership to the Department of Motor Vehicles (DMV) along with the required transfer fee, any sales tax that is due, and an application for registration in the name of the buyer. In addition to the certificate of ownership, fees and tax, a certificate of compliance regarding emissions levels of the vehicle is required before a new registration or certificate of ownership will be issued.

### REQUIREMENTS TO RELEASE SELLER FROM FUTURE LIABILITY

The seller of a vehicle must notify the DMV of the sale and transfer of ownership by completing a form provided by the DMV and mailing or delivering it to the department within a specified period of time (usually ten days) of the sale or transfer. The form must include the date of the sale or transfer, the name and address of the buyer or new owner, a description of the vehicle, and the actual mileage of the vehicle. A seller who fails to comply with the notification requirement may be liable for parking violations, civil liability, and criminal liability associated with ownership of the vehicle until he complies with the law or the new owner registers the vehicle.

## Obligations of Buyer

The buyer of a vehicle must endorse the certificate of ownership and forward the certificate and any fees to the DMV within a specified period (usually ten days) after the sale along with an application for registration. The buyer must write his driver's license number or identification card number on the certificate of ownership. If the vehicle registration will expire within thirty days of the time the buyer applies for title transfer and registration, he is required to submit the fees for renewal of the registration at the time he submits the transfer documents to the Department of Motor Vehicles.

## Types of Transfers of Motor Vehicles

A motor vehicle may be transferred by sale, gift, lease, auction, involuntary transfer, or in accordance with the probate laws upon the death of the owner.

## Sale of a Motor Vehicle by a Dealer

Motor vehicle dealers are required to comply with numerous laws, including motor vehicle laws and laws contained in the business and professions codes of the various states. Just as in a private sale, a dealer must notify the Department of Motor Vehicles when title to a vehicle is transferred.

## Antitheft Laws

### False Theft Report

It is illegal to make a false report of a stolen vehicle or license plate, and a person who has been previously convicted of filing a false vehicle theft report may be imprisoned.

### Penalty for Vehicle Theft

A person who is convicted of vehicle theft or is an accomplice or aids the thief may be imprisoned and fined. If the person has previously been convicted of vehicle theft, he or she may be imprisoned for an extended period (up to four years in California, for example). If the vehicle is an ambulance, a law enforcement vehicle, or a vehicle that has been modified to accommodate a disabled person, the offense is a felony in some states and is punishable, even on the first offense, by additional years in prison and a substantially increased fine.

## DRIVER'S LICENSES

### DRIVER'S LICENSE IDENTIFICATION REQUIREMENTS

The first step in obtaining a driver's license is filling out and filing an application with the Department of Motor Vehicles. Along with the actual application, most states require the applicant to provide one or more forms of identification usually to prove his or her name, date of birth, Social Security number, proof of residency, and proof of legal presence in the United States. Some forms of acceptable identification include but are not limited to the following:

Certified birth certificate

Valid identification card

Out-of-state driver's license or ID card

Valid passport

Naturalization certificate

Alien registration card ("green card")

Military ID card

Military driver's license

Voter registration card

U.S. Social Security card

In most states a person has to be sixteen years of age to obtain a driver's license. However, before he can obtain his first driver's license, most states require that he get a learner's permit. This allows someone, usually fifteen years or older, who has completed a drivers' education course to practice driving with a licensed driver over the age of eighteen. Driver training courses are usually offered through local high schools or colleges. Many states require people to practice driving for a specified amount of time before they can qualify to take the actual driver's license test.

Once a person is sixteen and has completed all the necessary training, he can apply for a driver's license. The Department of Motor Vehicles requires him to take a vision test, a written examination on traffic laws and road signs, and an actual driving test. If the applicant passes all three, he pays a fee and gets his picture taken. Usually a temporary license is issued until he receives his permanent license. Once he receives his permanent license, he is required to carry it when driving.

## Minimum Age to Obtain a Driver's License

Sixteen is the minimum age at which a person can obtain a driver's license in Arizona, California, Florida, Illinois, New Mexico, New York, and Texas.

## Denial or Refusal of Driver's License by DMV

The DMV may deny a driver's license to anyone who fails to meet all the requirements established by law, including those described under the sections above entitled "Driver's License" and "Examination of Applicants." The DMV may also refuse to issue or renew a license to anyone incapable of safely operating a vehicle because of alcoholism or excessive and chronic use of alcohol or drugs.

Any applicant for a license or renewal may be refused a valid license if he has failed to appear for a court hearing on a vehicle code violation or has failed to pay a fine for any violation of the motor vehicle laws. An applicant who has been refused a license for failure to appear must provide the DMV with a certificate of adjudication from the court before the department will reconsider the application.

An applicant for a new driver's license or renewal will be refused the license if he has failed to pay a parking violation and the violation notice has been transmitted to the DMV. An applicant who has been refused a license because of delinquent parking fines may pay the fines and any administrative penalties at the time he applies for a license or renewal; the license will be granted if all other requirements are met.

## Other Grounds for Denial or Refusal of a Driver's License

Driving a vehicle is a privilege, not a basic legal or constitutional right. Because it is considered a privilege, the state has considerable discretionary control over who may be granted a license. In most states the DMV may deny or refuse to grant a driver's license to any person

If the applicant fails to furnish the information required by the DMV.

If the DMV determines that the applicant has unlawfully used or allowed the use of a driver's license; the illegal use may include loaning a driver's license to another person for identification purposes or to gain access to alcoholic beverages when the other person is a minor.

If the person has used a fictitious name or impersonated another person while taking a test or has committed fraud in any application.

If the DMV determines that the applicant is negligent or incompetent to operate a vehicle as demonstrated by repeated accidents.

If the applicant has been convicted of transporting for sale any controlled substance or illegal drug with the use of a vehicle.

If the applicant has had his driving privilege placed on probationary status because of possession of drugs. The DMV may also refuse to renew the license if the applicant is subsequently convicted of another offense involving the use or possession of drugs, *whether or not the subsequent conviction involved the use or operation of a vehicle,* and a license refusal on this ground may be in effect for up to three years from the date of conviction in many states.

If the applicant has failed to appear on a citation for abandoning a vehicle on public or private property or has failed to pay the costs of removal of the abandoned vehicle.

## ADDITIONAL REQUIREMENTS FOR APPLICANTS UNDER TWENTY-ONE YEARS OF AGE

In many states, before a permit or license may be issued to anyone under the age of twenty-one, the DMV must inform the applicant that it is illegal to drive with a blood alcohol level that exceeds 0.01 percent, as determined by a preliminary alcohol screening—typically a breath analysis test. The penalty for violating this law is a one-year suspension of the driver's license; a refusal to take the test will result in a minimum one-year suspension of driving privileges. The applicant under age twenty-one must sign a statement acknowledging that he has been notified of this law.

## EMPLOYMENT-RELATED AGE RESTRICTIONS

In most states a person must be at least eighteen years of age before he can be employed in a job that requires him to drive. If the driving in the course of employment includes interstate commerce or the transportation of any hazardous materials, the person must in most cases be twenty-one years old.

## SUSPENSION AND REVOCATION

### SUSPENSION OR REVOCATION OF A DRIVER'S LICENSE

When a driver's license is suspended, his privilege to drive a vehicle is temporarily withdrawn. Usually a suspension is for a fixed period of time or until the license holder meets a specific requirement.

When a driver's license is revoked, his or her privilege to drive a vehicle is permanently terminated, and he or she must reapply for a license after the revocation time period has expired.

When a driver's license is suspended or revoked, the DMV notifies him by mail unless he has previously been notified by the court or a law enforcement officer. If the DMV is unable to notify the person by mail because he has moved and has left no forwarding address, as required by law, the DMV will notify him by personal service. The cost of the personal service will be charged to the party who failed to file a change of address. When he is eligible for reinstatement of his license, he will be required to pay the fees for personal service before the license will be issued.

## SUSPENSION OR REVOCATION BY THE COURT

The courts may suspend or revoke a driver's license for the following reasons, among others:

Speeding or reckless driving. Unless revocation is required by law, a license may be suspended for a brief period, usually for thirty days, for the first conviction, sixty days for the second conviction, and six months for a third or subsequent conviction.

Driving over one hundred miles per hour. Unless revocation is required by law, a license may be suspended for a brief period, usually thirty days.

A license may be suspended for up to six months for conviction of any of the following:

Failure of the driver of a vehicle involved in an accident to stop and seek out the owner of any property damaged in the accident

Reckless driving causing bodily injury

Failure to stop at a railway crossing

Evading a police officer

Knowingly causing or participating in a vehicle collision for the purpose of filing a false or fraudulent insurance claim

## SUSPENSION OR REVOCATION FOR CONVICTION OF DRUG USE OR POSSESSION

Any driver who has been convicted of any offense related to the use or possession of drugs, narcotics, or any other controlled substance, when that offense involved the use of a motor vehicle, may have his or her license suspended or revoked for up to three years in some states.

A driver convicted by any court of any controlled substance offense can be required to surrender his license to the court. Each conviction requires that the license be suspended for an additional term. If the license is suspended or revoked at the time of the conviction, an additional term shall be added to the time before the license may be reinstated.

## SUSPENSION OR REVOCATION OF LICENSES BY THE DEPARTMENTS OF MOTOR VEHICLES OF VARIOUS STATES

The departments of motor vehicles of various states must suspend or revoke the license of any person when the suspension or revocation has been ordered by the courts.

In addition to complying with court-ordered suspensions and revocations, the DMV in most cases may initiate a suspension or revocation when any of the following occur:

A conviction for failing to stop in the event of an accident where there is damage to property only

A second or subsequent offense of reckless driving

A conviction of manslaughter resulting from the operation of a vehicle

Failure to provide proof of insurance or financial responsibility

Convictions in another state that would result in suspension or revocation in the license-issuing state

Presenting a check in payment of a fine or fee or penalty that is not honored by the payor's bank

Violation of promise to appear or failure to pay a fine

Accrual of points in excess of the number permitted for a given time period

## FINANCIAL RESPONSIBILITY LAWS

The states require owners and drivers of motor vehicles to have liability insurance to cover any claims for damages that may be made against them in the event of an accident that causes death, injury to persons, or damage to property.

## COMPULSORY FINANCIAL RESPONSIBILITY

Every driver and every owner of a motor vehicle must at all times carry in the vehicle evidence of insurance or another form of financial responsibility. For most persons, financial responsibility is in the form of a policy of insurance. However, some corporations are "self-insured." A self-insured entity is issued a certificate or deposit number by the Department of Motor Vehicles. In either case the driver or owner must carry in the vehicle a written document that proves he meets the financial responsibility requirements.

## Minimum Insurance Requirements

Each state has laws requiring a minimum amount of liability limits.

### Table 13-1: Minimum Automobile Liability Insurance Requirements

| State | Minimum Amount for Bodily Injury or Death to One Claimant | Minimum Total Coverage for More Than One Person Who Is Injured or Killed | Minimum for Destruction or Damage to Property |
|---|---|---|---|
| Arizona | $15,000 | $30,000 | $10,000 |
| California | $15,000 | $30,000 | $15,000 |
| Florida | $10,000 | $20,000 | $10,000 |
| Illinois | $20,000 | $40,000 | $15,000 |
| New Mexico | $25,000 | $30,000 | $10,000 |
| New York | $10,000 | $50,000 | $20,000 |
| Texas | $20,000 | $40,000 | $15,000 |

## Accident Reports

Any driver involved in any accident on a street or highway in which the damage to the property of any one person is greater than a specified amount, usually five hundred dollars, or in which any person is injured or dies must report the accident to the Department of Motor Vehicles within a specified period after the accident (usually ten days), either personally or through an insurance agent.

## Penalty for Failure to File an Accident Report

The DMV will suspend the driving privilege of anyone who fails or neglects to report an accident as required, and his license will remain suspended until he proves that he has met the financial responsibility requirements by paying any damages arising from the accident. A nonresident may have his driving privilege suspended for failing to provide proof of insurance, while a resident of the state may have his driving privilege suspended if he has failed to meet the financial responsibility requirements of another state. Under some circumstances, a person who has had his driving privileges suspended because of his failure to provide proof of insurance may apply for a restricted license in order to drive to and from work or in the course of employment.

## DRIVERS INVOLVED IN AN ACCIDENT MUST EXCHANGE INFORMATION

Drivers involved in an accident, unless they are injured or unable to do so, are required by law to exchange the following information with each other:

Driver's name and current residence address

Driver's license number

Vehicle ID number

Current address of registered owner

Name and address of the vehicle's insurer

## PENALTY FOR FAILURE TO PROVIDE INFORMATION AFTER AN ACCIDENT

In most states any person who fails to comply with all these requirements is guilty of an infraction and is subject to a fine.

## SUSPENSION FOLLOWING UNSATISFIED JUDGMENTS

In most states any driver or owner of a vehicle who has been sued as a result of an accident and has had a judgment entered against him by the court will have his driving privilege suspended if the judgment is not paid within a specified period, usually thirty days from the date the judgment is entered. The suspension remains in effect until the person gives proof of financial responsibility and fully satisfies the judgment. If the trial court orders payment of the judgment in installments, a suspended license will be restored when the party proves financial responsibility for future damages and shows that no installments are in default. If the judgment debtor—the person required to pay damages—fails to pay any installment, he will have his driving privileges suspended until he is in compliance with the court order.

## CIVIL LIABILITY OF OWNERS AND OPERATORS OF VEHICLES

### PRIVATE OWNERS

Every owner of a motor vehicle is liable and responsible for the death or injury to any person or for damage to property resulting from a negligent or wrongful act or omission in the operation of his motor vehicle by any person using or operating the vehicle with his permission, whether that permission is expressed or implied.

### LIABILITY OF PERSONS SIGNING LICENSE APPLICATIONS OF MINORS

A minor is anyone under the age of majority under state laws for the purposes of the vehicle codes.

Before a minor's application for a driver's license may be granted, it must be signed and verified by the father and mother of the minor if both have custody of the minor. If only one parent is living or has custody, the application can usually be signed by that parent.

If the minor is a dependent or ward of the court, the application can usually be signed by a grandparent, an adult sibling, an aunt, an uncle, a foster parent with whom the minor resides, a probation officer, or a child protective services worker acting as an officer of the court.

A married minor may file an application signed by his or her spouse if that spouse is an adult.

An emancipated minor may file an application signed by his employer, in which case the minor may be granted a restricted license for use only in the course of his employment. No matter who signs or verifies the minor's application, the minor is required to provide proof of financial responsibility.

*The person who signs an application for a license for a minor will be held jointly liable for any damages caused by negligence, any illegal act, or the omission of any required act related to driving a motor vehicle.* An employer or official government employee who signs a minor's application for a license is exempt from this liability.

### LIABILITY OF PARENTS OR GUARDIAN

In most states any liability that arises from the operation by a minor of a motor vehicle, with the expressed or implied consent of his parents or guardian, will be imposed on the parents or guardian whether or not the minor is licensed.

### CANCELLATION OF THE LICENSE OF A MINOR

The license of a minor will be canceled by the Department of Motor Vehicles if the person who initially signed the application requests its cancellation. When it is canceled, the person who signed the application will be relieved of further liability for the acts of the minor.

If the father and mother or the guardian who signed the minor's application should die, the department will cancel the minor's license unless the guardian or person having custody of the minor consents to having the liability transferred to him.

## RULES OF THE ROAD

### PEDESTRIANS' RIGHTS AND DUTIES

If a pedestrian is crossing a street or road controlled by a traffic light, he may proceed to cross the street when the sign or symbol indicates "Walk." When a signal indicates a flashing or steady light that says "Wait" or "Don't Walk," it is illegal for a pedestrian to start to cross the roadway.

Where there are marked crosswalks controlled by traffic signals, pedestrians must cross the road only at the marked crosswalks. When walking along a roadway that does not have sidewalks, pedestrians are required by law to walk along the left-hand edge of the roadway, facing oncoming vehicular traffic.

Most states make it illegal for any person to hitchhike, that is to solicit a ride from the driver of a vehicle.

A pedestrian who is blind or partially blind and is carrying a white cane or is accompanied by a guide dog has the right-of-way, and any driver who fails to yield the right-of-way is guilty of a misdemeanor. Only a person deemed legally blind may carry a white cane with or without a red tip.

It is usually illegal for a pedestrian to use a bike path if there is a pedestrian sidewalk adjacent to the bike path.

Regulation of skateboards, in-line skating, and roller skating is usually the responsibility of the local governmental agency.

### SPEED LAWS

Basic speed laws state that no person shall drive a vehicle at a speed in excess of that which is reasonable and prudent, considering the weather, visibility, traffic, size and condition of the road surface, or circumstances that endanger people or property.

A speed limit is posted to indicate the maximum speed at which any vehicle may proceed on that road or street. Where no speed limit is posted, the following speed limits are typical of unposted speed laws in the various states:

Fifteen miles per hour:

When crossing a railroad crossing that is not controlled by a signal or flagman

When crossing a highway intersection where there is no signal, yield sign, or stop sign

In any alley

Twenty-five miles per hour:

When driving on any road that is not a state road and is in any business or residential area

When passing a school building at the time when children are going to or leaving the school or when they are present in the grounds around the school with no fence separating the grounds from the road and a sign is posted that says SCHOOL

When passing a senior center or other facility used primarily by senior citizens if that area is posted with a SENIOR warning sign

## MINIMUM SPEEDS

It is unlawful for anyone to drive on a road or street at such a slow speed that he impedes or blocks the normal movement of traffic, unless his slow speed is necessary for safe operation because of a steep grade or compliance with the law. If a minimum speed is posted for any road or street, that speed must be maintained by any vehicle operating on the road or street except when traveling at the minimum speed would be unsafe.

## DRIVING OFFENSES

The list of driving offenses is lengthy. Some of the more common ones are:

Reckless driving

Reckless driving causing bodily injury

Speed contests and exhibitions of speed

Throwing substances at vehicles

Littering

Spilling or releasing hazardous materials

Transporting a minor in the rear of a truck

Transporting an unrestrained animal in the rear of a truck

Operating a vehicle that exceeds the legal noise limits

Operating a vehicle when the driver has a blood alcohol level of 0.01 percent or more and is under twenty-one years of age

Driving with a blood alcohol level of 0.05 percent or more when the driver is under eighteen years of age

Driving with a blood alcohol level of 0.08 percent or more when the driver is an adult

Refusal to submit to intoxication test

Failure to pay a fine imposed by a court

Sale of a vehicle that has been declared a nuisance

Consuming alcoholic beverages while driving

Consumption of alcoholic beverages by a passenger

Open alcohol containers or marijuana in vehicle

Open alcohol container in vehicle in possession of person under twenty-one

Possession of unsealed alcohol containers in passenger compartment

Failure to yield the right-of-way

Unsafe lane change

Following too closely

Failure to stop at a stop sign or light

Excessive speed

## INFRACTIONS, MISDEMEANORS, AND FELONIES

Violations of traffic rules may be classified as infractions, misdemeanors, or felonies, depending on the seriousness of the violation and whether the driver has previously been convicted of the same offense.

## INFRACTIONS

Minor traffic violations are classified as infractions. Some violations that are classified as infractions include these:

Parking in a space reserved for a handicapped driver

Transporting an animal in the back of a truck when the truck is not enclosed or the animal is not tied so that it cannot be injured or ejected from the truck

Littering

Unlawful use of car pool lanes, including unlawful entrance and exit

Failure to yield the right-of-way to an emergency vehicle

Disconnecting or modifying a pollution control device

Failure to obey traffic signals by pedestrians

Driving a vehicle with too many occupants

Failure to keep a safe distance between vehicles

Failure to register a vehicle

Speeding up to one hundred miles per hour

The fine for an infraction varies with the offense, but in most states it is usually a minimum of fifty dollars and a maximum fine of one hundred dollars for the first offense. In addition to the fine, many states charge the violator a penalty assessment.

Whenever a driver pleads guilty to or is convicted of a second or third offense, the court may charge him with a misdemeanor or a felony if the charge is serious. Furthermore, whenever someone is injured or property is damaged as a result of a violation that would otherwise be charged as an infraction, the court may file misdemeanor charges against the driver. In addition to the charges imposed by the vehicle code, the driver may be charged with a criminal offense under the penal codes of various states.

The court may allow a person who is assessed a fine for an infraction to pay the fine in installments. However, the party must make each payment in full on or before the day it is due or appear in court on that day to explain why he cannot make the payment. Failure to make installment payments when they are due is punishable as contempt and may result in a warrant's being issued by the court for the arrest of the violator.

A person who has received a written notice to appear for an infraction may, prior to the time when he is required to appear, deposit bail with the clerk of the court and indicate his intention to plead not guilty to the violation. The case will then be set for arraignment and trial. When the violation is an infraction, the violator usually may submit a bail deposit and enter a plea by mail. If the person wishes to plead guilty to the violation, he may remit the required amount of bail to the court along with his guilty plea. In most cases, if the cited party does not appear in court on the scheduled day, the bail will be considered forfeited, and the violator's obligation will have been fulfilled.

## MISDEMEANORS

A misdemeanor charge is more serious than an infraction but less serious than a felony. Some of the violations that are misdemeanors include providing false information or making false statements to a law enforcement official, impersonating a police officer, fleeing from a patrol officer, using deceptive or false evidence of vehicle registration, altering or defacing vehicle ID numbers, allowing an unlicensed person to drive a vehicle one owns, reckless driving, engaging in speed contests, throwing items at vehicles, driving under the influence of drugs or alcohol, possession of marijuana, failing to secure children in child passenger seat restraints, turning back the odometer on a vehicle, failing to appear in court or pay a fine, using a fictitious name, failing to correct an equipment violation, and failure to attend traffic school. In some states some of these offenses may be treated as infractions.

An offense that would otherwise be an infraction is often treated as a misdemeanor if the person has been convicted of the same violation previously in the twelve-month period before the commission of the offense. Violations by pedestrians are usually not charged as misdemeanors even after the third violation within twelve months.

An individual convicted of a misdemeanor may be fined and imprisoned. For most misdemeanor offenses, the maximum fine is one thousand dollars and up to six months in jail. A driver convicted of a misdemeanor may be fined and sentenced to a jail term. If the person is unwilling or unable to pay the fine, in many states he or she may be jailed in lieu of paying the fine, at the rate of one day for a specified amount of the fine. However, some specific violations have penalties that exceed these limits, such as a misdemeanor conviction for the theft of a vehicle that has been modified for use by a disabled person or a misdemeanor charge of driving while under the influence of alcohol or drugs.

## FAILURE TO APPEAR

When a vehicle driver is given a citation by a law enforcement officer, the driver is required to sign a statement that he will appear in court at the time, day, and place stipulated on the ticket to enter a plea to the charges being alleged. If a driver refuses to sign the promise to appear, the officer will arrest him and take him to jail.

When a person has signed a promise to appear, he is required to do so. Prior to the date of his appearance, he may request a continuance—permission to appear at a later time. If the court grants his request, he will not be in violation of the promise to appear as long as he appears at the later time. If he wishes, he may hire an attorney to appear in court for him.

A person who fails to appear in court after promising to appear is guilty of a misdemeanor. The misdemeanor charge will be valid even if the charge on which he failed to appear is dismissed or he is found not guilty of it. In addition, the court may assess the violator a fine for the violation with which he was originally charged if a warrant for his arrest was issued after he had failed to appear. The court will usually suspend the violator's driving privilege until he has complied with the requirements of the court.

If the violation of a citation requires the person to post bail, he must do so on or before the date required by the court. Failure to post the required bail may result in the court's issuing an arrest warrant.

## Hit-and-Run/Failure to Stop/Leaving the Scene of an Accident

The driver of a vehicle involved in an accident causing death or injury to any person or resulting in damage to any property is required by law to stop immediately at the scene. Failure to stop at the scene of an accident in which the driver and his vehicle are involved is punishable by a fine and imprisonment. If a death or serious permanent injury results from the accident, a driver who leaves the scene may be punished by a sentence in state prison and a fine. If a driver leaves the scene of an accident where only property damage occurred, he may be punished by imprisonment in local jail and a fine.

## Misdemeanor Driving Under the Influence of Alcohol or Drugs

The law in all states has established that any adult who has a blood alcohol content exceeding a specified level is presumed to be under the influence of alcohol and is guilty of the offense of driving under the influence of alcohol. (See multistate compendium on drunk driving on page 222.)

By law any driver apprehended by a law enforcement officer who has reason to believe that the person may be under the influence of drugs or alcohol must submit to a test to determine the drug or alcohol level in his body. Failure to submit to and complete the test requires that the person's driving license be suspended or revoked from six months to one year. A suspension will usually be ordered by the court if this is the first time the person has refused to submit to a chemical test and he has no previous alcohol-related vehicle code convictions. Subsequent alcohol-related driving offenses will result in revocation of the person's driver's license for up to three years.

## Felonies

Felonies are the most serious violations and usually involve injury to persons, damage to property, repeated convictions, and wanton disregard for the safety of others. The penalty imposed by the court for conviction of a felony may include a substantial fine and confinement in state prison. A felony conviction usually results in the suspension or revocation of driving privileges in addition to the standard criminal penalties.

## Vehicular Manslaughter

Vehicular homicide occurs when a driver strikes and kills someone without intention while driving a car. Any person convicted of vehicular manslaughter may be charged with a felony if he is driving while his blood alcohol level exceeds the specified level, usually 0.08 percent, or if he is under the influence of a controlled substance and kills a person while committing an unlawful act that is not a felony, or if he commits an act that is not unlawful but might cause death. Gross negligence is not required. Felony vehicular manslaughter is punishable by up to four years in state prison in some states.

## The Point System

Some state departments of motor vehicles assign a point value to vehicle violations based on the seriousness of the violation. If a driver accumulates too many points in a specified period, the driver's license may be suspended or revoked, or driving privileges may be restricted, such as driving only to and from work.

Some of the point values typically assigned for violation of the vehicle laws in most states are:

- Failure to stop in the event of an accident          Two points
- Driving while under the influence of drugs or alcohol          Two points
- Reckless driving          Two points
- Responsibility for an accident          One point
- Driving on a suspended license          Two points

- Failure to use child safety restraints        One point
- Other violations        One point

## NEGLIGENT VEHICLE OPERATOR STATUS

A driver can be presumed to be a negligent operator of a motor vehicle if he accumulates points in increments as follows:

Four or more points in a twelve-month period

Six or more points in a twenty-four-month period

Eight or more points in a thirty-six-month period

Any person deemed to be a negligent operator of a motor vehicle may have his license suspended or revoked by the Department of Motor Vehicles. If a driver is notified of a pending suspension or revocation because he has accumulated too many points, he may request a hearing. In reaching a decision regarding suspension or revocation, the hearing officer will take into consideration the number of miles the driver travels.

If the facts allow, the DMV may permit the person to retain a probationary or restricted license. Before a suspended or revoked license may be reinstated, the applicant must usually submit proof of insurance or financial responsibility to the Department of Motor Vehicles.

## HABITUAL OFFENDER DESIGNATION

If a person convicted of vehicular manslaughter has been previously convicted for being intoxicated with a blood alcohol level exceeding the legal limit or for being under the influence of drugs or for driving in a reckless manner or for any combination of these offenses, he can be designated a habitual traffic offender under most state laws. That designation can remain in effect for up to three years after the conviction. A habitual traffic offender who is also convicted of driving with a suspended or revoked license can be punished by a substantial fine and imprisonment often up to 180 days.

A person may be designated a habitual traffic offender if he is convicted of driving while his license is suspended or revoked and he is involved in any combination of reportable accidents and convictions. On a first conviction, the habitual offender may be punished by a fine of at least one thousand dollars and imprisonment for 30 days. A second or subsequent conviction as a habitual offender often carries a penalty of a fine of two thousand dollars and imprisonment for 180 days. The penalties for being designated a habitual traffic offender are added to any penalties for the underlying convictions that led to the designation.

## OFFENSES INVOLVING ALCOHOL AND DRUGS

Driving while under the influence of alcohol or drugs is considered a serious violation. Although driving while intoxicated used to be considered strictly a vehicle violation, today most states have laws that impose criminal penalties on those convicted of serious alcohol- and drug-related vehicle offenses.

To prevent the high incidence of death and injury caused by drivers who consume alcohol and/or drugs and drive, states have enacted laws that are very strict and are aimed at both the punishment of the offender and his rehabilitation.

First offenses of driving while intoxicated may be charged as misdemeanors if the violations do not include an accident in which a person was killed or seriously injured or in which extensive property damage resulted. In deciding whether an offense should be charged as a felony or misdemeanor, law enforcement officials also evaluate the offender's prior driving record and his blood alcohol level at the time of arrest.

In most states persons convicted of alcohol-related offenses are required to attend court-approved rehabilitation programs.

Both adults and minors are treated strictly under current laws governing driving while intoxicated, but especially harsh laws have been established for minors in the hope that early intervention will prevent more serious incidents later in life.

The law provides extremely serious penalties for anyone convicted of an alcohol-related driving offense while working as a driver of a commercial vehicle, while transporting others for hire, when persons are injured or killed, when property is damaged, when another crime is committed by the driver while intoxicated, when the intoxicated driver has multiple convictions for similar offenses, when the convicted party has also been convicted of leaving the scene of an accident he was involved in as a driver, and when he fails to meet the financial responsibility laws.

## DETENTION BY A LAW ENFORCEMENT OFFICER ON SUSPICION OF DRIVING WHILE INTOXICATED

A law enforcement officer may detain any person whom he reasonably suspects of driving while under the influence of any alcoholic beverage or drug or any combination of alcohol and drugs. The officer may conduct a field sobriety test, usually a series of movements to evaluate the suspect's physical responses and coordination at the time of the initial detention. He may ask the person detained to submit to a preliminary alcohol screening test commonly known as a breath test. If the officer determines, after evaluating the results of the field sobriety test and the breath test, that the person is under the influence of alcohol or drugs, he will arrest him and take him into custody. If the person refuses to take the field sobriety test or breath test, he will be arrested if the officer reasonably suspects him of being under the influence.

## Arrest on Suspicion of Driving While Under the Influence of Alcohol or Drugs

A law enforcement officer who reasonably suspects someone of violating the law by driving a vehicle while under the influence of alcohol or drugs may arrest that person and transport him to the appropriate jail. At the jail he is required to give the authorized personnel information to establish his identity and is usually photographed and fingerprinted. The officer will inform the suspect of his obligation to submit to a chemical blood test.

The person arrested usually may choose to have either a blood test or a urine test, and the test is conducted at no charge to him. Even if he has taken a breath test, he usually must submit to either a blood or urine test.

## Penalty for Refusal to Submit to Blood or Urine Test

Anyone who refuses an officer's request to submit to a chemical test will have his driving privilege suspended for up to one year. If the driver has previously been convicted of driving while under the influence of alcohol or drugs, vehicular manslaughter, reckless driving, reckless driving with bodily injury to another person, or gross vehicular manslaughter while intoxicated, or if he previously has had his license suspended or revoked for refusing to submit to a chemical test of blood or urine, his license may be revoked for two years. Two or more convictions of the violations in this paragraph resulting in a two-year suspension can cause his license to be revoked for three years. Even if a person is not convicted of driving while under the influence of alcohol or drugs, these penalties can be imposed.

## Written Agreement to Submit to Chemical Test

In most states any person who applies for a driver's license or renewal of a license is required to sign, as part of the application process, a statement that he agrees to submit to a chemical test of his breath, blood, or urine when requested to do so by a law enforcement officer who suspects he is driving while under the influence. An applicant who refuses to sign the agreement will not be issued a license or have his license renewed.

## SUSPENSION OF LICENSE AT TIME OF ARREST AND TEMPORARY LICENSE

Under the more aggressive procedures implemented in most states today, if a person who has been arrested on suspicion of driving while under the influence of alcohol has a blood alcohol level greater than the legal limit or if he is under the influence of drugs, he receives a notice of order of suspension and has his driver's license confiscated by the arresting officer. The officer issues him a temporary license that is valid for a short period, usually thirty days from the date of arrest.

## PENALTIES FOR CONVICTION OF DRIVING WHILE INTOXICATED

### FIRST OFFENSE

Any person who is convicted, pleads guilty, or enters a plea of nolo contendere for driving under the influence of alcohol or drugs will be punished by any or all of the following:

1. Imprisonment in jail for the minimum period under state law, usually ninety-six hours and a maximum period usually of six months
2. A fine of up to one thousand dollars
3. Suspension of his driver's license for up to six months
4. Successful completion of a court-approved alcohol and drug education and counseling program
5. Probation for a prescribed period, usually for a minimum of three and up to five years, including items six through eight
6. A requirement that the person not drive with any measurable alcohol in his blood
7. A requirement that the person agree to submit to chemical testing if he is arrested for a future violation of driving while under the influence of alcohol or drugs
8. A requirement that the person not commit any criminal offense
9. Payment of an alcohol abuse education and penalty assessment

### SECOND OFFENSE

A person who is convicted of a second driving offense while under the influence of alcohol or drugs, if within the prescribed period of being convicted of reckless driving, driving while under the influence of alcohol or drugs, or driving while intoxicated and causing injury to another person, is subject to the following increased penalties:

1. Imprisonment for the prescribed minimum period of at least ninety days but no more than one year
2. A fine of up to one thousand dollars
3. Suspension of driver's license for up to eighteen months
4. Successful completion of a court-approved alcohol and drug education and counseling program as decided by the court
5. Probation for three to five years, including items six through eight below
6. A requirement that the person not drive with any measurable alcohol in his blood
7. A requirement that the person agree to submit to chemical testing if arrested for a future violation of driving while under the influence of alcohol or drugs
8. A requirement that the person not commit any criminal offense
9. Payment of an alcohol abuse education and penalty assessment

## Two Prior Convictions

Any person convicted three or more times within the prescribed period, usually seven years, of driving under the influence of alcohol or drugs, with previous similar convictions or for reckless driving with or without injury to another person, can be subject to the following penalties:

1. Imprisonment for no less than the prescribed period, usually 120 days and no more than 1 year
2. A fine of up to one thousand dollars
3. Revocation of his driving privilege for up to three years. After the license has been revoked for a minimum period, usually twenty-four months, the person may apply to the court for a restricted license if she has successfully completed an alcohol education program and agrees to have an ignition interlock device installed in her vehicle
4. Mandatory designation as a habitual traffic offender for up to three years
5. Successful completion of an alcohol and drug education and counseling program
6. Probation for three to five years, including items seven through nine below
7. A requirement that the person not drive with any measurable alcohol in her blood
8. A requirement that the person agree to submit to chemical testing if she is arrested for a future violation of driving while under the influence of alcohol or drugs
9. A requirement that the person not commit any criminal offense
10. Payment of an alcohol abuse education and prevention penalty assessment

## ADDITIONAL PENALTIES

In most states, if someone is injured or dies as a result of a first violation of driving under the influence of drugs or alcohol, the person convicted of the violation is guilty of a felony.

Multiple convictions of driving under the influence of alcohol or drugs in cases in which another person is injured often require mandatory imprisonment for up to seven years.

## IMPOUNDMENT OF VEHICLE UPON CONVICTION OF DRIVING WHILE UNDER THE INFLUENCE OF ALCOHOL OR DRUGS

The court in most states today may order any vehicle driven in an alcohol or drug violation impounded for a specified period, usually up to ninety days at the registered owner's expense.

## SEIZURE AND SALE OF VEHICLE USED IN COMMISSION OF OFFENSE

Any vehicle owner who is convicted of gross vehicular manslaughter while intoxicated, vehicular manslaughter, or driving under the influence of alcohol or drugs with or without injury to another person, and who has previously been convicted of one of the same offenses, may have his vehicle seized by the sheriff and sold as ordered by the court.

## SUSPENSION OR REVOCATION PERIOD TO BEGIN AFTER PRISON TERM IS COMPLETED

In some states whenever any person is sentenced to serve one year or more in jail or prison for a conviction for leaving the scene of an accident or for driving under the influence of alcohol or drugs with or without injury to another, the court may order that his driving privilege suspension or revocation be postponed so that the time period begins after the prison sentence has been served.

## ADDITIONAL PENALTIES FOR HIGH BLOOD ALCOHOL LEVEL

A few states have passed laws under which any person determined to have a blood alcohol level of 0.20 or greater at the time he committed an offense related to driving while under the influence of alcohol or drugs may be subject to penalties beyond those established for the basic offense, including probation.

## PENALTY FOR SPEEDING AND RECKLESS DRIVING WHILE DRIVING UNDER THE INFLUENCE OF ALCOHOL OR DRUGS

It is common for state laws to hold that any person convicted of driving under the influence of alcohol or drugs and also convicted of reckless driving by exceeding the specified speed limit by usually thirty miles per hour or more shall be required to serve an additional term of imprisonment.

## CONSUMPTION OR PRESENCE OF ALCOHOL IN A VEHICLE

It is routinely held to be illegal for a driver or passenger in a vehicle to drink any alcoholic beverage while the motor vehicle is being operated on any road, except for passengers in a bus, taxicab, or limousine for hire. It is also illegal for anyone while a driver or passenger in a vehicle to have in his possession any kind of container with alcohol unless it is in a sealed bottle or can. Usually a partially empty bottle that contains alcohol and is not sealed may be transported in the trunk of a vehicle.

## ALCOHOLIC BEVERAGE IN VEHICLE DRIVEN BY PERSON UNDER TWENTY-ONE

Most states provide that no container carrying any alcoholic beverage, whether or not it is sealed, may be carried in a vehicle driven by anyone under the age of twenty-one unless the driver is accompanied by a parent, responsible adult relative, or legal or temporary guardian designated by the parent.

## OFFENSES INVOLVING ALCOHOL BY PERSON UNDER TWENTY-ONE

In some cases it is against the law for any person under the age of twenty-one to drive a motor vehicle if he has a blood-alcohol level of 0.01 percent or greater as measured by a preliminary alcohol screening test and/or breath test. If any person under twenty-one years of age is detained under suspicion of driving after having consumed alcohol and refuses to submit to a breath analysis test, he can have his driver's license suspended or revoked. In California and a few other states, if a preliminary alcohol screening test or breath analysis test indicates that the person under twenty-one years of age has a blood alcohol level of 0.01 or greater, the law enforcement officer can immediately take possession of the driver's license. In that case the officer must issue a temporary license, which will be valid for a specified period, usually thirty days or until the Department of Motor Vehicles issues a notice of suspension to the driver. A driver whose license is suspended because he was under twenty-one years and had a blood alcohol level of 0.01 or greater is not subject to other penalties. The offense is not an infraction, misdemeanor, or felony but is strictly a civil action in most states.

## EQUIPMENT OF VEHICLES

### GENERAL REQUIREMENTS

It is generally unlawful to operate any vehicle that is unsafe or is not equipped as required by law. After a law enforcement officer has notified an owner or a driver that a vehicle is unsafe, it may not be driven until it is repaired and safe, except to return to the driver's or owner's residence or place of business or to a repair facility.

During darkness passenger vehicles must have two operating headlights, and the beams must be properly adjusted. Every passenger vehicle must have two red tail lights and two stop lights on the rear of the vehicle, and the rear license plate must be illuminated either by the tail light or by a separate light. A vehicle may be equipped with parking lights, but it is usually illegal to drive at any time with the parking lights on, unless the headlights are also on. Flashing lights are prohibited on passenger vehicles, except for intermittent turn signals, hazard lights on a disabled vehicle parked off the roadway as a warning of a hazard, or headlights on vehicles in a funeral procession. Emergency vehicles may use flashing lights as authorized by law.

Typically every passenger vehicle must be equipped with both service and parking brakes and must be capable of stopping within twenty-five feet while traveling twenty miles per hour.

Passenger vehicles must have windshields made of safety glass and must be equipped with windshield wipers.

It is illegal to obstruct the driver's vision with any object or material on the windshield or front door windows. It is illegal to install or affix any transparent material to a windshield or the side or rear windows of any motor vehicle if the material alters the color or reduces the light transmittance of the glass, except in those cases where the driver has in his possession a letter from a doctor or optometrist stating that he has a medical or visual condition that requires shielding from the sun.

Motor vehicles must have a horn in operating condition, but only authorized emergency vehicles may have sirens.

Vehicles must have mufflers that comply with the noise requirements established by the state. Manifolds, mufflers, and exhaust pipes must be maintained in a gas-tight condition. Vehicles are required to have proper emissions devices and a certificate of compliance in order to be registered or operated.

In most states any vehicle manufactured after a specified date, usually January 1, 1962, must be equipped with at least two seat belts in the front passenger compartment.

The tires on a vehicle must meet the minimum tread requirements. All vehicles must have fenders that are adequate to direct any debris or liquid on the roadway away from the vehicle.

Usually any television operated in a passenger vehicle must be placed so that it is not viewable by the driver.

## Mandatory Seat Belt Use

Most states have enacted a Private Passenger Motor Vehicle Safety Act, which states that no person shall operate a private passenger motor vehicle unless the driver and all passengers are properly restrained by safety belts or approved child safety restraint systems.

Exceptions to the mandatory seat belt law are usually allowed for taxicabs operated on city streets and limousines for hire, in which front seat occupants are required to use seat belts. An additional exception is made for drivers or passengers with medical conditions that prevent the use of a seat belt, if those conditions are certified by licensed physicians.

Violation of the mandatory seat belt law is punishable by a fine of twenty dollars and up for the first offense and substantially more for each subsequent offense. In addition, the courts may require a person convicted of violating this provision to attend a court-approved traffic school.

## Child Safety Belt and Passenger Restraint Systems

Most states today have laws which state that any child under a specified age, usually four years, *or* who weighs less than a specified amount, usually forty pounds, regardless of age must be secured in an approved child safety seat whenever he is in a passenger car, truck, or van. The driver, parent, or guardian of a child who is not properly secured may be fined. The fine for a first offense may often be waived by the court for a parent who is economically disadvantaged, and the court may refer the parent or driver to a program that provides child passenger restraints at a reduced cost. The violation will usually be reported to the Department of Motor Vehicles. A second violation of the child passenger restraint requirement can require the payment of a fine in excess of one hundred dollars plus penalty assessments. The fine for a second or subsequent violation usually cannot be waived.

A parent, guardian, or driver who permits a vehicle to be operated when a child is not fastened in an approved seat belt is subject to a moderate fine usually of fifty dollars for the first offense and one hundred dollars for any subsequent offense. If the parent of the child is present in the vehicle, he or she shall be liable for the fine even though he or she is not the driver.

In most states auto rental agencies are required to notify people renting vehicles of the child restraint requirements and to make available for rent child restraint systems that meet federal requirements and are less than five years old.

## TRAFFIC SCHOOL

The court may allow someone who has been cited for unsafe operation of a vehicle such as speeding to attend a special court-approved traffic school. After the driver has successfully completed traffic school, the court may dismiss the violation. The dismissal is important because vehicle insurance rates are based, among other things, on the number and frequency of driving violations. The person who receives the traffic ticket is usually required to pay a fee equal to the violation fine plus the cost of the traffic safety school instruction.

Traffic school usually is an eight- to twelve-hour class, and those attending are required to show identification before they will be permitted to enter. Some jurisdictions have a home study traffic school program available.

Someone who attends traffic school must obtain a certificate from the school and submit the completed certificate to the court. Failure to deliver the certificate to the court will result in a conviction for the offense, which is then entered on the person's driving record.

Some offenders may choose to attend traffic school voluntarily. However, the court may *order* a violator to attend traffic school. Any person who fails to comply with a court order to attend traffic school may be guilty of a misdemeanor.

## PLEADING GUILTY, NOT GUILTY, OR *NOLO CONTENDERE*

A plea of guilty, a plea of *nolo contendere,* a judgment of guilty, or a forfeiture of bail all constitute a conviction for any motor vehicle offense except a parking violation.

## TRIAL IN TRAFFIC CASES

In most states a traffic violation can be treated as an infraction or a misdemeanor. The difference is in degree of the offense and, in many states, entitlement or not of a jury trial. For example, a speeding ticket is an infraction with no right to a jury trial in most states. Driving under the influence in most cases is a misdemeanor with the right to a jury trial and the possibility of going to jail if one is convicted.

If someone chooses to fight the traffic ticket, there are certain steps he should follow. After pleading not guilty, he is given a trial date. He must appear at the scheduled time and on the scheduled date. In most states he is required to go to municipal court and appear before a judge, a commissioner, or a judge pro tempore. In court his case is called by the clerk or judge. He and any witnesses and the officer approach the table where all are sworn in. Then the officer presents his case by telling the judge the facts of the case as he believes them to be. Technically the officer has the burden of proof in a traffic trial. Once the officer has testified, the defendant may cross-examine him. Then it is the defendant's turn to present his case.

The defendant's goal is to discredit the officer's testimony by presenting evidence that disproves his case. If he has any defenses, he can raise them at this time. The judge may now ask if the officer wants to cross-examine, but this is rare. However, the defendant should be prepared for it just in case he is questioned about his testimony. Once both sides have been presented, the judge may or may not ask for a closing argument. After all testimony and evidence and final arguments have been given, the judge makes his decision.

In some states traffic infractions are handled by a prosecutor. The scenario is the same as outlined above, except that a prosecutor is there with the officer. The prosecutor presents the officer's case and will more than likely cross-examine the defendant after he has testified.

After you have been cited, and while the incident is still fresh in your mind, write down what happened. Try to be as detailed as possible. If possible, take pictures of the scene close to the time it happened so that they accurately reflect the scene.

Locate any maps or diagrams of the area where the incident occurred or make them yourself.

You have the right to bring witnesses. A witness is someone who was present during the incident and could testify about what happened. Go over the facts of the case with any witnesses to make sure the recollection of the facts are consistent. Then go over the questions you will ask in court. Always try to clarify the points of the case. If a witness does testify, he should be instructed to tell the truth, no matter what—even if it hurts your case.

If a witness has to be excused from work or school or has indicated that he is unwilling to testify, you have the right to subpoena him. A subpoena requires him to appear in court. If he does not appear, he can go to jail, be fined, or be held in contempt of court. To obtain a subpoena in most states, give the court clerk your name, case name, trial date, courtroom number, and the name and address of the person being subpoenaed. The court clerk will issue the subpoena; however, you are responsible for serving it.

A subpoena must be served on a witness by someone who is at least eighteen years old and is not a party to the action. To request documents, you can serve a subpoena duces tecum. It is similar to a regular subpoena except that you are asking for documents instead of a witness.

If you cannot appear on the scheduled date or need time to prepare, you may ask for a continuance to a later date. You should make a written request in advance, with a copy to the officer. If you do not get a response, call the clerk's office and show up on the scheduled date with your letter, and ask the court again for a continuance.

Testimony can be prepared by outlining what is to be said. Do not write it down verbatim or overrehearse. This can often make the testimony sound artificial or make it appear that you are lying. You should practice the testimony to avoid getting nervous while in court.

Prepare a final argument. This should consist of reasons why the officer has not met his burden of proof. Point out the weaknesses in the officer's testimony, and reiterate any defenses that have been raised. Be warned, however, that not all judges allow a final argument. If the judge denies this right, you may have grounds to appeal the case.

In most states misdemeanor cases are tried by prosecutors and are heard before juries. Because there are juries, these cases are very difficult to defend at trial, and I strongly recommend that you seek legal advice from an attorney. If you do not seek legal advice, use the above-mentioned infraction trial suggestions along with the following:

In most cases the first appearance in court is the arraignment. You agree to appear when you sign a notice to appear or when you are released from jail on bail. The purpose of the arraignment is to inform you of your rights so that you may enter a plea of guilty, not guilty, or nolo contendere. Before making a plea, you can ask the judge for a continuance in order to seek legal advice. If you decide to make a plea, be warned. If you plead guilty, and the case involves an auto accident, a guilty plea can be used against you in a separate civil action for money. Furthermore, in a guilty plea there are no negotiations for a lesser plea or for a reduced penalty. By pleading not guilty, you can try to reduce the charge and/or the penalty by negotiating with the prosecutor, or you can fight the misdemeanor at trial.

After you have made your plea of not guilty, a trial date is set, and you can and should request a jury trial if it is available. In some states a pretrial conference date is given instead of a trial date. At the conference a trial date is set. You must be sure to ask for a jury trial at the pretrial conference as well as ask for it when you first plead not guilty.

Because the courts are so backed up with cases, prosecutors are often encouraged to make deals with defendants. Usually a prosecutor will offer a defendant a "lesser" charge in exchange for a guilty plea. More than likely the deal is a lesser fine and/or less or no jail time. You may accept or reject the prosecutor's offer.

If you take the deal and plead guilty to a lesser charge, you go back to court, where the judge will make sure you understand what the deal is and what the consequences are. If you reject the deal, you go to trial.

The most important part about a jury trial is the selection of the jury. It starts when the potential jurors enter the courtroom. Usually a list of their names and occupations is given to the defendant ahead of time. In most states the judge then asks the potential jurors questions. However, some judges allow the prosecutor and the defendant or his lawyer to ask questions, so be prepared. Try to find out ahead of time who the judge is and which procedure he uses. If you are allowed to ask questions, make a list of questions that you want to ask in advance. The questions are intended to seek information about the jurors. The defendant wants to find out if they will be prejudiced against him. Once he has asked the questions, he must decide which jurors he wants to disqualify from the jury. He may disqualify a potential juror by using a peremptory challenge or a challenge for cause. Peremptory challenges can be used for any reason, and most states allow six to ten challenges per side. For example, the defendant may not like the person's attitude or appearance.

For cause challenges can be used when the potential juror seems prejudiced against the defendant. When he wants to excuse a juror, he should let the judge know which juror and what type of challenge he is using.

Once the jury is selected, the trial begins. However, at the end of the trial the judge must instruct the jury. The instructions will be submitted at the end of the evidence but before the closing arguments. Jury instructions in most states are found in jury instruction books that are in law libraries under "Jury Instructions." The instructions should include, at a minimum, the following:

Duties of the judge and jury

Which side has the burden of proof

Rules for determining the credibility of a witness

Elements of the crime the person is charged with

Presumption of innocence

Once the instructions are submitted, the judge reads them to the jury. The jury then deliberates and returns with a verdict.

# 14

# Criminal Law

## CIVIL LAWS AND CRIMINAL LAWS

Laws in the United States are divided into two basic types: civil law and criminal law. Civil laws cover noncriminal wrongdoing between individuals. The parties involved in a civil dispute have the right to bring legal action against each other.

Criminal law covers wrongdoing that is injurious to society at large. Violations of criminal laws are prosecuted by the district attorney if the law is a local or state law or by the U.S. attorney if the law is a federal law. The district attorney or U.S. attorney represents the people of the state or federal jurisdiction and prosecutes the violator on behalf of the people or society at large.

This procedure is well stated in a court case that held "that a criminal action being prosecuted by the people, and not in the interest of any injured person, is a fundamental principle of criminal law" (*People v. Clark,* 117 CA 2d 134).

## RIGHTS OF DEFENDANTS IN CRIMINAL CASES

A person who has been charged with having committed a crime has several rights under the U.S. Constitution.

### Fourth Amendment
The defendant has a right to be free from unreasonable searches and seizures. Any search and seizure must be based on probable cause and generally must be made pursuant to a search warrant. Probable cause is a legally sufficient basis to believe that evidence of a crime will be found on the person or property to be searched. Searches and seizures that are made without warrants are unconstitutional unless they qualify under one of the legal exceptions.

Exceptions are situations in which a search warrant is not required. No warrant is required when the search is incident to a lawful arrest or involving an automobile if there is probable cause to believe the vehicle contains evidence of a crime or when the evidence is in plain view to an officer who is legally present. Another exception exists to allow the police to stop and frisk (pat down outer clothes) for weapons when they have a reasonable suspicion that a person may be armed. Police can also search someone who consents if the consent is given voluntarily and intelligently. No warrant is required when the police are in hot pursuit of a dangerous suspect or when the evidence is of a type that could deteriorate or vanish in the time a warrant could be obtained; this includes blood samples with alcohol and fingernail scrapings.

### Fifth Amendment

The Fifth Amendment to the U.S. Constitution gives the defendant the right to refuse to answer questions whose answers may tend to incriminate him. Usually a person must assert the privilege at the time of questioning, but this is not the case in a trial. At trial the witness or defendant has the right not even to take the stand.

The Fifth Amendment further prohibits the government from requiring a person to stand trial twice for the same offense. Double jeopardy does not apply to cases in which a jury has not been able to reach a verdict (hung jury) or when the second trial is for a different offense or when a different state or the federal government was the prosecutor.

### Eighth Amendment

The Eighth Amendment prohibits cruel and unusual punishment by the government of those accused of or convicted of crimes. The length of a jail or prison sentence cannot be excessive in relation to the nature of the crime. The death penalty is not, in and of itself, considered cruel and unusual punishment if it is imposed in strict compliance with the requirements as stated by the U.S. Supreme Court. But it can be unconstitutional if it is disproportionate to the crime.

## HOW CRIMINAL LAWS ARE MADE

The people of the United States and of each state, county, and city elect or appoint officials who have the authority to draft and adopt the criminal laws that govern society. In the various states, state laws and the penalty for violation of those laws are listed in the state codes.

The states have no unwritten criminal laws; for an act or omission to constitute a crime, it must be a violation of a written statute. The statutes covering criminal law are found in the penal or criminal codes of various states.

## DEFINITION OF A CRIME

The penal codes usually define crime as "an act committed or omitted in violation of a law forbidding or commanding it," and to which is annexed upon conviction, one of the following punishments:

Death

Imprisonment

Fine

Removal from office

Disqualification to hold and enjoy any office of honor, trust, or profit in the state

## FELONIES AND MISDEMEANORS

Crimes are divided into felonies and misdemeanors. Infractions are sometimes associated with crimes but are less serious and do not subject the violator to imprisonment.

A felony is a crime punishable by death or by imprisonment in state prison usually for more than one year.

Every other crime or public offense is a misdemeanor, which may result in local jail time of up to one year.

## ELEMENTS OF A CRIME

For a crime to have taken place, there must be the criminal act, criminal intent, the capacity to commit the crime, parties to the crime, and the elements or characteristics (corpus delicti) of the crime. The party accused of the crime must not be exempt from criminal liability.

## THE CRIMINAL ACT

The criminal act alone is not sufficient evidence to convict a suspect of having committed a crime. To constitute a crime, there must be unity of act and intent. In every crime or public offense there must exist both act and intent together or criminal negligence. The intent or intention is manifested by the circumstances connected with the offense.

## CRIMINAL INTENT

Criminal intent is the second element necessary for the commission of a crime. *Intent* refers to the mental state of the offender and is often called by its Latin name *mens rea* or the "guilty mind." Not all crimes require the same intent.

## GENERAL INTENT

General intent can be inferred from the doing of an act or failure to act.

## SPECIFIC INTENT

Specific intent is not inferred from the act but must be proved through such evidence as testimony and physical effects.

## TRANSFERRED INTENT

An offender can be held liable for a crime under the doctrine of transferred intent. For example, if A, meaning to kill B, kills C by mistake, A can still be held liable for the murder of C through the doctrine of transferred intent.

## CAPACITY: PERSONS WHO ARE NOT LEGALLY CAPABLE OF COMMITTING A CRIME

The law usually provides that all persons are capable of committing crimes except in special circumstances.

1.    In Arizona, California, and Florida, children under the age of fourteen are incapable of committing a crime in the absence of clear proof that at the time of committing the act charged against them they knew it was wrong. In Illinois, children under thirteen and in Texas children under fifteen are incapable of committing a crime in the absence of clear proof that at the time of committing the act charged against them they knew it was wrong.

      If the prosecutor can establish clear proof that at the time of committing the act the person under the specified age knew it was wrong, that person may be tried for the crime. Relevant areas of inquiry into establishing clear proof may include the minor's age, intelligence, education, experience, and any prior police contacts. The court may also question the minor's parents, teachers, and friends if doing so would be helpful.

2.  An idiot is legally defined as one who is virtually without mentality, one who is without understanding and thus is incapable of committing a crime.

This defense is separate from an insanity plea and serves only to establish the defendant's mental state from birth. Such a person is said to be incapable of appreciating the character and significance of his acts. Mental retardation does not necessarily come within the scope of this defense unless it can be established that the defendant was incapable of knowing the wrongfulness of his acts.

3. Persons who commit a criminal act under ignorance or mistake of fact, without criminal intent, are incapable of committing a crime.

If an act that by law is a crime is committed accidentally or by mistake, the defendant may avoid a penalty if he can prove that his act was indeed an accident or mistake. Mistake of fact in a criminal proceeding is a matter for the jury to decide.

In the crime of receiving stolen property, a person must know that the property was stolen. He must have knowledge of the illegal means by which it was obtained. If he does not know the property was stolen, he is not guilty of the crime. For example, if a pawnshop owner accepts a ring that was in fact stolen but he does not know that it was stolen, he is not guilty of receiving stolen goods.

4. A defendant may enter a defense of unconsciousness if he can establish that his acts were not done voluntarily. For example, if a person suffers from a physical illness that he is unable to control and he commits an otherwise criminal act as a result of that illness, he could be considered unconscious at the time of that act and would not be liable. Unconsciousness does not require that a person be incapable of movement. People who commit the act without being conscious of what they are doing are incapable of committing a crime.

5. People who commit the act or make the charged omission through misfortune or by accident, when it appears that there was no evil design, intention, or culpable negligence, are incapable of committing a crime.

Misfortune or accident may be introduced as a defense when there is an absolute lack of criminal act, criminal intent, or criminal negligence. For example, a person is driving carefully and within the speed limit when someone runs in front of the vehicle, causing the driver to strike and kill the victim. This would be an accident, not a crime.

6. Unless the crime is punishable by death, persons who commit the act or make the charged omission under threats sufficient to show reasonable belief that their lives would be endangered if they refused are incapable of committing a crime.

If a person commits a crime because he fears for his life, the threat of loss of life must be immediate. Threat of future danger is not a defense. Also, in most states, if the crime committed is punishable by the death penalty, no amount of threats, coercion, or duress will relieve a person who cooperates in the commission of such crime.

### Table 14-1: Age Capacity to Commit a Crime

Age at which a person is considered legally capable of committing a crime:

| | |
|---|---|
| Arizona | Fourteen |
| California | Fourteen |
| Florida | Fourteen |
| Illinois | Thirteen |
| New Mexico | No statutory age, case-by-case determination |
| New York | Fourteen |
| Texas | Fifteen |

## DEFENSES TO CRIMES

### INTOXICATION

Unconsciousness may in some cases be a defense to a criminal charge. However, unconsciousness caused by voluntary intoxication is available only as a partial defense to an offense requiring specific intent and is no defense at all to a crime of general intent (such as assault with a deadly weapon). Both act and intent together or criminal negligence must exist in every crime and is deemed to exist regardless of unconsciousness arising from voluntary intoxication.

### INSANITY

When a defendant enters a plea of not guilty by reason of insanity, the jury first tries him to determine his guilt or innocence in the commission of the crime. If he is found not guilty, he is released, and there is no need for the jury to consider the insanity factor.

If he is found guilty, the jury then hears evidence to determine his mental state at the time of the offense. Most states require a defendant who enters a plea of not guilty by reason of insanity to prove he was insane at the time the crime was committed. Evidence for or against insanity usually comes from the testimony of psychiatrists who have examined the defendant.

If the jury determines the defendant was insane at the time of the offense and evidence indicates he is now fully recovered, the judge will dismiss criminal charges and release him. If the jury determines that the defendant was insane at the time of the offense and evidence indicates he is still not fully recovered, the judge will commit the defendant to a mental health facility as authorized by law. The judge may order the defendant committed as either an inpatient or an outpatient, depending on the situation and the defendant's mental health.

If, after hearing the evidence, the jury finds the defendant was sane at the time of the offense and has been found guilty, the defendant will be sentenced for the crime as allowed under the law.

## PARTIES TO A CRIME

Historically, people involved with a crime were classified according to a complicated balance of each one's relationship to the crime. Today most laws provide only two classifications for persons associated with the commission of a crime. *Principals* to a crime are all persons concerned in the commission of a crime, whether it be felony or misdemeanor or whether they directly commit the act constituting the offense, or aid and abet in its commission, or, not being present, have advised and encouraged *its commission*.

An *accessory* to a crime classified as a felony is any person who, *after a felony has been committed,* harbors, conceals or aids another in such felony, with the intent that the other may avoid punishment. Any person convicted as an accessory may be confined to state prison. Even if the principal accused in a crime is acquitted, a person charged as an accessory can be tried and convicted.

## STATUTES OF LIMITATIONS

*Statutes of limitations* apply to both civil and criminal offenses and limit the amount of time that may legally pass between the time the offense was either committed or discovered and the filing of criminal charges (see multistate compendium on statutes of limitation, pages 197 to 199).

There are different statutes for felonies and misdemeanors, and not all crimes in a classification have the same time limitation. In some cases a **grand jury** indictment must be returned or a criminal complaint filed within a certain time after the crime is discovered. In other instances the statute of limitations starts running when the crime is committed.

## Running and Tolling of the Statute of Limitations

Two terms often used in conjunction with the statute of limitations are *running* and *tolling*. When someone says that the statute of limitations has begun to run, he means that the time period within which a complaint must be filed has begun to be reduced by one day for each day that passes without the filing of the complaint. When the statute of limitations is tolled, the time period is temporarily stopped or suspended, and the number of days for which the statute of limitations is tolled may be added on to the end of the time period established by law.

## Statute of Limitations for Misdemeanors

In California misdemeanors carry a one-year limitation. That means a complaint must be filed in municipal court or a grand jury indictment must be returned within that one-year statute of limitation. If the suspect has been outside the state during any part of the one-year limitation, that time does not count. Thus, if a suspect is absent from the state for six months and then returns, the six months' absence does not reduce the one-year period still required before the statute of limitations expires (see multistate compendium below).

## Statute of Limitations for Felonies

In California, felonies have a three-year statute of limitations following the commission of the felony. However, some felonies carry a three-year limit following the discovery of the felony (see multistate compendium, below). In 1987 California law extended the statute of limitations to six years for all crimes punishable by imprisonment of eight years or more.

There are some serious crimes such as murder for which there is no statute of limitations. Charges may be filed at any time after the crime has been committed or discovered.

### Table 14-2: Statutes of Limitation in Criminal Cases

#### ARIZONA

| | |
|---|---|
| **Felonies** | There is no statute of limitations for murder, misuse of public funds, or falsifying public records. The statute of limitations for all other felonies is seven years. |
| **Misdemeanors** | Six months for petty offenses and one year for all other misdemeanors. |

## *Table 14-2: Statutes of Limitation in Criminal Cases (cont.)*

### CALIFORNIA

**Felonies**     There is no statute of limitations for murder or for offenses that are punishable by death or life imprisonment or for embezzlement of public funds. The statute of limitations is five years for crimes that are punishable by eight years or more in prison, and three years for crimes punishable by six years or more.

**Misdemeanors**     One year for noncapital offenses; two years for specified acts against minors under fourteen; and three years if the offense is punishable by confinement in state prison.

### FLORIDA

**Felonies**     There is no statute of limitations for crimes punishable by death or life imprisonment. The statute of limitations is four years for first-degree felonies and three years for all other felonies.

**Misdemeanors**     Two years for first-degree misdemeanors and one year for all others.

### ILLINOIS

**Felonies**     There is no statute of limitations for murder, manslaughter, arson, reckless homicide, treason, and forgery. For all other felonies it is three years.

**Misdemeanors**     Eighteen months.

### NEW MEXICO

**Felonies**     Fifteen years for murder and first-degree felonies, six years for second degree felonies, and five years for third- and fourth-degree felonies.

**Misdemeanors**     One year for petty offenses and two years for all other misdemeanors.

### NEW YORK

**Felonies**     There is no statute of limitations for murder or for class A felonies. Five years for all other felonies.

**Misdemeanors**     One year for petty offenses and two years for all other misdemeanors.

## TEXAS

**Felonies**
There is no statute of limitations for murder or manslaughter. Ten years for thefts involving fiduciaries, five years for theft, burglary, robbery, arson, and rape. It is three years for all other felonies.

**Misdemeanors**
Two years.

## FEDERAL CRIMES

A crime is prosecuted under federal law when it has been committed against an agency of the United States or an individual representing the United States. The term *United States* includes all places subject to the jurisdiction of the United States (18 U.S.C. 1 §5).

Federal jurisdiction applies to a crime committed against an agency, agent, or employee of the federal government. Bank robbery, as an example, is a federal crime because money is controlled by the federal government, not by any state. Mail fraud is also a federal crime because the postal service is an agency of the federal government. Crimes committed aboard a commercial airplane, train, ship, or other common carrier are prosecuted as federal crimes because interstate commerce is controlled by the federal government.

Federal crimes are resolved in federal district court and are prosecuted by the U.S. attorney for that district.

Federal criminal laws and procedures are explained in Title 18 of the U.S. Code. Any person who has questions about federal crimes and federal criminal procedure should consult an attorney.

## DETENTION AND ARREST

Detention and arrest have significant differences.

### DETENTION

*Detention* is the right vested in a law enforcement officer to question a person for a short period of time in order to determine if there is reason to classify the person as a suspect in commission of a crime. It does not involve taking a suspect into custody but may precede an arrest.

The courts have ruled that permitting temporary detention for questioning does not conflict with the Fourth Amendment of the U.S. Constitution, since it strikes a balance between a person's interest in immunity from police interference and the community interest in law enforcement (People v. Mickelson, 59 Cal 2d 448).

## *Miranda* WARNING RIGHTS

The U.S. Supreme Court ruled, in a famous 1966 case known as *Miranda v. Arizona,* that law enforcement officers must warn a suspect that any statements he makes at the time of his arrest or afterward can be used to assist in prosecuting him for a crime. The purpose of the *Miranda* rights warning is to protect a suspect's constitutional right against self-incrimination.

When a suspect is arrested, the arresting officer must recite the *Miranda* warning before questioning the suspect. If the suspect speaks a language other than English, the *Miranda* rights warning must be recited in the suspect's language.

The *Miranda* warning states: "You have the right to remain silent. Anything you say can and will be used against you in a court of law. You have the right to talk to a lawyer and have him present with you while you are being questioned. If you cannot afford to hire a lawyer, one will be appointed to represent you before any questioning, if you wish one."

## FAILURE TO RECITE *Miranda* RIGHTS DOES NOT BAR PROSECUTION

If a law enforcement officer fails to read or recite the *Miranda* warning before questioning a suspect, that suspect may still be prosecuted for the crime with which he is charged. Failure to recite the *Miranda* warning means only that any statements made by the arrested suspect before the *Miranda* warning is read, or before the suspect consults an attorney, cannot be used in court as evidence to convict the suspect of the crime.

## WAIVER REQUIRED BEFORE QUESTIONING

After an arresting officer recites the *Miranda* warning, he must also ask the suspect two questions: "Do you understand each of these rights I have explained to you?" and "Having these rights in mind, do you wish to talk to us now?"

If the suspect answers yes to both questions, the officer may proceed to question him about the alleged offense. The suspect may refuse to answer any question and may stop talking and exercise his right to remain silent at any time during the questioning. He may also refuse to answer any further questions until his attorney can be present.

## Exceptions to the *Miranda* Warning and Waiver

A law enforcement officer is not required to recite the *Miranda* warning or secure a waiver from a suspect under three conditions:

When a suspect walks into a police station and states that he or she wants to confess to a crime

When a person calls the police to offer a statement or other information

When an officer is conducting a general investigation at the scene of a crime and asks bystanders if they heard or saw anything that might relate to the crime

## Booking

A suspect who has been arrested is fingerprinted and photographed, and a record of his or her arrest is recorded with the law enforcement agency.

## Filing of the Criminal Complaint

When a suspect has been arrested and processed, or booked, the arresting officer must then present the information available to him either to the district attorney, in a state matter, or to the U.S. attorney, in a federal matter. The prosecutor decides if the charges against the suspect should be filed as a misdemeanor or felony complaint.

When a prosecutor elects to file felony criminal charges against a suspect, he either presents a criminal complaint to a judge or submits a bill of indictment to the grand jury.

## Criminal Complaints Issued by Judges

In asking a judge to issue a warrant of arrest against a suspect, the prosecutor must present a complaint that explains the crime with which the suspect is being charged and the circumstances surrounding his detention and arrest. If the judge agrees, on the basis of the information provided by the officer, that the suspect should be tried for the crime, he will issue a warrant for suspect's arrest. If the crime is minor, the judge may order that a simple summons be issued instead of a warrant. If the suspect fails to appear as ordered in the summons, a warrant will be issued.

## EXECUTION OF THE WARRANT AND ARREST OF THE SUSPECT

Once a judge has issued a warrant for the arrest of a suspect, a law enforcement officer arrests the suspect.

## ARRAIGNMENT

When a suspect is arraigned, he appears before a judge and is formally presented with the charges made against him. After hearing the charges, he is asked by the judge if he understands the charges and is asked to plead guilty or not guilty to those charges.

If the suspect pleads not guilty to the charges, the judge will order that a trial be held to determine his guilt or innocence. If the charges against the accused are to be tried as a felony, the trial will be held in the state superior court.

## THE GRAND JURY

The institution of the *grand jury* dates back to ancient England. There, and for many years in the United States, a person accused of a crime could not be tried unless the grand jury first heard evidence and, on the basis of that evidence, ordered the suspect arrested and tried for the crime.

In some states the grand jury is still an important part of the process of indicting anyone accused of a criminal offense. However, most states have some provision for a suspect to be charged with less serious offenses without involvement of the grand jury.

If the prosecutor seeks an indictment against someone through the grand jury process, he must prepare a bill of indictment and present it along with any evidence he may have. After hearing the evidence against the accused, the grand jury determines if there is probable cause to indict, arrest, and try the suspect. If the grand jury believes that the state has established probable cause, it issues an indictment and the suspect will be arrested and arraigned. In most states the prosecutor can therefore choose either to go to the grand jury or to conduct a preliminary hearing only before a judge.

## REQUIREMENT OF GRAND JURY INDICTMENT
## IN FEDERAL CRIMINAL MATTERS

Unless a state's constitution requires a grand jury indictment, the prosecutor may indict a suspect by presenting a complaint to a judge and obtaining a warrant for the suspect's arrest and arraignment. In a matter where a suspect is being charged with a federal crime, however, the U.S. attorney must secure a bill of indictment from the grand jury unless the accused waives that requirement.

A grand jury indictment must be used in federal criminal matters because the Fifth Amendment to the U.S. Constitution states: "No person shall be held to answer for a capital, or otherwise infamous crime, unless on a presentment or indictment of a grand jury, except in cases arising in the land or naval forces, or in the militia. . . ."

If the grand jury endorses the *bill of indictment* submitted by the U.S. attorney, the accused is indicted and will subsequently be arrested, arraigned, and tried.

## THE PRELIMINARY HEARING

When a defendant is arrested for a felony charge, he is brought before a judge for a preliminary hearing to determine if there is adequate evidence to establish probable cause and proceed with the prosecution of the suspect. *Probable cause* means the existence of facts and/or circumstances making a reasonable person believe that a crime had been committed. At the preliminary hearing the prosecutor presents evidence of probable cause, a synopsis of the charges against the suspect, and the reason why the prosecutor thinks the defendant is guilty of the crime charged. The defendant may be represented by an attorney at the preliminary hearing. The defendant or his attorney will give the judge a brief statement on why the suspect should not be charged with the crime. At the preliminary hearing the judge may find that there is adequate reason to suspect the defendant is guilty of the crime he is accused of, or he may reduce the criminal charge against the defendant from a felony to a misdemeanor. The judge will order that the defendant be arraigned and allowed to enter a plea of guilty or not guilty to the charges.

At the preliminary hearing the judge also determines if the suspect may be released on his promise to appear in court at a later time to plead to the charges. When a judge allows a suspect to be released upon his promise to appear, it is said that the suspect is released on his own recognizance (OR). If the seriousness of the crime or the criminal history of the accused supports it, the judge may order the suspect to post bail with a deposit of money left with the court, or if the charges are very serious and the suspect is considered a danger to the community, the judge may order the suspect confined to jail until his arraignment and thereafter with no bail.

## PLEA BARGAINING

Not all cases result in jury trials. *Plea bargaining* is a process whereby the prosecutor and defense counsel agree to a less serious charge or to a reduced sentence for the original charge, in exchange for a guilty plea. A plea bargain is advantageous to the defendant especially when the evidence against him is substantial and the outcome of a jury trial may be uncertain. Plea bargains are also often advantageous to the state because a guilty plea saves the taxpayers the expense of a lengthy trial and possible acquittal or dismissal of the charges against the accused.

Either side may suggest a plea bargain, but it is the prosecutor's decision as to whether a plea bargain will be allowed and on what terms. The prosecutor makes a formal offer to the defendant's attorney, who conveys the offer to the defendant. The defendant has the final choice about whether or not to accept the prosecutor's offer. If he rejects the prosecutor's plea bargain offer, the matter will be tried in court, and a judge or jury will decide if the suspect is guilty.

## JURY TRIALS

The Sixth Amendment, as well as Article II, Section 2 of the U.S. Constitution, gives anyone accused of a crime the right to a jury trial. The U.S. Supreme Court has interpreted this right to be limited to serious offenses for which a term of incarceration can be imposed. The right to a jury trial was created to protect individuals from improper, abusive, and arbitrary accusations by law enforcement. Juries are given the responsibility of fairly deciding the facts in a case and of determining who is telling the truth. Juries allow the public to participate significantly in the criminal justice system. Juveniles are not given the right to a jury trial unless they are tried as adults.

In federal trials and in most state trials there must be twelve jurors and a unanimous vote in order to convict a defendant. In state courts juries can be composed of fewer than twelve jurors. In a U.S. Supreme Court case against the state of Florida, the Court declared that a trial of only six jurors is valid in state court cases, and in a later case it ruled that five jurors are not enough. The high court also decided that when twelve jurors are required in state courts, the verdict does not have to be unanimous but that in six-juror cases a unanimous verdict is required. The Supreme Court has stated that the reason for requiring at least six jurors is to provide enough members to allow meaningful deliberation and group discussion.

A defendant in a criminal case can waive his right to a jury trial if it is done in an informed and intelligent manner and expressed in clear and certain terms. The prosecutor also has to waive the jury in order to proceed without one.

The right to a jury trial includes the right to a public trial although in some cases the public may be excluded to protect the interests of rape victims or to protect witnesses from intimidation or retaliation. This involves very controversial constitutional issues and conflicts since defendants have a right to cross-examine witnesses and the media have a right under the First Amendment to be present at a public trial in order to report on it unless their presence would interfere with producing a fair trial.

Civil jury trials under the Seventh Amendment do not require the same standards. Fewer than twelve jurors are permitted, and cases can be decided by less than a unanimous verdict.

## BURDEN OF PROOF

The burden of proof includes two separate legal principles. The first is the burden of persuasion, in which the party with the burden must produce sufficient evidence to prove a fact. The second is the burden of introducing evidence. In a criminal case the prosecutor has the burden of introducing evidence. If he does not, he has not met the burden and the case is dismissed. The defendant need not introduce any evidence. If the prosecutor does introduce evidence, he must then meet his burden of proof to persuade the jury to believe the evidence he has introduced.

In criminal cases the prosecutor must prove the guilt of the accused beyond a reasonable doubt. *Reasonable doubt* has been defined as follows: "It is such a doubt as would cause a juror, after careful and candid and impartial consideration of all the evidence, to be so undecided that he cannot say that he has an abiding conviction of the defendant's guilt. It is such a doubt as would cause a reasonable person to hesitate or pause in the gravest or more important transactions of life" (*Moore v. United States,* 345 F. 2d 97, 98 [D.C. Cir. 1965]).

In civil cases the burden of proof is by a preponderance of the evidence which is often referred to as "50% plus 1." A preponderance of evidence is "evidence which when compared to that opposed to it, has more convincing force, and thus the greater probability of truth" (93 A.L.R. 155).

The defendant has a right to counsel in a criminal case and to have counsel appointed at no charge if he cannot afford one. A federal law also permits a defendant in a federal case to have the assistance of investigators, experts, and other services necessary for an adequate defense (18 USC Sec. 3006A[e]).

A defendant can waive his right to counsel, and he has an equally protected right to represent himself. Waivers must be made intelligently and voluntarily. The right to counsel applies once criminal proceedings have been initiated, not only at trial. Violation of the defendant's right to counsel requires an automatic reversal of the conviction.

The defendant has the right under the Sixth Amendment to be confronted with the witnesses against him at trial. He also has the right to compel witnesses in his favor to appear and testify.

## EVIDENCE

In presenting the case to the judge or jury, the prosecutor and the defense attorney present the evidence to be evaluated in reaching a decision. Evidence may be divided into two basic classifications: direct and circumstantial.

## DIRECT EVIDENCE

Direct evidence is that which applies immediately and directly to the facts and does not require inferences or interpretations. Physical evidence is direct evidence.

### Physical Evidence
Physical evidence may be presented during a trial. It includes witnesses who may identify the suspect, blood samples extracted from a suspect or his victim, fingerprints, handwriting samples, and voice identification. To be used in a trial, any evidence must have been lawfully obtained.

### Witnesses and Testimony
Testimony by witnesses or others who have knowledge that may assist in reaching a conclusion about the guilt of the accused is one form of physical evidence. Witnesses may be questioned by both the prosecution and the defense.

### Subpoenas
The court may require that a witness appear to testify in a trial. A *subpoena* is issued by the court, demanding that the witness appear and stating the location, date, and time of the court appearance. It is an official court order, and anyone who fails to comply with a subpoena may be arrested. A witness who fails to appear after being subpoenaed may be arrested on a bench warrant and brought into court to testify. He may also be charged with a criminal offense of contempt of court.

A subpoena may also be used to require a person to provide documents to the court to be used as evidence in a trial.

### Depositions
If it is not possible for a witness to be present at trial, his or her testimony may be taken before the trial begins and presented to the judge or jury during the trial. Only the defense may depose witnesses, and only witnesses unable to attend the trial personally may provide testimony by means of depositions. At the deposition the witness must swear to the truth of his statements and answers; a reporter certified by the court records what is said. The defense and prosecution

may have representatives present to ask the witness questions. Witnesses for the prosecution may not be deposed but must appear in person in court, or their testimony cannot be heard.

## Circumstantial Evidence

Circumstantial evidence is more subtle. It requires the jury to use analysis, interpretation, and inference in order to reach a conclusion. The prosecution must prove each element of circumstance beyond a reasonable doubt. For example, a person is charged with robbing a bank, and stolen currency from the robbery is later found in his room. The currency is circumstantial evidence.

## Inadmissible Evidence

Evidence that is inadmissible in court often falls under the exclusionary rule. The exclusionary rule was designed to discourage law enforcement agencies from using unlawful means to obtain evidence. This means evidence unlawfully obtained as a violation of the searches and seizures clause of the Fourth Amendment. For example, if a person is stopped for a traffic violation, he cannot be forced to open the trunk of his car unless the police have probable cause to suspect some illegal substance is in the trunk. If the police force the person to open the trunk without probable cause, under the exclusionary rule nothing they find in the trunk can be admitted as evidence.

## Witnesses

When a case goes to trial, both the prosecution and the defense are allowed to call in witnesses to testify. There are several classifications of witnesses. Character witnesses, who are often friends of the victim or defendant, tell the court about the person's character. Eyewitnesses tell the court what they saw at the scene of the crime. Police witnesses and expert witnesses who are specialists in a particular field serve to clarify points that the lay jury might otherwise not understand.

# Crimes and Penalties

## Assault and Battery

The crimes of assault and battery are often referred to jointly. *Criminal assault* is defined as "an unlawful attempt, together with a present ability, to commit a violent injury on another person." It is not necessary for the person being assaulted to have actual physical harm done to him. It is the *attempt* to injure another person that constitutes an assault.

Thus, if a person throws a rock at someone and misses, he is guilty of assault because he attempted to harm the other person by throwing the rock. If, however, the person throwing the rock is such a long distance from the intended victim that it is absolutely impossible to hit him by throwing the rock, no assault has taken place. Throwing the rock is the unlawful attempt, but unless the distance the rock has to travel is such that the intended victim could actually be harmed, the element of present ability is missing.

*Battery* is willful and unlawful use of force or violence upon another person. Battery requires the physical touching of another, either directly or indirectly. In the rock-throwing example, if the person throwing the rock hits the other person with the rock, he has committed both assault and battery. Hitting someone with a rock is an unlawful use of force against another person. The amount of force is not important, and the victim does not need to suffer a visible wound or mark. Every touching of another person in a hostile or offensive manner is a battery. If a person is convicted of battery, the law assumes that the victim was damaged, but the victim does not have to prove any physical injury.

Depending on the nature and extent of the crime, a conviction for assault and battery can be a misdemeanor resulting in a fine or confinement in county jail or both, or it may be a felony punishable by a fine or confinement in state prison or both.

## ASSAULT WITH A DEADLY WEAPON

Defining what constitutes a deadly weapon is sometimes difficult. In California the courts have ruled that regardless of the originally intended use of a particular object or instrument, if the object is used in a manner likely to cause death or great bodily injury, it is a deadly weapon (*People v. Robertson,* 217 C. 671). While most of us recognize firearms as deadly weapons, other less obvious objects may also fall within the accepted legal definition. For example, if the driver of an automobile attempts to run over someone with his vehicle, he will be guilty of assault with a deadly weapon because the automobile, if it is intentionally used in a manner likely to cause death or great bodily injury, can be considered a deadly weapon.

There are some federal laws regarding the use and possession of firearms, but each state is permitted to make its own laws regulating most firearms. In California certain guns are considered illegal, and their mere possession is a felony. For example, it is a felony to be in possession of a shotgun that has a barrel less than eighteen inches long or a total length of less than twenty-six inches. It is also a felony to be in possession of a rifle that has a barrel less than sixteen inches long or a total length less than twenty-six inches.

In most states any person convicted of a felony or addicted to narcotics is not permitted to own or be in possession of a firearm. A minor usually may not purchase or possess a firearm without prior written permission of his parent or legal guardian. A minor under sixteen years of age may not purchase a concealable firearm.

In most states it is illegal to carry any concealed weapon, either on one's person or in a vehicle, unless the person in possession of the concealed weapon has a special permit allowing it. Handguns and Mace are examples of concealed weapons. Misdemeanor penalties for possession of a concealed weapon include a fine and possible incarceration in the county jail. Frequently, if a person carrying a concealed weapon without a permit has a previous felony conviction, the concealed weapon possession charge will be tried as a felony offense in most states, and the penalty may include incarceration in a state prison. Recently many states like Texas have passed laws that make it much easier to obtain permits to carry concealed weapons.

There are also laws regulating the sale and possession of knives. In California every person who carries and every person who sells, loans, or gives to anyone a switchblade knife with a blade over two inches long is guilty of a misdemeanor. Furthermore, any knife used in a manner likely to cause death or great bodily injury is considered a deadly weapon, and the possessor is subject to felony prosecution for assault with a deadly weapon.

## HOMICIDE

Homicide is a category composed of six crimes:

First-degree murder

Second-degree murder

Voluntary manslaughter

Vehicular manslaughter

Involuntary manslaughter

Felony murder

## MURDER

*Murder* is the unlawful killing of a human being by another human being with malice aforethought. Murder may be first-degree murder or second-degree murder.

*First-degree murder* is an unlawful killing that is willful, deliberate, and premeditated. First-degree murder is classified as a felony and can be punishable by death, confinement in state prison for life without possibility of parole, or confinement in state prison for a specified number of years to life.

*Second-degree murder* is an unlawful killing with malice aforethought but without deliberation and premeditation. Second-degree murder is classified as a felony and is punishable by confinement in the state prison for a specified term of years to life.

*Felony murder* is the unlawful homicide that occurs in the commission or attempted commission of a felony. In most states the felony must be a serious or violent one such as burglary, arson, rape, and kidnapping. Felony murder is usually considered first-degree murder.

## CAPITAL PUNISHMENT, OR DEATH PENALTY

Capital punishment, or the death penalty, refers to the sentence of death for a crime. The Supreme Court has held that the death penalty is not cruel and unusual punishment. Each state has its own laws regarding punishment.

## MALICE

*Malice aforethought,* either expressed or implied, refers to the state of mind of a person who commits a wrongful act. It is an elusive concept that lends itself more to an explanation than to a definition. In fact, no simple definition of *malice aforethought* has ever been formed. Malice is the hostile way a person feels toward another, a feeling of hatred or desire to injure another; it is the requisite mental state of mind for murder. The word *malice* is used to denote the purpose and design of the assaulting party. Malice means "a wish to vex, annoy, or injure another person, or an intent to do a wrongful act, established either by proof or presumption of law." The definition suggested by Perkins in *Criminal Law,* 2d ed., is that "malice aforethought is an unjustifiable, inexcusable and unmitigated man-endangering-state-of-mind."

The concept of malice aforethought as found in the penal codes of various states may be expressed or implied. "It is *expressed* when there is manifested a *deliberate* intention unlawfully to take away the life of a fellow creature. In other words, there is no justification, excuse, or mitigation for the killing recognized by the law. It is implied when no considerable provocation appears, or when the circumstances attending the killing show an abandoned and malignant heart." In either case, it is manifested by the doing of an unlawful or felonious act intentionally and *without legal cause or excuse. It does not imply a preexisting hatred toward the individual injured.* Malice is found when a person shows wanton disregard for human life by committing an act that involves a high probability that it will result in death.

When an intentional killing is shown, malice aforethought is established. Example one: A defendant, with premeditation and deliberation, buys a gun, robs a liquor store, and kills the clerk. Example two: A defendant, after having a relationship that motivates the killing, plans to kill the victim and intentionally kills the victim according to the preconceived plan. Both are examples of expressed malice aforethought, the *deliberate* intention to take away the life of another human being unlawfully.

Malice aforethought may also be implied. The classic example is the drive-by shooting: Without provocation, a defendant shows a conscious disregard for human life by firing a bullet through a window, not knowing or caring whether anyone is behind it. An innocent person is killed. No provocation is necessary. The mental component of malice aforethought is present if the defendant knows that his conduct endangers the life of another and acts with conscious disregard for life.

If there is a legally recognized justification or excuse for the killing, there is no malice aforethought. Example one: A defendant is attacked and in self-defense kills his assailant to save himself from being murdered. There is no malice aforethought. Example two: A man discovers his wife's adultery and, in the heat of passion, kills her lover. While there would be no malice aforethought, hence no murder, this would very likely at least be voluntary manslaughter, a serious felony punishable by confinement in state prison.

## MANSLAUGHTER

Manslaughter is the unlawful killing of a human being by another human being, with an absence of malice. Manslaughter is divided into the following three classifications:

*Voluntary manslaughter* is the killing of a person caused by heat of passion or prompted by a sudden quarrel. Voluntary manslaughter is punishable by confinement in state prison for a specified period usually ranging from two to fifteen years.

*Involuntary manslaughter* is the death of a person resulting from the commission of an unlawful act other than a felony as a result of negligence except when the death involves a motor vehicle. Involuntary manslaughter is punishable by confinement in state prison for a specified period usually ranging from one to five years.

*Vehicular manslaughter* is the death of a person resulting from the driving of a motor vehicle. A driver who kills a pedestrian or causes a fatal accident by failing to yield the right-of-way may be convicted of vehicular manslaughter.

A boat is considered a vehicle under the law, and the operator of a boat may be convicted of manslaughter if he causes the death of another while operating a boat. Vehicular manslaughter is punishable by confinement in either state prison or county jail.

## Kidnapping

Any person who forcibly steals, takes, or arrests anyone in one state and carries him into another country, state, or county or into another part of the same county is guilty of kidnapping. Kidnapping includes enticing or seducing a victim by false promise or misrepresentation. If someone entices a person to go to another city or state on the promise of some reward when the perpetrator's real intention is for unlawful or immoral purposes, he can be charged with kidnapping. Kidnapping is a felony punishable by confinement in state prison.

Usually, if the kidnapped person is under a certain age at the time of being kidnapped, the crime is punishable by increased prison time.

## Sexual Battery

Sexual battery is often referred to as sexual assault. Any person who touches an intimate part of another person without the latter's consent, when the touching is for the purpose of sexual arousal, sexual gratification, or sexual abuse is guilty of sexual battery. In most states sexual battery may be charged as a misdemeanor or a felony and may be punished by a fine or imprisonment or both.

## Rape

Rape, whether committed by force, fraud, or enticement, is punishable by confinement in county jail or state prison. The law requires only that the rape be against the victim's will. The sexual history of the victim is irrelevant, and the victim does not need to prove additional physical injury, such as wounds, cuts, and bruises. Consensual sex with a minor is rape with permission.

Recent changes in the law in most states now allow one spouse to bring an action for rape against the other spouse. This is the case in Arizona, California, Florida, Illinois, and New Mexico.

Statutory rape is unlawful intercourse between an adult and a minor. The age that determines who is a minor differs from state to state (see multistate compendium on statutory rape and sexual assault, below).

## *Table 14-3: Statutory Rape/Sexual Assault*

### ARIZONA

Charge        Sexual assault.

Definition    Sexual conduct with a minor by intentionally or knowingly engaging in sexual intercourse with any person under the age of fifteen is a Class 2 felony. Any person who engages in sexual intercourse with a person fifteen years or older is guilty of a Class 6 felony.

Punishment    State prison up to one and a half years.

Defense       The victim's lack of consent was based on incapacity because the victim was fifteen, sixteen, or seventeen years old and the defendant did not know the age of the victim.

### CALIFORNIA

Charge        Rape.

Definition    a. Unlawful sexual intercourse with a female not his wife when the female is under eighteen years.

b. Unlawful intercourse with a minor not more than three years younger than the perpetrator is a misdemeanor.

c. Engaging in sexual intercourse with a minor three or more years younger than the perpetrator, depending on the circumstances, is by definition a felony or misdemeanor.

d. Any person over twenty years who engages in unlawful sexual intercourse with a minor under the age of sixteen years is guilty of either a misdemeanor or felony.

Punishment    a. County jail or state prison up to one year.

b. County jail or state prison up to one year.

c. County jail or state prison up to one year.

d. County jail or state prison up to four years.

Defense       A good faith, reasonable mistake as to age.

## Table 14-3: Statutory Rape/Sexual Assault (cont.)

### FLORIDA

Charge        Sexual assault.

Definition    Sexual intercourse with an unmarried person of previous chaste character under the age of eighteen is a second-degree felony.

Punishment    Jail up to fifteen years.

Defense       None. Ignorance of age is no defense nor is misrepresentation of age by the victim nor is a bona fide belief that the victim is of a specific age.

### ILLINOIS

Charge        a. Sexual assault.

                b. Criminal sexual abuse.

                c. Aggravated criminal sexual assault.

Definition    a. When a perpetrator commits an act of sexual penetration with a victim under the age of eighteen at the time of the act and the accused is a family member, or when a perpetrator commits an act of sexual penetration with a victim who is at least thirteen years but under eighteen years and the accused is seventeen years of age or over and holds a position of trust, authority, or supervision in relation to the victim.

                b. When the accused is under seventeen years of age and commits an act of sexual penetration with a victim who is at least nine but under seventeen years of age at the time the act is committed, or when the accused commits sexual penetration on a victim who is at least thirteen years of age but under seventeen years of age, and the accused is less than five years older than the victim.

                c. When the accused is seventeen years of age or older and commits an act of sexual penetration on a victim who is under thirteen years of age, or when the accused is under seventeen years of age and commits an act of sexual penetration with a victim who is under the age of nine.

Punishment    a. Class 1 felony.

                b. Class A misdemeanor.

                c. Class 2 felony.

Defense    Consent of the victim or that the accused reasonably believed the person to be seventeen years of age or over.

## New Mexico

Charge    Criminal sexual penetration.

Definitions    a. Criminal sexual penetration is the unlawful and intentional causing of a person to engage in sexual intercourse, cunnilingus, fellatio, or anal intercourse or the causing of penetration, to any extent and with any object, of the genital or anal openings.

b. Sexual penetration on a child under thirteen years of age.

c. Sexual penetration on a child thirteen to sixteen years of age when the perpetrator is in a position of authority over the child and uses his authority to coerce the child to submit.

d. Sexual penetration on a child thirteen to sixteen years of age when the perpetrator is at least eighteen years of age and at least four years older than the child and is not the spouse of the child.

Punishment    a. N/A

b. First-degree felony.

c. Second-degree felony.

d. Fourth-degree felony.

Defense    Consent; impotency (not a complete defense).

## New York

Charge    Rape.

Definitions    a. A male is guilty of rape when he engages in sexual intercourse with a female less than eleven years old.

b. When a person eighteen years or older engages in sexual intercourse with another person whom the actor is not married to and who is less than fourteen years old.

c. When a person engages in sexual intercourse with another person who is not married, who is incapable of consent by reason.

d. When twenty-one years or older, he/she engages in sexual intercourse with another person to whom the actor is not married and is less than seventeen years old.

## *Table 14–3: Statutory Rape/Sexual Assault (cont.)*

### NEW YORK

| | |
|---|---|
| Punishment | a. Rape first degree. |
| | b. Rape second degree. |
| | c. Rape third degree. |
| | d. Class E felony. |
| Defense | None. A person is incapable of consent if he is less than seventeen years. |

### TEXAS

| | |
|---|---|
| Charge | Sexual assault. |
| Definition | When a person intentionally or knowingly causes the penetration of the anus or female sexual organ of a child by any means. A child is a person less than seventeen years of age. |
| Punishment | Second-degree felony. |
| Defense | It is an affirmative defense that the actor was not more than three years older than the victim, and the victim was a child of fourteen years or older. |

## ROBBERY, BURGLARY, AND THEFT

Robbery is the taking of personal property from someone against his will by the use of force or fear. Theft is an offense against property, whereas robbery is an offense against a person and his property. Burglary is the act of entering with the intent of committing a felony.

### Robbery

If a person threatens another with bodily injury and forces him to hand over his wallet, a *robbery* has been committed. Robbery is a felony punishable by confinement in state prison.

If a firearm is used in the commission of a robbery or the attempt of a robbery, an additional charge of assault with a deadly weapon can be made, and more years will be added to the prison sentence.

It is not necessary for the perpetrator of a crime to take actual possession of the property of his victim in order to be guilty of a crime. Attempted robbery also carries a penalty of confinement in state prison. Plus, more prison time can be imposed if a firearm was used in the attempt.

Robbery of a pharmacy or against a person who has legal custody of narcotics at the time of the robbery carries the maximum sentence allowed under the laws of many states.

## Burglary

*Burglary* is the entering of a building, vehicle, or other structure with the intent to commit a theft or felony within the structure or vehicle. The elements of both entry and intent must be met to convict a person of burglary.

While burglary is often referred to as *breaking and entering,* no breaking is necessary for commission of the crime. Any entry, no matter how slight, satisfies the legal requirement for entry. Entry does not actually need to be made by the person committing the crime. An animal trained to pick up items at its master's request may be used to commit a burglary. If an animal is used in the commission of a burglary, liability for the burglary transfers to the person having control of the animal.

The requirement of specific intent to commit a theft or felony can often be inferred from the unlawful entry. If a suspect enters the victim's home and assaults or batters a woman who is inside, the court often infers that the suspect entered the structure with the intent to commit rape, a felony. This establishes the prosecution's charge of burglary as well as a charge for the attempted felony, in this case rape.

A person can be charged with burglary if he enters a vehicle or structure legally when it can be proved that he did so with the specific intent to steal or commit a felony.

Every burglary of an inhabited dwelling is considered burglary in the first degree, punishable by confinement in state prison. An inhabited building may be a home, trailer, boat, or other place regularly occupied by a person. Burglaries of other structures are considered second degree, punishable by confinement in either county jail or state prison.

## Theft

*Theft* means stealing, taking, or carrying away the property of another with the intent of denying him or her of it temporarily or permanently. Larceny, embezzlement, and stealing are all theft. Theft may be classified as grand theft or petty theft (see multistate compendium, "Table 15-4: Petty and Grand Theft," page 218).

*Grand theft* is, among other things, the theft of (1) real or personal property with a value in excess of the amount set by each state, for example, four hundred dollars in California; (2) property taken from another that is either held in the hand or attached to the victim at the time of the theft; (3) or an automobile, a firearm, or, in some states, a farm animal of any value. Grand theft is usually punishable by confinement in county jail or state prison.

*Petty theft* covers all other unlawful taking of personal property and is usually punishable by a fine and/or confinement in county jail (see multistate compendium below).

### Table 14–4: Petty and Grand Theft

#### ARIZONA

| | |
|---|---|
| Petty theft/misdemeanor | Up to $250 |
| Grand theft/felony | $250 or more, a motor vehicle or firearm |

#### CALIFORNIA

| | |
|---|---|
| Petty theft/misdemeanor | Up to $400 |
| Grand theft/felony | $400 or more, a motor vehicle, firearm, or horses |

#### FLORIDA

| | |
|---|---|
| Petty theft/misdemeanor | Up to $300 |
| Grand theft/felony | $300 or more, a will, firearm, motor vehicle, or farm animal |

#### ILLINOIS

| | |
|---|---|
| Petty theft/misdemeanor | Up to $300 |
| Grand theft/felony | $300 or more or a firearm |

#### NEW MEXICO

| | |
|---|---|
| Petty theft/misdemeanor | Up to $250 |
| Grand theft/felony | $250 or more |

#### NEW YORK

| | |
|---|---|
| Petty theft/misdemeanor | Up to $1,000 |
| Grand theft/felony | $1,000 or more, property worth over $1,000, or a motor vehicle worth over $100 |

#### TEXAS

| | |
|---|---|
| Petty theft/misdemeanor | Up to $1,500 |
| Grand theft/felony | $1,500 or more or a firearm |

## BRIBERY AND PERJURY

*Bribery* is any unlawful attempt to reward another person in exchange for a favor. The favor may be an act or a failure to act. Bribery includes the asking, giving, or receiving of anything of value for the purpose of corruptly influencing a person or an official in the performance of his duties. Bribery can be a felony or a misdemeanor, depending on the circumstances. In Arizona, California, Florida, Illinois, New Mexico, New York, and Texas, any attempt to bribe a witness to keep him from testifying at a trial, to give false testimony, or to abstain from giving testimony is a felony. Bribery is a serious crime and may be a federal or state crime.

*Perjury* is the giving of false testimony under oath. An oath is a pledge taken before testifying in court that the statements a witness makes are true. Any person who knowingly, and under oath, gives false testimony is guilty of perjury. Usually perjury is punishable by confinement in state prison.

There are many federal and state crimes that carry serious penalties. The crimes listed above are only a sampling of felonies and their penalties. Any person who has questions about state or federal crimes should consult with an attorney who specializes in criminal law.

## HATE CRIMES

California, Florida, and Illinois have statutes that prohibit hate crimes. The statute in California states: "All persons within the jurisdiction of this state have the right to be free from any violence, intimidation by threat of violence, committed against their persons or property because of their race, color, religion, ancestry, national origin, political affiliation, sex, sexual orientation, age, disability, or position in a labor dispute, or because another person perceives them to have one or more of those characteristics. . . ."

In Florida a felony or misdemeanor is reclassified if the crime shows prejudice based on race, color, ancestry, ethnicity, religion, sexual orientation, or national origin of the victim. For example, if the crime is normally punishable as a felony in the second degree and if the above is proved, then the crime is now punishable as a felony in the first degree.

In Illinois a person commits a hate crime when "by reason of the race, color, creed, religion, ancestry, gender, sexual orientation, physical or mental disability, or national origin of another individual or group of individuals, he commits assault, battery, aggravated assault, misdemeanor theft, criminal trespass to residence, misdemeanor criminal damage to property, criminal trespass to vehicle, criminal trespass to real property or mob action." A hate crime is a Class A misdemeanor for the first offense and a Class 3 felony for a subsequent offense.

In both Florida and Illinois, the state allows for civil cause of action for damages and injunction or other appropriate relief, in addition to the criminal cause of action.

## THREE STRIKES

Both California and New Mexico have *three strikes laws*. In California, if a defendant has been convicted of a felony and it has been pleaded and proved that the defendant has one or more prior violent felony convictions, the court adheres to the following:

1. There shall not be a collective term limitation for consecutive sentencing for any subsequent felony conviction.
2. Probation for the current offense shall not be granted, nor shall the execution or imposition of the sentence be suspended for any prior offense.
3. The length of time between the prior felony conviction and the current felony conviction shall not affect the imposition of the sentence.
4. There shall not be a commitment to any other facility other than state prison.
5. The total amount of credits awarded shall not exceed one-fifth the total term and shall not accrue until the defendant is physically placed in the state prison.
6. If there is a current conviction for more than one felony not committed on the same occasion and not from the same set of facts, the court shall sentence the defendant consecutively on each count.
7. If there is a current conviction for more than one serious or violent felony as described in number 6, the court shall impose the sentence for each conviction for which the defendant may be consecutively sentenced.
8. Any sentence imposed pursuant to this section will be imposed consecutively to any other sentence which the defendant is already serving.

A violent felony may be any of the following but not limited to them: murder, manslaughter, mayhem, rape, sodomy by force, oral copulation by force, lewd acts on a child, a felony punishable by death, any felony in which the defendant inflicts great bodily harm, shooting at or from a motor vehicle, kidnapping, or robbery with a deadly weapon.

If a defendant has a prior felony conviction that has been pleaded and proved, the punishment for an indeterminate term shall be twice the sentence otherwise imposed as punishment for the current felony conviction.

If a defendant has two or more prior felony convictions that have been

pleaded or proved, the term for the current felony conviction shall be an indeterminate term of life imprisonment with a minimum term calculated as the
greater of these two: three times the sentence for each current felony conviction
after prior convictions or twenty-five years.

The prosecuting attorney shall plead and prove each prior felony. He may also
move to dismiss or strike a prior felony conviction as justice requires if there is
insufficient evidence to prove the prior conviction.

In New Mexico, when a defendant is convicted of a third violent felony and
each violent felony conviction is in New Mexico, the defendant shall, in addition
to the punishment imposed for the third *violent* conviction if that sentence does
not result in death, be punished by a sentence of life imprisonment. A violent
felony in New Mexico means murder in the first degree; shooting from a motor
vehicle, resulting in great bodily harm; kidnapping resulting in great bodily
harm inflicted upon the victim by his captor; criminal sexual penetration; and
robbery while the suspect is armed with a deadly weapon, resulting in great bodily harm.

Three strikes and similar laws designed to impose much more severe punishment on criminals are the result of extreme and growing frustration and
anger by the public at a crime rate that is out of control. There is, however, a great
deal of opposition to these laws by judges, lawyers, and even prosecutors who
think that the results in some cases are ridiculous and far too costly. In California a man was convicted of his third strike for stealing a piece of pizza and was
sentenced to a term of twenty-five years to life in prison. Obviously the cost to
the public to feed, cloth, and keep him in good health while he is in prison will
be extremely high. It is estimated that the average cost of keeping one person in
state prison in California is between twenty thousand and thirty thousand dollars per year and is even more for maximum security prisoners.

In California a shortage of jail and prison space has resulted in the early
releases of many prisoners in order to accommodate the large numbers of new
arrivals. This too has caused a negative reaction from those who believe that
criminals should serve their entire sentences.

Despite the rapidly increasing need for more jails and prisoners, few people
are glad to pay the enormous costs of additional prisoners. This raises once again
the age-old debate about whether or not prisoners should be "rehabilitated" or
merely punished. In California a federal appeals court ruled that judges have the
authority to strike prior convictions in order to avoid the harsh sentencing
requirements of the three strikes law. Prosecutors and a very large percentage of
the public do not agree with the ruling.

## Table 14–5: Drunk Driving

### ARIZONA

| | |
|---|---|
| Blood alcohol content limit | 0.10 percent. |
| Rehabilitation required | Yes. |
| Driver's license suspension | Ninety days for first DUI. License revoked for second DUI in five years. |
| Jail/fines | First DUI minimum: twenty-four hours in jail and $250 fine and eight to twenty-four hours of community service. Second DUI within five years: sixty days in jail and minimum of $500 fine. |

### CALIFORNIA

| | |
|---|---|
| Blood alcohol content limit | 0.08 percent (for adults). |
| Rehabilitation required | Yes if the defendant is granted probation. |
| Driver's license suspension | Six months for first DUI, ninety days if probation is granted; sometimes driving to and from work and to educational and rehabilitation programs is allowed. One-year suspension of license for a second DUI. |
| Jail/fines | First DUI: ninety-six hours to six months in jail and $390 to $1,000 fine. For second DUI: ninety days to one year in jail and $390 to $1,000 fine. |

### FLORIDA

| | |
|---|---|
| Blood alcohol content limit | 0.08 percent. |
| Rehabilitation required | Yes. |
| Driver's license suspension | Suspension or revocation of the defendant's driver's license upon conviction. |
| Jail/fines | First DUI: up to six months and $250 to $500 fine. Second DUI within three years: up to nine months in jail and $500 to $1,000 fine. |

## ILLINOIS

| | |
|---|---|
| Blood alcohol content limit | 0.10 percent. |
| Rehabilitation required | If deemed necessary after professional evaluation. |
| Driver's license suspension | For up to one year upon conviction. |
| Jail/fines | First DUI: up to one year in jail. Second DUI within five years: minimum of forty-eight hours in jail or minimum of ten days of community service. |

## NEW MEXICO

| | |
|---|---|
| Blood alcohol content limit | 0.08 percent. |
| Rehabilitation required | Court can order defendant to have a professional evaluation and complete treatment program if deemed necessary or helpful. |
| Driver's license suspension | One-year loss may be avoided by attending a rehabilitation program. |
| Jail/fines | First DUI: thirty to ninety days in jail and/or $300 to $500 fine. Second DUI within five years: ninety days to one year in jail and/or up to $1,000 fine. |

## NEW YORK

| | |
|---|---|
| Blood alcohol content limit | 0.10 percent. |
| Rehabilitation required | The court can order the defendant to attend a victim impact program. |
| Driver's license suspension | First DUI: six months' suspension. Second DUI within ten years: one-year suspension. |
| Jail/fines | First DUI: up to one year in jail and/or $350 to $500 fine. Second DUI: a minimum of one year in jail and/or a $500 to $1,000 fine. |

## *Table 14-5: Drunk Driving (cont.)*

### TEXAS

| | |
|---|---|
| Blood alcohol content limit | 0.10 percent. |
| Rehabilitation required | Yes if the blood alcohol level is 0.17 percent or higher. |
| Driver's license suspension | First DUI: 90 days to one-year suspension. Second DUI: 180 days to two years' suspension. |
| Jail/fines | First DUI: seventy-two hours to two years in jail and $100 to $2,000 fine. Second DUI: fifteen days to two years in jail and $500 to $2,000 fine. |

## *Table 14-6: Illegal Firearms*

### ARIZONA

| | |
|---|---|
| Illegal firearms | Automatic weapons, rifles with barrels less than sixteen inches in length, shotguns with barrels less than eighteen inches in length, any modified rifle or shotgun with an overall length less than twenty-six inches. |
| Waiting period | None. |
| Prohibited owners | Persons convicted of felonies involving violence or possession and use of a deadly weapon or dangerous instrument whose civil rights have not been restored. Persons in jail or prison and anyone the court finds to be a danger to himself or others while in treatment. |

### CALIFORNIA

| | |
|---|---|
| Illegal firearms | Cane or wallet gun, plastic firearms, short-barreled shotgun, short-barreled rifle, zip gun, nunchaku. |
| Waiting period | Mandatory waiting period to receive a gun after purchase is fifteen days. |
| Prohibited owners | Persons under twenty-one may not carry concealed weapons. Persons under eighteen, convicted felons, drug addicts, persons whose probation conditions prohibit gun ownership, and those convicted of violent crimes and certain misdemeanors may not own guns. |

## FLORIDA

Illegal firearms        Short-barreled shotguns and rifles and machine guns.

Waiting period          Mandatory waiting period to receive a gun is three days.

Prohibited owners       Minors and convicted felons whose civil rights have not been restored.

## ILLINOIS

Illegal firearms        Machine guns, rifles with barrels less than sixteen inches, shotguns with barrels less than eighteen inches, or any modified rifle or shotgun that has an overall length of less than twenty-six inches.

Waiting period          Mandatory waiting period to receive a gun is seventy-two hours.

Prohibited owners       Persons under twenty-one may not carry concealed weapons if convicted of misdemeanors and persons declared delinquents by the court. Persons under eighteen cannot carry concealed weapons. Drug addicts, mentally retarded persons, and persons who were in a mental hospital within the previous five years may not own guns.

## NEW MEXICO

Illegal firearms        None.

Waiting period          None.

Prohibited owners       Convicted felons.

## NEW YORK

Illegal firearms        Machine guns and the use of a silencer.

Waiting period          None.

Prohibited owners       Convicted felons, aliens, and persons under sixteen years of age.

## TEXAS

Illegal firearms        Machine guns, short-barreled firearms, and silencers.

Waiting period          None.

*Table 14-6: Illegal Firearms (cont.)*

TEXAS

Prohibited owners    Felons convicted of violent crimes or where violence was
threatened and minors under eighteen may not own
firearms. Intoxicated persons may not use or possess
firearms.

## VICTIMS OF CRIME

While statistics vary and even conflict with respect to whether crime has
increased or decreased, the majority of people feel that crime has reached
extreme and dangerous levels. Our lives are filled with a daily supply of reports
and descriptions of an ever-escalating number and variety of violent crimes.
Accounts of vicious and gruesome murders involving torture and mutilation
seem to be routine subjects of news stories.

On any given day a visit to your local criminal court will reveal an almost end-
less number of people pleading guilty or being convicted of criminal conduct.
Sadly there are always more victims than criminals since most criminals commit
numerous violations before finally being arrested.

The almost constant reporting of new incidents of crime has caused an under-
standable reaction from the public. Organizations such as MADD (Mothers
Against Drunk Driving), law enforcement agencies, and high-profile politicians
have become vocal advocates for "victims' rights." As a result, most states have
passed laws that provide certain basic rights to victims in criminal cases. In most
cases these include the right of the victim and family members to make written
victim impact statements and to be heard at the time the criminal is sentenced. A
victim is usually entitled to be paid restitution by the criminal for expenses caused
by the crime. This can include hospital and doctor bills, loss of earnings, and damage to property (cars, home, etc.). Many of the rights relate to the increased punishment for repeat offenders and those guilty of certain types of offenses such as
drunk driving that causes injuries and sexual abuse crimes. Other laws deal with
expanding the type of evidence permitted in court, reducing or eliminating certain defenses previously allowed to defendants, and the right to be notified before
a defendant is released from custody. A few states have actually added the victims' rights to their constitutions; this gives the new law a higher level of authority since it cannot be easily repealed like a law passed by a state legislature.

The U.S. Congress is considering a proposed constitutional amendment that,
if passed and ratified by at least two-thirds of the states, would make victims'
rights constitutionally guaranteed rights equal to those contained in the Bill of

Rights. The proposed amendment is known as the Victims' Rights Amendment. The rights that it would provide include these:

Being notified of and not excluded from any public proceedings relating to the crime (not just sentencing)

Being heard and being permitted to submit a statement at pretrial or trial proceedings to determine the accused's release from custody and acceptance of a negotiated plea (plea bargain)

Notice of release on parole or after escape

Proceedings that are free from unreasonable delay

Receiving an order for restitution from the sentencing judge against the defendant

Consideration of the victim's safety in determining the release of the defendant

Notice to victims of all the rights included in the amendment

Victims of crime should promptly notify the police. They should also quickly identify and make contact with any witnesses to the crime and write down their names, addresses, and telephone numbers. While many victims feel understandably threatened by the criminal and may be reluctant to press charges for fear of retaliation, it is important to realize that none of the victims' rights is available unless the incident is properly reported and processed.

As noted above, a convicted criminal can be ordered to pay the victim restitution. In most states that restitution order can be enforced as a civil judgment for collection purposes. A separate civil lawsuit can be filed against the criminal for pain and suffering, loss of earnings, future medical bills, and even the interruption to the victim's marital relationship. The victim's spouse can also file suit for interruption to the marital relationship (called loss of consortium). In the civil case the court can issue injunctions, or orders that compel or prohibit certain conduct by the defendant. Typically they include orders not to contact the victim— that is, not to go to the victim's home or place of employment and not to contact the victim by phone.

Finally, most states have created victim assistance programs. These programs provide social and financial assistance to the victims of crime. In a criminal case victims and witnesses are provided information about proceedings, and their participation is made more convenient. Transportation to and from the proceedings is often provided, status updates are given, and moral support is provided during the victim's statements and/or testimony.

A major part of any victims' assistance program provides financial assistance.

Substantial amounts can be paid to hospitals, doctors, psychiatrists, and other mental health providers for services to the victim and to certain family members for services relating to the crime. If the injury caused the victim to be disabled, the programs usually pay for loss of salary (sometimes for up to two years). These financial payments are usually limited to out-of-pocket expenses. This means the program will pay only for expenses due from the victim directly after payment to the providers of services from all other sources. So, if the victim has a thousand-dollar hospital bill and his insurance company has paid eight hundred dollars, the victim assistance program would pay only the victim's out-of-pocket amount of two hundred dollars.

As can be seen, victims of crime have many remedies available to them. None of these remedies will ever completely compensate a victim for the pain, suffering, emotional trauma, fear, and other injuries and losses suffered. However, unlike victims in other countries or in this country in earlier years, victims today can at least have the satisfaction of participating in the process to convict and punish criminals, and they can receive some financial assistance to pay medical bills and recover lost income.

Victims should always take immediate action. The law provides for certain time periods called statutes of limitations within which claims and lawsuits must be filed. In criminal cases the defendant has very strict constitutional rights including the right to a speedy trial and to have charges filed within a reasonable period of time. This can be a very short period in criminal cases.

# 15

# Immigration and Naturalization

The United States has always been a nation of immigrants. For more than two hundred years people have immigrated here from every country in the world.

## Immigration Is Exclusively a Federal Matter

The laws governing immigration and naturalization are exclusively under the control of the federal government. The Immigration and Naturalization Service (INS) is the federal agency responsible for administering the Immigration and Nationality Act (INA). In 1990 the immigration act was rewritten and new major provisions were enacted in 1996. The INA is contained in Title VIII of the U.S. Code, the primary body of law for federal matters.

## Purpose of Immigration Laws

The purpose of the immigration act is to protect the health and welfare of both citizens and noncitizens by limiting the number of those who may permanently enter the country each year and to prevent an adverse effect on the American labor market. With the 1990 amendments to the immigration act, virtually all immigrant categories have numerical annual limits placed on them except for the parents, spouses, and children of U.S. citizens. The main purpose of the 1996 changes was to toughen the laws against terrorists, criminal aliens, and aliens unlawfully residing in the United States.

## ALIENS

An alien is a foreign-born person who has not become a citizen of this country. Aliens within the United States have certain constitutional rights. The Constitution and Congress determine what rights and privileges will be granted to aliens. Individual states have laws governing aliens as well.

The Fifth Amendment to the U.S. Constitution protects all "persons" from deprivation of life, liberty, or property by the federal government without due process of law. This includes aliens. The Fourteenth Amendment protects aliens from deprivation of life, liberty, or property by the states. In addition, aliens are afforded the protection of the Bill of Rights through the Fourteenth Amendment. These rights apply as well to undocumented aliens. For example, undocumented aliens are entitled to just compensation if they are victimized or injured as a result of negligence.

The Fifth and Fourteenth Amendments do not provide aliens the same advantages as those afforded U.S. citizens. Although aliens are entitled to equal protection of the laws under the due process clause, Congress can classify aliens on the basis of nationality and make laws accordingly. For example, our laws forbid aliens from becoming senators or members of the House of Representatives. In addition, the federal government may draw distinctions between lawful and unlawful aliens when determining eligibility for federal benefits (*Matthews v. Diaz,* 426 U.S. 67 [1976]). A state, however, may not create alien classifications unless it can show a compelling government interest for such discrimination.

### BORDER SEARCH

At the border or its functional equivalent (meaning stations near the border, checkpoints, international airports, and roads extending from the border), no suspicion or probable cause is needed for a brief stop and questioning (*Martinez v. Fuerte* [1976], 428 U.S. 543). Probable cause, consent, or a search warrant is necessary if someone is stopped at a place not considered the border or its functional equivalent (*United States v. Brignoni-Ponce* 422 U.S. 873 [1975]).

### INTERROGATION BY AN INS AGENT

An INS officer may interrogate any alien or person reasonably believed to be an alien without a warrant, about his citizenship, immigration status, or right to remain in the United States. An INS agent also has the right to arrest any alien who in his presence or view is entering or attempting to enter the United States in violation of the immigration laws. The agent may arrest any alien in the United States if the agent has reason to believe that the alien is in violation of these laws and is likely to escape before a warrant can be obtained. Furthermore, an agent may search any alien vessel in U.S. territorial waters and any railway car, aircraft, or vehicle within twenty-five miles of the border. This does not include dwellings (8 U.S.C.S. 1357).

## ALIENS AS IMMIGRANTS OR NONIMMIGRANTS

Lawfully admitted aliens by law are classified as either immigrants or nonimmigrants.

### IMMIGRANTS DEFINED

Immigrants are people who intend to remain in the United States and become permanent residents. An alien permanent resident is sometimes called a green-card holder.

There is a strict limit on the number of immigrant visas issued each year for each classification of immigrants. A priority system for the issuance of immigrant visas permits some applicants to immigrate quickly while others may wait for years.

### NONIMMIGRANTS DEFINED

Nonimmigrants are people who are in the United States for a limited time, usually for a specific purpose, but plan to return to their home countries. This category includes those traveling on vacation and those in the United States for business reasons. Nonimmigrant visas are not subject to the same strict limitations as immigrant visas, but one may be denied because of the inability of the applicant to show an unrelinquished foreign domicile or restricted because of the political relationship between the home country of the applicant and the United States.

## IMMIGRANT CLASSIFICATIONS

### PERMANENT RESIDENT VS. RESIDENCE

In legal terms, *residence* usually means the place where a person lives at any one time and is not affected by his intent to remain in that place. However, the term *permanent resident* as it applies to the immigration laws refers to the legal status accorded to an immigrant who is lawfully permitted to live permanently in the United States and is based on the person's intent to remain in the United States (8 U.S.C. §1101[a][20]).

## IMMIGRANT CATEGORIES AND ANNUAL VISA ALLOTMENTS

The 1990 act significantly revised the way in which immigrants are classified and established limits on the numbers who may immigrate in each category and subcategory in any single year.

| | |
|---|---|
| Family-sponsored immigrants | 480,000 |
| Employment-based immigrants | 140,000 |
| Diversity immigrants | 55,000 |

There is currently an annual refugee quota of 50,000 or more, set each year from designated countries by the president in consultation with the Congress.

### Family-Sponsored Immigrants
Family-sponsored immigration is based on the relationship with a person who is a U.S. citizen or a lawful permanent resident and on a family member's wish to immigrate from another country. There are five categories of family-based immigrants:

1. Immediate relatives of U.S. citizens such as spouses, unmarried children under the age of twenty-one, parents of U.S. citizens over the age of twenty-one, and spouses of deceased citizens, with certain restrictions (8 U.S.C. §1151[b][2][A][1])
2. Unmarried sons and daughters (twenty-one or older) of U.S. citizens
3. Spouses and unmarried sons and daughters of permanent residents
4. Spouses and unmarried children under the age of twenty-one; unmarried adult sons and daughters; married sons and daughters of U.S. citizens
5. Brothers and sisters of adult U.S. citizens

The current backlog of applicants in the last category is eight years.

### Employment-Based Immigrants
There are five categories of preferences for people who wish to immigrate under the employment-based immigration provisions (8 U.S.C. §1153[b]):

1. Priority workers, who are defined as persons with extraordinary abilities in the sciences, arts, education, business, or athletics, including outstanding professors or researchers and some top-level corporate executives. Most priority workers must have employment offers before they will be granted immigrant visas (forty thousand annual visas).
2. Aliens with advanced degrees in professional fields and aliens with excep-

tional abilities in the sciences, arts, or business. Specific job offers are usually required for visas in this category (forty thousand annual visas).

3. All other aliens seeking to immigrate on the basis of offers of permanent skilled or unskilled employment (forty thousand annual visas) and a labor certification establishing that there are not sufficient able, skilled, and qualified workers immediately available in the geographic area of employment and that the employment will not have an adverse effect on the American labor market.

4. "Special immigrants," including religious workers, U.S. employees of fifteen years serving abroad, persons serving in armed forces on active duty for twelve years, and returning permanent residents.

5. Alien investors who invest in new commercial enterprises in the United States with the amount of the investment being one million or five hundred thousand dollars in targeted high-unemployment areas, resulting in permanent full-time employment for at least ten U.S. citizens. This visa is conditional and is reviewed after two years with the possible result of an unconditional grant of permanent resident status.

## DIVERSITY IMMIGRATION

### QUALIFYING FOR DIVERSITY IMMIGRANT STATUS

Only natives of countries with fewer than fifty thousand immigrants to the United States over the preceding five years can qualify for a visa based on diversity (there are fifty-five thousand of these visas available each year).

Under this program there are six international divisions, and each area is categorized as a low-admission or high-admission area. Only those from low-admission countries within a low-admission region can qualify for a visa based on diversity. No more than 3,850 visas may be granted for natives of any one country in any one year. Visas based on diversity are distributed through a random selection from all applications submitted during the annual application period.

To be eligible for a visa under the diversity category, an applicant must have at least a high school education and at least two years' work experience in an occupation that requires at least two years' training or experience (8 U.S.C. §1153[c]).

### ADJUSTMENT OF STATUS

The original application process for applying for an immigrant status requires the applicant to complete a detailed application at a U.S. consulate office outside the United States (8 U.S.C. §§1201, 1202). However, changes over the years allow a permanent resident to apply without leaving the United States if certain specific eligibility criteria are met (8 U.S.C. §1255). For example, if an alien has entered the United States legally and has either maintained lawful status or is the parent, spouse, or minor or unmarried child of a U.S. citizen, he may file an application to adjust his status at the local INS office. All others must have paid a fine of one thousand dollars until this procedure of fining expired.

Adjustment of status may also be granted to an alien who has been in the United States continuously since before January 1, 1972, under what is called the registry provision. To be eligible for permanent resident status under the registry provision, an alien does not have to prove that he entered the United States legally (8 U.S.C. §1259).

## COUNTRY FROM WHICH AN ALIEN EMIGRATES

Diversity-based immigration depends on how many immigrants have previously been granted visas from any particular country. When a visa is granted to a person from Brazil, for instance, it reduces the number of visas that may be granted to people from Brazil for the rest of that year. When a visa is granted to a person on the basis of his coming to the United States from another country, it is said to be charged to that country.

The general rule regarding which country an alien visa will be charged to is that an alien will be charged to the country of his birth, regardless of his country of citizenship or residence (8 U.S.C. §1152[b]). There are four exceptions to this rule:

1. A spouse may be charged to the country of his spouse's birth when a visa is not available for the first spouse's country.
2. Unmarried minor children may be charged to the country where either parent was born if they are accompanying the parent to the United States.
3. Former U.S. citizens who were born in the United States may be charged to their countries of citizenship or their countries of last residence if they are not citizens of any country.
4. An alien born in a country that was not the birthplace of either of his parents may be charged to the country of birth of either parent if his parents did not intend to remain permanently in the country of the child's birth at the time he was born.

## NONIMMIGRANT VISAS

Any alien who does not fit into one of the nonimmigrant classifications is considered by law to be an immigrant alien. Because of this legal presumption, the burden of proving he is a nonimmigrant falls on the applicant. Proof that a nonimmigrant plans to stay temporarily in the United States and that he qualifies as a legitimate nonimmigrant must be provided to both the consular officer in his home country and to the immigration officer at the border. To accomplish this, the alien needs to establish that he fits into one of the nonimmigrant classifications and is not classified as excludable. For example, an applicant will be excluded if he is unable to prove an unrelinquished foreign domicile. The two exceptions to this dual-intent preclusion are the HIB temporary foreign professional and the L-1 intracompany transferee manager. (Refer to Table 15–1, page 257.)

The length of time for which a visa is granted depends on the purpose of the applicant's visit. Those who wish to enter the United States on a nonimmigrant status must first apply for a visa at the U.S. consulates in their home countries.

## THE NONIMMIGRANT APPLICATION PROCESS

The applicant must give his full and true name, date and place of birth, nationality, the purpose and length of his intended stay in the United States, a personal description, photographs, and any additional information necessary to establish his identification and intentions.

Once the visa application has been completed, the applicant must remain in his home country until his application is approved and he has been informed by the consular office that he is authorized to travel to the United States. The nonimmigrant visa will be evidenced by a stamp placed in the alien's passport by the consular office.

Nonimmigrant visas are issued only for temporary visits and do not allow aliens to remain in the United States permanently. Once the time period specified on the visa has expired, the nonimmigrant must return to his home country.

For all other applicants requesting permanent resident status, the availability of visas is based on priority by the filing dates of immigrant visa applications or labor certifications.

## ADJUSTMENT OF STATUS

*Adjustment of status is available only to those who have entered the United States with proper documentation and complied with the inspection process at a port of entry.* Inspection means the alien presents his visa to a U.S. immigration officer at a port of entry and meets all requirements for admission to the United States. His visa will be stamped at a port of entry, and unless he is excludable, he will be admitted into the United States.

In some cases people who enter the United States unlawfully are subject to deportation unless they pay a thousand-dollar penalty when applying for adjustment of status.

## EXTENDING THE EXPIRATION DATE ON A TEMPORARY VISA

In some situations it is possible to have the expiration date on a nonimmigrant visa extended. Someone who enters the United States as a temporary visitor on a nonimmigrant visa and has not completed his purpose by the date his visa expires may apply for an extension in order to finish his business.

## APPLYING FOR WORK AUTHORIZATION

Some nonimmigrants may apply for work authorization, and if it is granted, their employment is restricted to a specific employer or for a specific purpose. A nonimmigrant who enters the United States as a student, on an F-1 visa, may not work more than twenty hours per week when school is in session, but he may be granted twelve months' practical training, usually upon conclusion of his degree.

## EXCLUDABLE ALIENS

The concept of exclusion of aliens is an important one because an applicant is evaluated several times during the petition and application process, and a finding of excludability at any time will result in a determination of ineligibility to enter the United States.

The United States has laws designed to protect citizens and noncitizens from immigrants who may be harmful to the health and welfare of the nation. To accomplish that objective, some aliens are excluded from admission to the United States and are ineligible to receive a visa. Under the 1990 Immigration Act there are nine categories of grounds for exclusion of aliens.

### 1. Persons with Health-Related Problems

Aliens are excluded if they have communicable diseases of public health significance or if their medical conditions may result in their being dependent on public-supported medical care. The responsibility for establishing the list of qualifying diseases rests with the secretary of health and human services. The list currently includes gonorrhea, infectious leprosy, infectious-stage syphilis, and active tuberculosis. AIDS and HIV have been removed from the list of diseases that create grounds for exclusion. In some cases the INS may grant a discretionary waiver of exclusion based on medical grounds.

Aliens are excluded if they have physical or mental disorders that may manifest themselves in the form of a threat to the property, safety, or welfare of the aliens or others.

Aliens are excluded if they have physical or mental disorders and behaviors associated with the disorders that have posed a threat to them or others and are likely to recur. The earlier act required exclusion of anyone who had previously had a psychotic episode or had been classified as mentally retarded or insane. Under the amended act of 1990, people with mental retardation such as Down's syndrome are no longer excluded.

The 1990 act eliminated several nonmedical exclusions, such as insanity, now considered a legal, not a medical, matter.

Aliens determined to be drug abusers or addicts are excluded from admission. Previously persons who were determined to be alcoholics were excludable. Under the 1990 act, persons who are alcoholics may now be classified within the medical classification. The distinction is important because aliens who fall into the category of drug abusers or addicts cannot receive discretionary waivers.

An alien, whether an immigrant or a nonimmigrant, may be required to submit to medical examination to verify that he is not excludable for health reasons.

### 2. Persons with Criminal Backgrounds

These criminal acts will exclude aliens from the United States:

Conviction or commission of a crime involving moral turpitude

Violation of laws relating to controlled substances

Conviction of multiple criminal offenses with combined sentences of five years or more but not including political offenses

Engaging in illicit trafficking in a controlled substance with no conviction but not to include experimental use of drugs by minors or drug smugglers caught at the border

Engaging in prostitution or recent past prostitution activities including habitual prostitution

Commission of a serious criminal offense for which diplomatic immunity has been asserted as the result of which the alien has left the United States

### 3. Persons Who May Pose Security Risks to the United States

These types of persons are excluded from admission into the United States:

Persons seeking entry to engage in sabotage, espionage, export of prohibited technology, activities with a purpose of violent overthrow of the U.S. government, or "any other unlawful activity"

Persons with a history of terrorist activity or the likelihood of engaging in such activity after entry, including conducting fund-raising activities for terrorist groups or activities

Persons who pose potentially serious adverse foreign policy consequences by their entry

Persons who are members of the Communist or any other totalitarian party

Persons participating in Nazi-era persecution or other activities meeting international definitions of genocide

**4. Persons Who May Become Dependent on Public Support**
The earlier act required that certain people not capable of earning livings were to be excluded on medical grounds. In the 1990 act this category was eliminated, but these people may still be excluded because of the probability that they may become dependent on public support.

For an applicant to overcome the exclusion based on likelihood of his becoming a public charge, he must be able to establish income and resources which prove that he is able to live above the poverty limits established by the federal Department of Health and Human Services. Failure to establish incomes above that level will result in a determination of ineligibility.

**5. Persons Who Have Specific Employment-Based Restrictions**

**6. Persons Who Have Been Illegal Entrants and Immigration Law Violators**

**7. Persons Who Have Submitted False Documentation in Relationship to Their Applications**

**8. Persons Who Would Eventually Be Ineligible to Become U.S. Citizens**
The two subcategories of this exclusion class are (1) persons who deserted as military service personnel or evaded military service by leaving the United States and (2) aliens who have applied for and received exemptions from military service on the basis of their alienage.

Persons in category 1 will not be granted any type of visa, including a nonimmigrant visa. Persons in category 2 may be granted nonimmigrant visas but will be excluded from receiving immigrant visas.

## 9. Miscellaneous Grounds

Some of those grouped into this category include the following:

Persons who actively practice polygamy and intend to practice it in the United States

Aliens who act as guardians while accompanying a helpless alien who has been ordered excluded because of health reasons or infancy (§212[a][9][B])

Aliens whose home countries have not signed the Hague Convention of the Civil Aspects of International Child Abduction and that fail to recognize a custody order of a child outside the United States when the child has a lawful claim of U.S. citizenship and a court has entered an order granting custody to a U.S. citizen

Aliens who fall within any of the above categories will not be granted visas to enter the United States unless they can obtain waivers of exclusion. An attorney who specializes in immigration law can advise an alien on matters of exclusion and waivers.

## Some Previous Grounds for Exclusion Eliminated by the 1990 Act

The 1990 act eliminated some classifications of exclusion that had previously existed including:

1. Sexual deviates (homosexuals)
2. Paupers, beggars, and vagrants
3. Aliens coming to the United States to engage in any immoral sexual act
4. Illiterate immigrants over the age of sixteen

## Deportable Aliens

Until an alien becomes a U.S. citizen, he can be deported if convicted of certain deportable offenses. Both nonimmigrants who are visiting on a temporary basis and immigrants who are permanent residents but have not yet become U.S. citizens are subject to deportation. Under the 1990 act there are five categories of persons having deportable offenses:

1. Persons excludable at entry who entered without inspection or who have violated status
2. Persons who have been convicted of certain criminal offenses

3. Aliens who have failed to comply with the registration requirements of the Immigration and Naturalization Act while present in the United States, including those who have knowingly made false statements in registration applications or other forms required by the immigration laws
4. Persons who pose security risks to the United States, these grounds for deportation being the same as the grounds for exclusion based on being a security risk
5. Aliens who, within five years after entry to the United States, become public charges from circumstances that the attorney general believes arose prior to entry though unforeseen circumstances cannot give rise to deportability (a "public charge" being anyone who has received public assistance)

## PREVENTING EXCLUSION AND DEPORTATION THROUGH WAIVERS

The Immigration and Naturalization Act contains several provisions for granting waivers of excludability and deportability.

A waiver of excludability is granted for longtime permanent residents returning to the United States from a temporary trip abroad to a home in the United States, where they have lived for at least seven consecutive years. This category of waiver may be granted at the discretion of the attorney general of the United States, and it covers all grounds for exclusion except those who are excluded for security risks and aggravated felonies.

A permanent resident of seven years who is granted a waiver in deportation proceedings based on his having proved he has been rehabilitated after conviction for a crime other than aggravated felony is returned to the status of a permanent resident.

Nonimmigrant aliens may be granted waivers of exclusion based on three criteria: (1) a risk to security, (2) the seriousness of aliens' violation of immigration or criminal law, (3) the nature of the applicants' reason for seeking entry.

A waiver can be limited in any manner, and a departure bond may be required. In the limiting of a waiver, the alien may have a time limit placed on his visit, may be limited to specific geographical sites, or may be restricted from certain activities.

Aliens who would otherwise be excluded because of health issues, fraud, smuggling immediate relatives, being public charges, certain crimes, prostitution, and possession of thirty grams or less of marijuana may be granted discretionary waivers if they are the spouses or unmarried sons or daughters of citizens, permanent residents, or aliens who have been issued immigrant visas. Failure of an alien to comply with the conditions of the waiver is grounds for deportation. Waivers are most often based on family reunification and require that the alien demonstrate that failure to grant the waiver will result in "extreme hardship" to the U.S. citizen or permanent resident and that the alien has been rehabilitated. To prove extreme hardship, the alien is required to establish equities and family economic and emotional interdependency.

Under certain circumstances, a waiver may be granted to an alien who has been excluded because he or she committed fraud or misrepresented information on a visa application or other document required by the INS. Certain family relationships must exist for this waiver to be granted unless the fraud or misrepresentation occurred at least ten years before the application for a visa, entry, or adjustment of status.

## REMOVAL PROCEEDINGS (FORMERLY DEPORTATION)

All aliens facing removal have a right to a fair hearing under the due process clause of the U.S. Constitution. The federal government must prove that an alien is removable. An alien has the right to be advised of the charges filed against him, sufficient time to prepare his case, and the right to be represented by legal counsel, although not at government expense because deportation is a civil, not a criminal, matter (see "Criminal Law" chapter on page 190).

An alien is protected against self-incrimination, but he may produce evidence and witnesses in his behalf. For example, an employer may come forward and testify to the character of the alien and explain how deporting the alien employee would hurt the employer's business.

Aliens and U.S. citizens are protected from unreasonable searches and seizures under the Fourth Amendment, but search warrants and probable cause are not required for border searches by immigration officials.

In some cases an alien may be allowed to leave the United States voluntarily before an official order of removal is issued. The advantage of voluntary departure is that the alien will be allowed to return to the United States with a new visa without being excluded under the law that prohibits reentry within indicated periods for aliens who have been involuntarily removed.

At a removal hearing the alien may ask the judge to let him leave the United States at his own expense rather than have the U.S. government transport him. The advantage of voluntary departure is that the alien can avoid having an official order of deportation filed against him, and he will be allowed to reapply for a new visa. It is a crime to return to the United States after deportation without prior approval.

Removal can be withheld in the case of any alien whose life or freedom would be threatened by his being returned to his home country. He can, however, be deported to another country where he would be safe. At a removal hearing the judge will ask the alien to which country he wishes to be removed. If possible, the alien will be removed to the country of his choice. The alien can, however, be removed to any country that has agreed to take him.

In some cases removal may be avoided by filing an application for adjustment to permanent resident status. This remedy is available to qualified aliens already in the United States wishing to adjust their residency status without leaving the country. An alien will not qualify for adjustment in status if he is in categories 1, 3, and 4 below unless a thousand-dollar penalty was paid before October 1, 1997:

1. A ship's member
2. An exchange visitor who has not satisfied the two-year foreign residence requirement or had it waived
3. A person who entered while in transit to another country
4. A person who entered the United States without inspection or under fraudulent circumstances

## NONWAIVABLE EXCLUSIONS

A waiver of excludability may be granted to applicants who would otherwise be excluded unless they are excluded because they are aggravated felons; because they participate, or have participated, in espionage or sabotage activities with a purpose to overthrow the U.S. government by violent or unlawful means; because they engage in the illegal export of goods, technology, or sensitive information; because they participate in activities related to genocide such as Nazi-era persecution; or because granting the waiver would result in adverse foreign policy consequences.

Examples of aggravated felonies are the following:

Rape and sexual abuse of a minor

Money-laundering of property transactions if the funds exceed ten thousand dollars

Violent crimes for which one year or more is served

Theft, for which one year or more is served

Alien smuggling, for which a term of one year or more is served (exception: smuggling a spouse, child, or parent)

Falsifying a passport, for which a term of one year or more is served

It is very important to note that this is a poison pill to all future immigration, regardless of equities, and guarantees removal from the United States of permanent residents.

## SPECIAL LEGISLATION TO PREVENT DEPORTATION

Relief from deportation may also be requested through a process known as the private bill. In this process a special request (private bill) is introduced in either the House of Representatives or the Senate, asking Congress to intervene and halt the deportation proceeding. The introduction of a private bill does not automatically stop deportation proceedings.

An alien who seeks relief from deportation under a *private bill* must present his case to a member of the Senate or House of Representatives. If the senator or representative believes that the alien has a bona fide reason to be relieved from deportation, he will introduce the private bill on behalf of the alien. If the alien is represented by an attorney, his attorney may discuss the matter with the judiciary committee of whichever house introduced the bill and submit documented evidence to support his case. The bill will then be reviewed by that committee. Most private bills are introduced in the House of Representatives.

If an alien is already in the United States and is requesting a private bill to avoid deportation, it will contain the following information: the alien's name, age, place of birth, address in the United States, the date, place of his last entry into the United States, the location of the U.S. consulate at which he obtained his visa, and his immigration status at the time of the request. Documentation must also be presented regarding the alien's occupation and employment record, the names and addresses of all relatives in the United States and abroad, the immigration status of those relatives, and the dates of all entries (legal and illegal) into the United States.

If Congress approves the private bill, it will be enacted into law and become a legislative mandate enforced by the INS. That means the alien will be relieved from removal and granted a visa. If Congress is not favorable to the private bill, the alien will be removed in accordance with the laws of deportation. If the alien is outside the United States and Congress does not approve the private bill, his request for a visa will be denied in accordance with immigration laws.

Private bill procedures are not permitted unless all other immigration remedies have been exhausted. In other words, the alien must start with immigration procedures before he seeks relief through the private bill process.

Congress has stringent criteria requiring proof of extreme hardship and is usually unwilling to assist in drug cases.

The introduction of a private bill may result in the termination of an alien's lawful nonimmigrant status. In such a case, if Congress is not favorable to the bill, the alien will be permitted to withdraw the private bill and retain his nonimmigrant status for the length of time stated on his visa, or he may voluntarily leave the United States. In most cases a private bill will not be allowed for an alien who has applied for an adjustment in status or who entered the country unlawfully without inspection.

For more information about the private bill process, see the Senate and House rules reprinted in "70 Interpreter Releases 597-602 (5-3-93)," or contact an attorney who specializes in immigration law.

## IMMIGRATION AND MARRIAGE

An alien who seeks permanent resident status through marriage to a U.S. citizen or permanent resident, or who comes to the United States as a nonimmigrant fiancé or fiancée of a citizen in order to apply later for permanent resident status, will now be granted only a conditional resident status of two years. If after two years the couple is still married, the alien may apply for an adjustment to permanent resident status. This must be done within ninety days before the second anniversary. If the marriage is dissolved prior to the two-year anniversary other than through the death of a spouse or because of the spouse's being the victim of battering and physical or emotional abuse, the marriage is judged to have been a fraud entered into only for immigration purposes. The alien's resident status is terminated, and deportation proceedings begin.

Failure to file the application for adjustment in status results in termination of the resident status and initiation of deportation proceedings. The couple is called for an interview and must demonstrate that the marriage is solvent and was not entered into solely for immigration purposes.

Marriage fraud carries heavy penalties. A person convicted of marrying to evade the U.S. immigration laws could be fined and sent to prison. Anyone convicted of marriage fraud will be denied permanent resident status even if he later enters into a bona fide marriage to a U.S. citizen or permanent resident.

U.S. immigration law places a restriction on adjustment to permanent resident status for aliens who marry while they are in deportation or exclusion proceedings. Aliens who marry during this time are presumed by law to have married only for immigration purposes, and to overcome that presumption, the petitioner must attach to his petition a request for an exemption accompanied by documentation establishing the sincerity of the marriage.

U.S. law takes immigration marriage fraud very seriously. An alien who is considering marriage to a U.S. citizen or permanent resident or who enters as a nonimmigrant fiancé must be sure to comply with all requirements for alien marriage and file all necessary applications and documents on the appropriate filing date. If necessary, he should consult an attorney who specializes in immigration law.

## RIGHTS AND OBLIGATIONS OF ALIENS

Aliens are not necessarily entitled to the same rights and protection afforded U.S. citizens under the Constitution. While the federal Civil Rights Act of 1964 made it illegal to discriminate against persons because of age, race, sex, religion, or national heritage, it does not offer protection to aliens as a group.

### EMPLOYMENT RIGHTS

The Immigration and Control Act (IRCA) of 1986 was implemented to allow aliens who had been in the United States for an extended period of time to gain legal permanent resident status. Commonly known as the amnesty program, IRCA legalized the temporary status of qualified alien residents, refugees, and persons in the United States who were seeking asylum and confirmed the status of permanent residents as "intending citizens"—the legal definition given to those groups. As part of IRCA, those persons who were granted legal status were further protected by laws that prohibit employers from engaging in unfair immigration-related employment practices based on citizenship.

Aliens must have authorization from the INS to work in the United States, and any alien who works without first obtaining the required authorization may be removed for violating the rules governing his status as an alien.

Under IRCA, every employer in the United States is prohibited from hiring any alien who has not received from the INS the necessary authorization to work (8 U.S.C. §1324a). Stringent record keeping is required of employers, and any employment applicant is required to provide proof of his right to work within three days of being hired. Any employer who hires someone and later discovers that he or she is not authorized to work in the United States is required to terminate that person's employment unless the alien was hired before November 6, 1986 (8 U.S.C. §§1324a[a][3], 1324a[1][3]). If an alien uses a fraudulent document to obtain employment, he is subject to removal. If an employer hires an alien, knowing that the alien used a false document to verify his work authorization status, the employer will be punished as provided by federal law with a fine of up to three thousand dollars per violation and up to six months' imprisonment (8 U.S.C. §1324c).

The courts have determined that it is permissible for the federal government to refuse to hire anyone who is not a citizen, and aliens are prohibited from employment in some jobs at the state and local levels, particularly when the jobs involve public trust or the political community.

Private employers may refuse to hire aliens if the employer has three or fewer employees, if he is prohibited from hiring aliens because of a contractual agreement with the federal, state, or local government, or if he gives preference to a U.S. citizen over an equally qualified alien who is protected under IRCA (8 U.S.C. §1324b[a][2], [4]).

All aliens, even those who are in the United States illegally and are often referred to as undocumented aliens, are protected by the Fair Labor Standards Act and must be paid the minimum wage established by federal law.

## ALIEN EMPLOYMENT CLASSIFICATIONS

There are three classifications of aliens authorized to work in the United States:

1. Aliens who are authorized to work for any employer in accordance with their lawful status and who then must apply for an employment authorization document (EAD) to prove that they are authorized to work; a receipt indicating that the alien has applied for an EAD is valid evidence of his right to work for ninety days (permanent and temporary residents do not need to apply for EADs).
2. Aliens who are authorized to work for a specific employer including those who have been sponsored by a specific employer; aliens in this category do not need to apply for EADs since their entry documents are stamped with the required authorization.
3. Aliens who must obtain explicit permission to work at a particular job but do not have any inherent work authorization cannot work until they have obtained approved EADs from the INS.

## RIGHTS TO SOCIAL WELFARE BENEFITS AND EDUCATION

Social welfare programs in the United States are administered sometimes by the federal government and sometimes by the individual states. The Welfare Reform Act of 1996 made specific provisions for aliens who were admitted to permanent status not to be allowed access to social welfare programs, including the preclusion of aged permanent residents from SSI. Aliens may be restricted from access to social welfare programs at both the federal and state levels; several states have passed laws that prohibit them from receiving welfare benefits. The courts have upheld state restrictions on benefits for aliens when the state has been able to show that the restrictions served a substantial state interest.

The Supreme Court has been reluctant to uphold state laws that prohibit undocumented aliens from attending public schools. While this matter is far from settled, the prevailing attitude has been that the best interests of the nation are served if all residents, illegal as well as legal, are afforded an education.

## PROPERTY OWNERSHIP

The rights of aliens to own real estate in the United States have not been firmly decided. Since the laws in the United States leave the regulation of land use and ownership to the states, each state has its own laws regarding restrictions of alien property ownership and ownership of property by nonresident and absent aliens and alien corporations. Some bar any alien ownership of property, and others limit the percentage of ownership interest an alien may hold.

Aliens may be prohibited from owning radio and television stations.

State regulations concerning alien ownership of property are subject to the federal Constitution. In Arizona there are no statutory provisions regarding property ownership. In Florida ownership, inheritance, dispositions, and possession of real property by aliens not eligible for citizenship may be regulated or prohibited by law (Const. Art. 1 §2); however, an undocumented alien in Florida is permitted to take property by inheritance. In California, Illinois, New Mexico, New York, and Texas any alien may hold property just as if he were as a citizen; an alien's right to inherit property may be restricted.

## FIREARMS

It is illegal for an alien not lawfully in the United States to ship or transport into interstate or foreign commerce or to possess or affect commerce with any firearm or ammunition or to receive any firearm or ammunition that has been shipped or transferred in interstate or foreign commerce. Aliens unlawfully in the United States may not as employees receive, possess, or transport any firearms or ammunition in or affecting interstate commerce.

Any alien who, at any time after entry into the United States, is convicted under any law of purchasing, selling, offering for sale, using, owning, exchanging, possessing or carrying, or attempting or conspiring to purchase, sell, offer for sale, exchange, use, own, possess, or carry any weapon that is in violation of any firearm law is deportable.

## HOMESTEAD EXEMPTION

Any person residing in the United States is eligible for the homestead exemption. Homestead laws allow a person to register a portion of his real and personal property as a homestead exemption so that creditors may not take away the property when economic conditions are bad (for homestead exemptions, see Table 8-1 on page 96).

## RIGHT TO WORK

Aliens lawfully admitted into the United States have the right to work and to engage in business and trade. A nonimmigrant form I-94 classification assigned by INS determines if a nonimmigrant alien is permitted to work (20 C.F.R. 422.§105). Nonimmigrants are lawfully admitted for fixed temporary stays for specific purposes.

States, under the Fourteenth Amendment, may require citizenship as a qualification for certain public positions that involve discretionary decision making. For example, a citizenship requirement has been upheld in order to become a police officer (*Foley v. Connelie,* 435 U.S. 291), a public schoolteacher (*Ambach v. Norwick,* 99 S. Ct. 1589), and a peace officer (*Cabell v. Chavez-Salido,* 454 U.S. 432).

## SOCIAL SECURITY NUMBER

Social Security numbers may be assigned to aliens lawfully admitted into the United States for permanent residency, to aliens admitted as refugees, and to aliens granted asylum or temporary parole status (20 C.F.R.§422.104).

## UNEMPLOYMENT BENEFITS

Arizona, California, Florida, Illinois, New Mexico, New York, and Texas all require a person to be either a citizen or a lawfully admitted alien while the services to be eligible for unemployment benefits are performed.

## ACCESS TO COURTS

Aliens lawfully admitted to the United States have the same rights and access to state courts as do U.S. citizens. Aliens who are not lawfully in the United States may also sue in state courts because the issue is residence, not nationality. Therefore, if a person resides in a particular county, he may sue in the appropriate state court in his jurisdiction.

## WELFARE REFORM ACT

Recently Congress made this statement concerning national policy with respect to welfare and immigration: "Self-sufficiency has been a basic principle of United States immigration law since the earliest of immigration statutes." It continues to be the immigration policy of the United States that aliens within the nation's borders not depend on public resources to meet their needs but instead rely on their own capabilities, the resources of their families, their sponsors, and private organizations. The availability of public benefits should not constitute an incentive for immigration to the United States.

An alien who is not a qualified alien is not eligible for federal public benefits. A *qualified alien* within the United States means:

An alien who is lawfully admitted for permanent residence under the Immigration and Naturalization Act

An alien who is granted asylum under section 208 of this act

A refugee who is admitted to the United States under section 207 of this act

An alien who is paroled into the United States under section 212(d)(5) of this act for at least one year

An alien whose deportation is being withheld under section 243(h) of this act

An alien who is granted conditional entry pursuant to section 203(a) (7) of this act prior to April 1, 1980

Federal public benefits are defined as any grants, contracts, loans, professional licenses, or commercial licenses provided by an agency of the United States or by appropriated funds of the United States, and any retirement, welfare, health, disability, public or assisted housing, postsecondary education, food assistance, unemployment benefit, or any other similar benefit for which payments or assistance are provided to an individual, household, or family by an agency of the United States or by appropriated funds for the United States.

Aliens who are not qualified aliens are eligible for the following benefits:

Medical assistance under Title XIX of the Social Security Act, for care and services that are necessary for the treatment of an emergency medical condition of the alien involved and are not related to an organ transplant procedure, if the alien otherwise meets the eligibility requirements for medical assistance under the state-approved plan under this title

Short-term, noncash, "in kind" emergency disaster relief

Public health assistance for immunizations with respect to immunizable diseases and for the testing and treatment of symptoms of communicable diseases whether or not these symptoms are caused by communicable diseases

Programs, services, or such assistance as soup kitchens, crisis counseling and intervention, and short-term shelter specified by the attorney general

Programs for housing or community development assistance or financial assistance administered by the secretary of housing and urban development, Program V of the Housing Act of 1949, or under the Consolidated Farm and Rural Development Act, to the extent that an alien was receiving the benefit on the date of the enactment of this act

A state is authorized to determine the eligibility of a qualified alien for any designated federal program. Designated federal programs are Temporary Assistance for Needy Families, Social Services Block Grant, and Medicaid. Qualified aliens are not eligible for any specified federal programs that include food stamps and Supplemental Security Income. The following are qualified aliens who are eligible for designated federal programs:

Refugees and asylees: up to five years after entering the U.S.

an alien admitted to the United States as a refugee under Section 207 of the INA

an alien granted asylum under Section 208 of such act

an alien whose deportation is withheld under Section 243(h) of such act

Certain permanent resident aliens

who are lawfully admitted to the United States for permanent residence under the INA

who have worked forty qualifying quarters of coverage as defined under title II of the Social Security Act or can be credited with such qualifying quarters as provided under Section 435, and in the case of such qualification beginning after December 31, 1996, did not receive any federal benefit during any such period

Veterans and service personnel such as:

those discharged with an honorable discharge and not because of their alien status

an armed forces person on active duty

his or her spouse or unmarried dependent child.

## FIVE-YEAR EXCLUSION OF BENEFITS FOR LEGAL IMMIGRANTS

A qualified alien who enters the United States on or after the date of the new Welfare Reform Act is not eligible for any federal benefits for a period of five years beginning at the alien's entry into the United States. This limitation will not apply to the following:

Refugees and asylees up to five years after entering the U.S.

an alien admitted to the United States as a refugee under Section 207 of the INA,

an alien granted asylum under Section 208 of such act, or

an alien whose deportation is withheld under Section 243(h) of such act

Veterans and service personnel discharged with an honorable discharge and not because of their alien status

Armed forces personnel on active duty

Spouses or unmarried dependent children of refugees and asylees

The limitations for qualified aliens will not apply to the following assistance or benefits:

Medical assistance under Title XIX of the Social Security Act, for care and services that are necessary for the treatment of an emergency medical condition of the alien involved and are not related to an organ transplant procedure, if the alien otherwise meets the eligibility requirements for medical assistance under the state-approved plan under this title;

Short-term, noncash, "in kind" emergency disaster relief

Assistance or benefits under the National School Lunch Act

Assistance or benefits under the Child Nutrition Act of 1996

Public health assistance for immunizations with respect to immunizable diseases and for the testing and treatment of symptoms of communicable diseases whether or not these symptoms are caused by communicable diseases

Payments for foster care and adoption assistance under the Social Security Act for a parent or a child who would, in the absence of restrictions, be eligible to have these payments made on the child's behalf, but only if the foster or adoptive parent of the child is a qualified alien

Programs, services, or assistance specified by the attorney general

Programs of student assistance under the Higher Education Act of 1965 and the Public Service Health Act

Benefits under the Head Start Act

Benefits under the Job Training Partnership Act

## TAXATION

All aliens, whether here legally or illegally, are required to pay tax on any income they earn while living and working in the United States. Aliens considered to be permanent residents are required to pay income tax to the U.S. Treasury for any income they receive from any source worldwide. Once a person becomes a permanent resident alien, he is obligated to pay taxes on any income he receives (even if he is not present in the United States for a single day in a given tax year). Before a permanent resident can be released from his obligation to pay income tax on worldwide income, he must officially surrender his permanent resident status.

A permanent resident alien becomes responsible for payment of income taxes to the United States on the first day that he enters the United States as a permanent resident, and every applicant for permanent residence must file a statement regarding his tax status with his application.

An alien who holds a green card is considered a permanent resident. However, nonimmigrant aliens may also be classified as permanent residents for tax purposes under one of several formulas contained in the Internal Revenue Code. Those formulas are complicated and usually require the assistance of an attorney or professional tax adviser for interpretation. In general, however, there are two basic tests that are used:

1. The 183-day test. Under this test any alien who was present in the United States for any 183 days in the year is taxable as a U.S. resident; the 183 days do not have to be continuous; some exceptions apply and anyone who is unsure if he falls into this classification should seek professional advice.
2. The cumulative presence test. This test requires any alien who has been present in the United States for a certain number of days over a three-year period to pay taxes on worldwide income.

Nonresidents pay 30 percent for taxes on income received from U.S. sources, profit from the sale of real property, and income associated with a trade or business in the United States, including rents and dividends.

## Aliens Employed as Personal Service Workers in the United States

All aliens who are employed as personal service workers—housekeepers, nannies, private caretakers, etc.—are required by law to pay income taxes including Social Security taxes and unemployment compensation premiums. Whether the alien is a resident or nonresident for tax purposes, the alien's employer is required to deduct the required taxes from the employee's pay and submit the monies deducted to the appropriate government agency.

## Military Service and Registration

Aliens can serve in the U.S. armed forces, and any alien who serves in the U.S. military is allowed to become a citizen under special provisions and allowed to enter the United States without a visa during the time he is on active military duty (8 U.S.C. §§1439, 1440, 1354).

Since aliens may be drafted for military service, any alien who leaves the United States to avoid being drafted may be permanently excluded from entering the United States (8 U.S.C. §1182[a][22]).

An alien who has been granted permanent resident status and is between the ages of eighteen and twenty-six is required to register with the Selective Service System. If he does not, he will be prohibited from naturalization until he is thirty-one years old because of the requirement of five years of good moral character immediately preceding the application for naturalization.

## POLITICAL RIGHTS

U.S. citizenship is restricted to persons who have been born in the United States, who have become naturalized citizens, and who have been granted citizenship by Congress.

State citizenship is governed by each individual state; however, no state permits a noncitizen to vote, hold political office, or sit on a jury.

## NATURALIZATION AND CITIZENSHIP

Aliens who come to the United States often come with a desire to become citizens, but there is no requirement that an alien become a citizen, no matter how long he or she intends to live in the United States. Some aliens choose not to become U.S. citizens because their home countries may not allow them to retain their native citizenship.

Naturalization is the process whereby any person not born in the United States becomes a citizen. The INS provisions for naturalization govern those who were not born in the United States.

The requirements that must be met before an alien can become a naturalized citizen are these:

1. Lawful admission as a permanent resident of the United States unless the alien served on active duty in the military during a period of hostilities.
2. Continuous residence in the United States for at least five years immediately preceding the filing of an application for naturalization; the residence requirement for the spouse of a U.S. citizen is three years. Continuous residence is a legal concept and is not the same as being physically present; however, a physical absence of one year or more will violate the continuous residence requirement except for specifically defined situations.
3. Physical presence in the United States for a total of at least half of the time required for residence. For most aliens this is equal to two and one-half years prior to filing the application; for the spouse of a citizen, the time is one and one-half years.
4. Residence for at least three months in the state in which the naturalization application is filed.
5. Ability to read, write, and speak ordinary English. People who are physi-

cally unable to learn English, those who are over the age of fifty years and have lived in the United States as lawful permanent residents for at least twenty years prior to filing an application for naturalization, and those over the age of fifty-five who have lived in the United States for at least fifteen years since becoming permanent residents may be exempt from the English-language requirement. Blindness and deafness are considered legitimate physical disabilities, but advanced age and limited intelligence are not.

6. Knowledge and understanding of the fundamentals of the history and government of the United States. The *Federal Citizenship Textbook Series,* available from the Government Printing Office, is the preferred source for questions used by INS examiners in establishing that applicants have complied with this requirement.

7. Good moral character and an attachment to the principles of the U.S. Constitution and proper disposition to the good order and happiness of the United States. Communists are prohibited by law from becoming naturalized citizens. An applicant for naturalization who is eligible to register for military service must present proof that he has registered with the Selective Service.

8. Continuous residence in the United States from the date of filing the naturalization application to the actual admission to citizenship. Continuous residence does not mean that the applicant must be physically present during the entire time, but only that he maintain a permanent domicile in the United States to which he intends to return.

9. The intention to reside permanently in the United States. A naturalized citizen who is found to have lacked the intent to reside permanently in the United States at the time he was admitted to citizenship may be denaturalized.

10. Be eighteen years of age at the time the naturalization application is filed except a child who is naturalized with his or her parents (8 U.S.C. §§1423, 1427, 1429, 1451, 1455).

## ALIENS WHO ARE INELIGIBLE FOR NATURALIZATION

The immigration laws define three categories of persons who are not eligible for naturalization:

1. Anarchists and Communists. Aliens who advocate the overthrow of the U.S. government or who publish such a philosophy or actively support a group that does so may not become naturalized citizens (8 U.S.C. §1424); prior or passive affiliation with a Communist organization will not automatically bar admission as a naturalized citizen.

2. Military deserters and draft evaders. Aliens who were convicted by court-martial as military deserters or aliens who left the jurisdiction of the United States to avoid being drafted are barred from becoming naturalized citizens. Some exemptions apply for persons who served the military in their native countries.

3 Aliens in deportation proceedings or subject to a final order. Any aliens who have been served with final orders of deportation are barred from naturalization unless they are currently in the U.S. armed forces and have served honorably for three years or have served in the military on active duty during a period of hostilities.

## APPLICATION PROCEDURE TO BECOME A NATURALIZED CITIZEN

The Immigration Act of 1990 changed the procedures for naturalization, from a judicial proceeding that could be performed only by a federal court to an administrative proceeding under the authority of the attorney general and the INS (8 U.S.C. §§1443–1450).

The procedure for seeking naturalization requires that the alien complete and file an application with the INS (information in the application will allow the INS to determine if the applicant meets the legal requirement for naturalization) and complete an interview with an INS naturalization examiner. At the interview the examiner questions the applicant about information on his application and confirms his ability to speak, read, and write English and his knowledge of U.S. government and history. During the interview the examiner asks the applicant to execute an oath in which he swears to the truth of the information contained in his application. If the examiner approves the application, the applicant may take the oath of naturalization at that time, or he may participate in a judicial ceremony where the oath is administered.

## DENIAL OF AN APPLICATION FOR NATURALIZATION

If an application for naturalization is denied, the applicant may appeal the decision through a hearing with the INS. If the INS again denies the application, the applicant may appeal the matter to a federal district court.

## CITIZENSHIP RIGHTS AND RESPONSIBILITIES

The Fourteenth Amendment to the Constitution defines U.S. citizenship: "All persons born or naturalized in the United States, and subject to the jurisdiction thereof, are citizens of the United States and of the State wherein they reside."

Once a person qualifies for and becomes a citizen of the United States, he is free to enter the United States without obtaining permission and has an absolute right to live and work in this country.

A naturalized citizen is issued a certificate of naturalization by the INS as evidence of his U.S. citizenship. After the certificate of naturalization is issued, the citizen may apply for a passport, allowing him or her to travel outside the United States and return without needing a visa.

A naturalized citizen may vote in local, state and national elections and may sit on juries.

## LOSS OF CITIZENSHIP

### DENATURALIZATION

An alien who commits fraud, omits any important information, or misrepresents any information in applying for naturalization may have his naturalization status terminated by a process called denaturalization. Denaturalization proceedings are initiated by the attorney general and are filed in a U.S. district court. There is no statute of limitations on the government's ability to institute a denaturalization proceeding. Even if a citizen has been a naturalized citizen for a number of years, he may be denaturalized if the government learns that he provided false information on his naturalization application.

### EXPATRIATION

Expatriation is the loss of U.S. citizenship. A U.S. citizen may become subject to expatriation by his intentions and acts that validate those intentions. The INS lists several categories of acts that constitute expatriation and that are expatriative only if they are committed voluntarily and with the intention of relinquishing citizenship. These include the following:

Naturalization in another country when the person is over the age of eighteen and he requests the naturalization

Serving in the military of a foreign country engaged in hostilities against the United States

Serving in a foreign government position that requires an oath of allegiance to the foreign state

Making a formal renunciation of U.S. citizenship before a consular officer outside the United States or anywhere if the United States is in a state of war

Committing an act of treason or attempting to overthrow the U.S. government or bearing arms against the United States

## DUAL CITIZENSHIP

The United States does not support affirmative dual citizenship of its citizens. The Immigration and Naturalization Act considers the naturalization of a U.S. citizen in a foreign country to be expatriating. When a person is naturalized in the United States, that person has to take an oath that contains a renunciation of allegiance to all foreign states.

When a U.S. citizen becomes a naturalized citizen of another nation, he is subject to being expatriated—losing his citizenship. However, some U.S. citizens may be dual citizens simply because the laws of the foreign nation allow a person born in the United States, who is by law a citizen of the United States, also to be a citizen of his or her parents' nation or nations.

A person born abroad to two parents who are both citizens of the United States may be both a citizen of the country in which he was born and a citizen of the United States.

## CONCLUSION

Issues of immigration, naturalization, and citizenship are complex and have gone through significant changes in recent years. Anyone who is confronted with an immigration or naturalization issue is encouraged to consult with an attorney who specializes in immigration law.

In California immigration consultants—*who are not attorneys*—are regulated by the state Department of Consumer Affairs. Please refer to the section on "Immigration Consultants" in the chapter entitled "Professional Ethics," page 84.

### *Table 15-1: Nonimmigrant Visas*

| Classification | Visa Type | Duration and Extensions Available |
| --- | --- | --- |
| A | Foreign government employees and their immediate family members | Indefinite, dependent on State Department. Determination of duration of their official status. Exclusions often do not apply. |

## Table 15-1: Nonimmigrant Visas (cont.)

| Classification | Visa Type | Duration and Extensions Available |
|---|---|---|
| B | Visitors who have permanent foreign residences and plan on returning to their native countries | Temporary basis. |
| B-1 | Business visitors | The list of permissible activities includes participation in conferences and taking orders or selling goods for the businesses they work for in their native lands. Duration is actual time needed to complete transaction but is usually no more than three months. |
| B-2 | Tourists, aliens visiting relatives and friends, aliens coming to the United States for medical treatment | Under the Visa Waiver Pilot Program (VWPP) citizens of some countries may visit the United States without first obtaining a visa. However, all Latin American citizens must obtain visas in order to enter the United States legally. The visa is valid until the alien presents himself at the border. The INS will determine how long he will be allowed to stay in the United States. Most B-2 nonimmigrants may stay for up to one year. Extensions may be granted in six-month increments. Aliens admitted as VWPP nonvisa holders may not receive extensions and may not remain in the United States for more than ninety days. |
| C | Transients passing through the United States on their way to another country | Duration is period required for transit only for a maximum of twenty-nine days. Extensions are possible but are unlikely. |

## Table 15-1: Nonimmigrant Visas (cont.)

| Classification | Visa Type | Duration and Extensions Available |
|---|---|---|
| D | Crew members of ships or aircraft | Maximum of twenty-nine days to land temporarily. No extensions are possible, and status cannot be changed. |
| E | Citizens of countries that have treaties or whose policies grant U.S. citizens reciprocal privileges to engage in trade or invest-ment | Alien need not maintain a foreign residence as long as he has an affirmative intention to leave when the period of stay expires. The dura-tion is initially one year but may be indefinite depending on alien's rela-tionship to the trade or investment that qualified his entry to the United States. |
| F | Students entering the United States to study full-time | Requires that the study be approved by attorney general, there are full courses of study, the students have sufficient funds to support them-selves, they maintain residences abroad, they are proficient in English or enrolled in courses to become pro-ficient, their programs are academic, and they intend to return to their homelands. Duration is as long as alien remains in qualified student status, plus periods of practical train-ing. Part-time student employment may be permitted. |
| G | Aliens who are represent-atives of international organizations and their personal attendants or servants | Indefinite, depending on State Department certification of status. Similar to A visa. |

## Table 15-1: Nonimmigrant Visas (cont.)

| Classification | Visa Type | Duration and Extensions Available |
| --- | --- | --- |
| H-1A | Professional nurses | Restricted to registered nurses; professional certification must be proved; petition must be filed by employer; valid for up to three years with extensions for up to five years; no presumption of immigrant status. |
| H-1B | Workers of distinguished merit and ability, "Special Occupation" | Requires special skill and at least a bachelor's degree in the qualifying subject or a degree equal to a U.S. bachelor's degree or an unrestricted state license or certification that will allow immediate employment, education, or special training, or experience equal to a bachelor's degree. Employer must petition. Maximum of six years. No presumption of immigrant status. |
| H-2A | Temporary agricultural workers | Employer must petition for permission to hire temporary workers. Workers must depart after time period has expired. Extensions for up to one year are available. |
| H-2B | Temporary nonagricultural workers | Skilled or unskilled workers. Initial period is determined by the services needed up to one year, with extensions in one-year increments, not to exceed three years. |
| H-3 | Trainees in authorized employment training | May be classroom or on-the-job training. Training must not be available in aliens' home countries. Duration may be up to two years. |
| I | Information media representatives | Bona fide members of foreign press, radio, or film while engaged in their professions. Duration is dependent on employment status. |

## Table 15-1: Nonimmigrant Visas (cont.)

| Classification | Visa Type | Duration and Extensions Available |
| --- | --- | --- |
| J | Exchange visitors | Participants in foreign exchange visitor programs. Duration of status. |
| K | Fiancés and fiancées | An alien entering the United States to marry a U.S. citizen. The marriage must take place within ninety days of entry. There are no extensions once alien is married, but he may apply for permanent resident status. |
| L | Intracompany transferees | Depending on the employer's need, the initial period may be up to three years. For extraordinary circumstances the stay may last seven years. |
| M | Vocational students | Students engaged full-time in an approved vocational education program and their families. Duration is for term of program, plus thirty days or one year, whichever is shorter. Extensions may be granted for thirty days or one year, whichever is shorter, to finish studies. |
| N | Family members of G-4 special immigrants | Duration is three years with extensions in increments up to three years. |
| O | Extraordinary ability entertainers, athletes, and others | Aliens of extraordinary ability in the sciences, arts, education, business, or athletics; persons assisting those of extraordinary ability; families of those who qualify. Duration is time to complete the event or activity, up to three years with extensions in one-year increments to complete the event. |

### Table 15-1: Nonimmigrant Visas (cont.)

| Classification | Visa Type | Duration and Extensions Available |
|---|---|---|
| P | Entertainers and athletes | Entertainers and athletes who cannot qualify under Classification O. Requires that the individual be coming to the United States to compete in or perform in a specific event. Duration is for term of event but may be up to five years, with a total of ten years, with extensions available in one-year increments. |
| Q | International cultural exchange aliens | Duration is to complete the exchange or for fifteen months, whichever is shorter. |
| R | Ministers and religious workers | Initial period is three years, with extensions in two-year increments, up to a maximum of five years. |
| S | Witness in criminal or national security investigation-prosecution | Admission maximum of three years—good until September 3, 1999. |
| TN | Canadian and Mexican professionals | Persons engaged in activities at a professional level, at least B.A. degree. No statutory limitation on stay. |
| WT or WB | Visitors without visas | Persons coming for business (WB) or pleasure (WT) for less than ninety days from designated low-fraud countries. |

# 16

# Accidents
# and Personal Injury

Personal injury is a specialized area of law that provides someone who has been injured as a result of negligence with legal remedies that enable him to recover money damages (compensation) from the person who caused the injury or from that person's insurance carrier.

## TYPES OF PERSONAL INJURY MATTERS

There are several types of personal injury cases. The most common ones involve injuries from automobile accidents. Some other types require serious consideration.

## MEDICAL MALPRACTICE AND PRODUCT LIABILITY

Medical malpractice involves a patient who has been injured as a result of negligent medical treatment. Product liability covers injuries sustained from defective merchandise. Both are highly specialized fields and should always be handled by attorneys who are experts in these areas of law.

Malpractice and product liability cases are very complicated and usually take several years to resolve. Anyone who has been injured by negligent medical treatment or a defective product should consult an attorney for advice. Some attorneys specialize only in medical malpractice or product liability cases.

## DOG BITES

Dog bites that are the result of negligence on the part of the dog's owner or handler may be compensated under personal injury law. Some restrictions apply to the recovery of damages for dog bites, however, so anyone who has been injured by a dog bite should discuss all the facts with an attorney before filing a claim. A person who teased a dog before it bit him may find that his right to recover is affected. Any contribution the injured party makes toward his own injuries will reduce his chances of being able to receive compensation for his injuries. However, anyone who is attacked by a dog without provocation will probably be able to receive compensation.

## SLIP AND FALL INJURIES

A person injured in a slip and fall accident as the result of someone else's failure to maintain an area in a safe and appropriate manner may recover damages under personal injury law. In order to receive compensation for a slip and fall accident, the accident must happen somewhere other than on the injured person's property. Many slip and fall accidents occur in stores or shopping malls when a floor is slippery or wet or has not been properly cleaned. Anyone involved in such an accident should report it immediately to the store manager or property management office or to an employee, security guard, or other authorized person if a manager is not available. The injured person should write down the names and addresses of people who witnessed the accident, so that their statements may be used to substantiate a personal injury claim.

## EVALUATING A PERSONAL INJURY CASE

Many factors determine the value of a personal injury case, and it takes experience to evaluate it properly. A person who has sustained an injury should always discuss the situation with an attorney before signing anything or agreeing to a settlement because the claim may be worth more than he is being offered. Some accidents result in delayed reactions or additional injuries that may not be immediately apparent. Someone who is injured may not realize he has been seriously hurt until several days or weeks after the accident.

Anyone who is injured should be examined by his physician even if he or she does not think he has been seriously injured. An attorney who specializes in personal injury can advise someone who is injured and recommend a doctor if the person does not have a personal physician.

## AUTOMOBILE ACCIDENTS

To illustrate how a personal injury case is handled, we will examine a typical automobile accident case.

The law requires that anyone involved in any type of accident involving a motor vehicle stop even if he is not at fault. Failure to stop, or hit-and-run, violations are serious criminal offenses and carry stiff penalties, including fines, imprisonment, suspension, and revocation of one's driver's license.

At the scene of an accident the parties have certain obligations:

1. They should check for injuries to any drivers, passengers, or pedestrians who may be involved. The law requires anyone involved in an accident to assist the injured. Do not move a severely injured person unless he is in extreme danger. For example, if someone is lying in a traffic lane, it may be necessary to move him to the side of the road so he will not be hit by passing vehicles.
2. They should call for an ambulance or ask someone else to do so while one of the parties stays with the injured person. Be assertive; do not hesitate to tell bystanders to call for an ambulance immediately.
3. They should cover an injured person with a blanket or coat and, if possible, stop any bleeding by applying gentle pressure to the wound or wrapping it with a clean cloth.
4. They should place flares around the accident site and along the road in the direction of oncoming traffic, to avoid additional collisions. If flares are not available and if it is safe to do so, send someone to warn approaching vehicles.
5. They should turn on emergency flashing lights on the vehicles and tell other drivers to do the same.

At an accident the first thing to do is to take care of anyone injured. As soon as possible, the driver of any vehicle or a bystander, if the driver is unable to do so, should telephone the police or highway patrol and report the incident.

The only circumstance under which someone involved in an accident should leave the accident scene is if he is the only one there and must leave to take an injured person to the nearest hospital. In that case the driver should contact the police or highway patrol as soon as the injured person arrives at the hospital. When reporting the accident, the party should tell the law enforcement agent the place he is calling from, where the accident happened, and why he left the accident scene.

Once any injured persons have been cared for, the drivers must exchange information including their names, addresses, telephone numbers, driver's license numbers and states of issuance, and the insurance carriers for the drivers and the vehicles. The drivers should write down the make, model, year, and license plate number of each vehicle involved. If the driver is not the owner, the name and address of the owner must be provided. Participants in the accident should also write down the names, addresses, and telephone numbers of all the passengers in all the vehicles involved and of all the witnesses, and should insist that the police or highway patrol be called to take an official accident report. The accident report may be needed later to help resolve any legal claim arising from the accident.

Everyone involved in an accident should cooperate with the officer investigating the accident and answer his questions, but it is important not to admit guilt even if a person thinks he might be at fault. The parties should ask where they can get a copy of the police report. When an officer prepares an investigation report, the parties to the accident should write down his name and badge number so that an attorney may question him about the accident.

If the police officer issues a ticket, the person receiving it must sign the ticket. In doing so, the party receiving the ticket is not admitting any guilt but is simply signing a promise to appear in court at a specified time to enter a plea on the charges being alleged. Anyone who refuses to sign a citation or ticket may be immediately arrested and taken to jail. Before appearing in court to answer the charges alleged in the ticket, the driver should consult with an attorney for advice on how to plead to the charges.

If any driver involved in an accident attempts to drive away or refuses to provide the information required by law, the others involved should write down his license plate number. The Department of Motor Vehicles will use that information to assist the police in finding the owner of the vehicle.

If there are any witnesses to the accident, their names, addresses, and telephone numbers should also be written down. In a personal injury trial an attorney may want to ask witnesses to testify about what they saw. Witnesses should be asked to remain at the scene until a law enforcement officer arrives so that the officer may question them.

Finally, each person involved in the accident should write down the weather and road conditions at the time. The exact time and place of the accident should be recorded, and a simple drawing of the roadway or intersection that indicates the direction each vehicle was traveling at the time of the accident may be very valuable. While these suggestions may seem unimportant at the time, such details can be crucial in determining who is liable for damages.

If someone hits a parked car or damages someone's property, he must try to locate the property owner. If the property owner cannot be found, the person who caused the damage must leave a note with his name, address, telephone number, a place where he can be reached, and an explanation of what happened.

It is illegal to leave the place where the damage occurred unless an appropriate note is left for the property owner. The person who caused the damage should also contact the local police, county sheriff, or highway patrol to inform them that the accident took place and that a note was left as required by law.

Anyone involved in an accident should never offer to pay for any damage or make any threats against the other driver or drivers. Resolving the issues of liability or damages and compensation should be left to attorneys.

Any person involved in an automobile accident should be examined promptly by his doctor even if he does not need emergency medical treatment and has no apparent injuries. He may have sustained injuries that he is not yet aware of, and his doctor's evaluation may be important to any future personal injury claim.

If the doctor requires payment prior to treatment, the victim should contact his attorney to explain the situation. The attorney may be able to refer the injured person to a doctor who will treat him and await payment of his fee until the claim is settled.

If the person who caused the accident does not have insurance, the victim's own policy may pay for his claim for personal injury if he has uninsured motorist coverage. If the value of the claim exceeds the available insurance, the injured person can sue the person who was at fault for the difference.

## MEETING WITH A PERSONAL INJURY ATTORNEY

Once the emergency medical needs of the parties have been taken care of, anyone involved in the accident should contact an attorney. Before releasing any information to anyone else, it is important that the parties fully understand their rights and obligations under the law. The attorney will take care of contacting the claimant's insurance company and the defendant's insurance company and will assist the claimant in completing any forms required to process his claim.

Personal injury claims should be filed only by those who have been injured as the result of an accident. If a person has not suffered any injury, he should not file a personal injury claim.

During the initial visit to an attorney's office the claimant may first be interviewed by a member of the attorney's staff. The interviewer will ask such questions as the claimant's name, address, telephone numbers where he can be reached, birthplace, birth date, age, marital status, and the names of his spouse and dependents. The interviewer may take photographs to attach to the file; they may be used to substantiate visible injuries such as bruises or cuts as well as the nature and extent of the damage to the vehicle.

If a doctor certifies that someone is unable to work as a result of an accident, the injured person's employment record will be important. At the first meeting with an attorney, the claimant should be prepared to answer questions about where he works, the date he was hired, his job title or classification, current earnings, dates he was absent from work because of the accident, and the amount of wages he lost because of the accident. He may also be asked for the names and addresses of previous employers.

The interviewer will ask the claimant to discuss his medical history including dates and descriptions of any prior injuries, hospitals or clinics where he was treated, names of attending physicians, and, if a claim was filed, whether the case was tried in court or settled out of court. For an attorney to evaluate a claim properly, he needs this background information, and it is important that the claimant answer all questions as completely and accurately as possible.

In addition to getting information about the claimant's medical history, the interviewer will ask questions about the most recent accident and the nature of the person's injuries; the names of any doctors, hospitals, or clinics that first treated those injuries; the names of any specialists who have rendered follow-up treatment or therapy; and the dates of treatment.

After this first interview the claimant meets with the attorney to discuss the types of personal injury claims available. The attorney answers any questions and explains the legal concepts of negligence, comparative negligence, testimony, and physical evidence that can be used in proving the claim and any potential problems that are apparent from the beginning. He also explains how the law firm plans to investigate the accident to help determine the facts, and he may recommend that the claim be settled out of court. If the attorney does not recommend accepting the final settlement offer, he will explain why the case should go to trial and whether the case should be tried before a jury or heard by a judge alone.

The circumstances of the case may permit adjudication in more than one court. The attorney advises the client which court is best and assists in deciding where to file the claim.

It is important that a client be completely honest in disclosing the facts of the accident to his attorney. An attorney is prohibited by a code of professional ethics from disclosing any sensitive or incriminating information regarding his clients. The code of ethics also prohibits an attorney from taking a case when he may have a conflict of interest and thus be unable to represent a client's best interest.

## DAMAGES: COMPENSATION FOR A LOSS

The basic principle of a personal injury case is that one party has breached the duty of due care owed to another and caused damage or injury to that person. There may be more than one person (defendant) accused of causing damage or injury named in a personal injury claim, and there may be more than one injured party (plaintiff) filing a claim against any defendant, but the concept of breach of duty remains the same.

When the plaintiff has suffered an injury, he is entitled to recover damages from the defendant and/or his insurance company. *Damages* means compensation in the form of money for a loss or injury. There are many kinds of damages, and the evaluation of damages is a highly complex and detailed area of law. The following is a brief summary of three basic damages frequently awarded in civil cases:

1. *Nominal damages:* a small sum of money awarded to the plaintiff for the purpose of having the judgment on record. Nominal damages are usually reserved for cases in which a plaintiff has suffered no substantial loss or injury to be compensated but in which the law recognizes a technical invasion of his rights and a breach of duty on the part of the defendant to exercise due care.
2. *Compensatory damages:* a sum of money intended to compensate the plaintiff for the loss or injury suffered and to restore him to his state of being before the injury. The majority of damages awarded in personal injury cases are compensatory damages.
3. *Punitive damages:* an additional sum of money awarded to the plaintiff to punish the defendant and deter others from committing similar offenses. Punitive damages are frequently awarded when it can be proved that the defendant showed a reckless disregard for the plaintiff's safety.

The calculation of damages is an extremely complicated area of law. Each case is unique, and there are many factors to consider in determining a dollar amount. The calculation of damages is something that should be left to an attorney to determine with the participation and consent of the injured party.

## TYPES OF PERSONAL INJURY CLAIMS

Seven basic types of claims that may apply in an accident case are clearly identified:

1. A *property damage* claim asks for compensation for the repair or replacement of one's vehicle. If a vehicle has to be replaced, the standard set for determining its replacement cost is the market value of the vehicle immediately before it was damaged. This may not be equal to the price the person originally paid for it or the amount still owed on it. Market value is

calculated according to industry-accepted publications that list suggested values for vehicles on the basis of age, mileage, condition, and the numbers and types of accessories on the vehicle as well as surveys of comparable vehicles for sale.

A party who has sustained damages or injuries may also be compensated for the loss of use of his vehicle during the time it takes to repair or replace it. Even if a party was unable to drive the vehicle during that time because of injury or damage to the vehicle, he is still entitled to compensation for the loss. Loss of use compensation is generally calculated at the cost of renting a similar vehicle for the number of days it takes to make the repairs.

2. *Medical expenses* are compensation for the cost of reasonable and necessary medical expenses that were actually incurred as a result of the accident. Medical expenses are frequently divided into two categories: diagnostic and treatment. Diagnostic expenses include ambulance, emergency room fees, X rays, and blood tests, while treatment expenses include regular follow-up office visits, therapy, and surgery.

Many insurance companies base their settlement offers only on the treatment costs of a claim. The diagnostic portion, however, is often the greater expense and should also be considered in claim evaluation.

3. *Loss of earnings* compensation may be available to a person who is employed by someone else, and it is calculated by the number of days lost from work and the person's pay rate at the time of injury. A self-employed person's loss of earnings is calculated by the estimated income he would have earned during his medical disability. In order to collect loss of earnings, two conditions must be present:

   a. A doctor must certify that the injured person is unable to work.

   b. The injured person must actually not work.

A person can collect for loss of earnings only for the period of time that both these conditions exist. An employee who regularly receives pay for overtime may be able to collect for that also.

An employee who continues to have an income by using accumulated sick or vacation time is still entitled to collect for loss of earnings as long as he does not actually work.

Property damage, medical expenses, and loss of earnings are often referred to as special damages because they have a precise and identifiable value, a specific dollar amount—for example, medical expenses that total fifteen hundred dollars.

Another type of damages is known as general damages, paid for pain and suffering. It is more difficult to attach a dollar value to general damages since there is no precise bill to present.

4. *Pain and suffering* compensation is classified as general damages. Com-

pensation is awarded for the pain and suffering the plaintiff endured above and beyond the actual cost of treating his injuries.

Damages can be awarded for emotional as well as physical injury and trauma. The largest part of any personal injury claim is for pain and suffering damages, and generally each person involved in the claim will be compensated individually. There are many factors that affect the value of a pain and suffering claim, including, but not limited to

   a. the nature and severity of injuries

   b. the likelihood of the plaintiff's recovering

   c. the effect of injuries on the plaintiff's ability to earn a living

   d. the scope and nature of the plaintiff's employment

   e. the earning potential or earning capacity of the plaintiff

   f. the effect of injuries on the plaintiff's ability to function as a whole person, including physical, mental, and emotional health.

5. *Loss of consortium* is compensation for the loss of the conjugal fellowship and company of one's spouse. It is awarded when there has been serious injury to or wrongful death of a spouse. In appropriate cases both the injured spouse and an uninjured spouse can receive compensation for loss of consortium.

6. *Injuries to others* compensation is awarded for emotional damage the plaintiff suffered as a result of having watched physical pain inflicted on an immediate family member. If a mother sees her child struck and injured by a motorist, she may be entitled to recover from the defendant for the emotional pain she suffered from what she saw in addition to her child's claim for the physical injuries.

7. *Wrongful death* compensation is paid to immediate surviving heirs for the wrongful death of the victim. Until the nineteenth century common law prohibited this kind of recovery entirely on the ground that it was immoral to place a monetary value on a human life. Since the nineteenth century the law has provided for wrongful death damages payable to the victim's family to lessen the economic hardships caused by the death. The recovery was originally enacted to benefit widows who lost their husbands, but the law soon evolved to allow recovery for widowers, children, parents, illegitimate children, and other surviving next of kin. The law now allows recovery not only for economic loss but for loss of companionship.

Compensation for a wrongful death is generally held to cover damages for the following:

   a. Loss of support: the financial support that the decedent would have supplied to his dependents had he lived.

   b. Loss of services: the monetary value of services that the decedent provided and would have continued to provide if he had not died, including services he performed at home or elsewhere for his spouse.

Loss of services also applies to the training, education, and guidance that a child would have received had it not been for the wrongful death of a parent.

c. Loss of society: a broad range of mutual benefits each family member receives from the other's continued existence, including love, affection, care, attention, companionship, comfort, and protection.

d. Damages for funeral expenses: recovery of costs in some cases when the decedent's dependents have either paid for the funeral or are liable for its payment.

## INSURANCE

The basic purpose of insurance is to protect against financial loss resulting from death, damage, or liability. The insured is the person or persons covered by the insurance policy, and the insurer or underwriter is the insurance company that issued the policy.

*Personal injury liability* coverage protects the insured against financial loss when he causes an accident that injures or kills others. The maximum amount that will be paid by the insurance company is dependent upon the amount of coverage the insured purchased when he bought the policy.

*Property damage liability* coverage protects the insured against financial loss when he or she causes an accident that results in damage to another person's property. Some insurance carriers pay for car rental expenses of the victim under property damage liability coverage while others pay under general liability coverage.

When someone is injured in an accident that is not his fault and the defendant has liability coverage, the defendant's insurance carrier will pay the value of the injured party's claim up to the limits of his policy. The minimum vehicle liability coverage required by law for bodily injury and property damage varies from state to state (see Multistate compendium on Minimum Automobile Liability Insurance Requirements on page 167).

In addition to paying medical expenses, the defendant's liability insurance carrier must compensate injured parties for loss of earnings, for pain and suffering, and/or for wrongful death.

The defendant's property damage liability coverage will pay for repairs to a damaged vehicle up to the limits of his policy and will compensate the injured party for the loss of use of his vehicle. The defendant's insurance may also cover related expenses such as towing, storage, and mechanical damage.

A person involved in an accident caused by an uninsured or underinsured motorist may have to recover all or part of his damages from his own insurance carrier.

The types of coverage available under an insurance policy include certain standard categories:

*Collision* coverage pays for damage to an insured's vehicle when that damage is caused by a collision. Many collision plans have deductibles. A deductible is the amount the insured must pay toward the damage before the insurance company is required to make any payment. For example, a person who has a five-hundred-dollar deductible is required to pay for the first five hundred dollars of repair costs, and his insurance carrier pays the rest. Collision coverage is limited to the market value of the vehicle immediately before the accident.

If the cost of repairs exceeds the market value, the vehicle will be considered "totaled." Many insurance companies do not offer collision coverage for very old vehicles, and if they do, the cost may make such coverage impractical.

*Comprehensive* coverage pays for damage to a vehicle caused by something other than a collision, up to its actual market value. This usually covers damage caused by fire, windstorm, hail, snow, vandalism, theft, glass breakage, and other noncollision incidents. It may also cover damage to or loss of personal items inside the vehicle and, on some policies, towing fees.

*Medical payments* coverage pays for medical expenses incurred by the driver and his passengers up to the policy limits. Payments under the medical coverage portion of an insurance policy are available even if a portion of the medical expenses has been paid by another policy. If the defendant's liability insurance pays the bills, the plaintiff is entitled to recover the medical costs again from his own auto medical payments coverage. For example, if a plaintiff has a thousand dollars in medical bills and the defendant has liability insurance, the defendant's insurance will pay the medical bills. In addition, the plaintiff is legally entitled to collect the thousand dollars again from his medical payments coverage.

If the defendant does not have liability coverage and the plaintiff must collect from his own insurance company under an uninsured motorist claim, the insurance carrier may be entitled to reduce the amount owed by an amount equal to what has previously been paid under any medical payments coverage. For example, if the total uninsured motorist claim is worth twelve thousand dollars and the carrier has already paid two thousand in medical payments, the insured may receive only ten thousand dollars as a final payment. Medical payments benefits may also be available when an insured or a relative who lives with the insured is injured in an accident that involves a motor vehicle, even if that claimant is a pedestrian, a bicycle rider, or a passenger in a car that belongs to someone other than the insured.

*Uninsured motorist* coverage pays damages, up to the policy limits, for personal injury or death caused by an uninsured driver. This coverage also applies to personal injury or death caused in a hit-and-run accident. In the event of a hit-and-run accident, most policies require the insured to file a police report within twenty-four hours of the accident and to produce physical evidence that the insured's vehicle was "touched" or damaged by the hit-and-run vehicle. Evidence usually takes the form of paint scrapings or other tangible material. Some carriers require the insured to notify his or her agent within twenty-four hours when there has been a hit-and-run accident.

In some states uninsured motorist coverage must be offered to anyone who purchases auto insurance, unless he specifically waives the coverage in writing. The insured is charged if he wants this coverage.

Uninsured motorist payments are limited to the maximum amount indicated on the policy. Before an insured person can collect damages under the uninsured motorist part of a policy, he must prove that the accident was not his fault and that the other person was uninsured.

Each state has established a procedure for proving that a defendant is uninsured. Usually the first step is to contact him to ask him if he has insurance. If he does not and will not sign a declaration to that effect, or if he refuses to answer, the plaintiff can file an accident report form (available at any DMV office) and mail it to the state Department of Motor Vehicles. In addition to uninsured motorist forms, all drivers must file accident report forms when the damage to any vehicle exceeds a specified amount or if anyone was injured or killed in the accident. The DMV prepares a report that indicates whether or not the defendant had liability insurance on the day of the accident. The plaintiff can then take the form to his insurance carrier, thus establishing his right to collect uninsured motorist benefits.

*Underinsured motorist* coverage protects the insured and his passengers when the defendant is insured but his or her personal liability limits or property damage limits are inadequate to cover the value of the claim. In this case, underinsured motorist coverage will pay the difference between what the defendant's coverage pays and the policyholder's underinsured coverage up to a maximum of the value of the loss. Usually underinsured motorist coverage is included on any motor vehicle insurance policy, and the insured is charged for it unless he specifically waives his right to this coverage in writing.

*Uninsured motorist property damage* coverage protects a vehicle owner if his vehicle is hit and damaged by an uninsured motorist. If an insured has uninsured motorist property damage coverage, he does not have to pay the deductible that would be required if he used his collision coverage.

*Car rental* coverage pays car rental costs up to the daily or total limits stipulated in the policy. Car rental coverage is not available from all carriers. If the defendant in an accident claim has liability insurance, his company should pay the car rental costs.

*Credit disability* coverage applies if an injured party is so severely injured that he is certified by a doctor as being medically disabled. Under the provisions of credit disability coverage, the insurance company continues to make the insured's car payments until he is no longer certified disabled or until the benefit maximum amount has been paid.


## BENEFIT CONDITIONS AND LIMITATIONS

Many medical payment benefits under automobile and group insurance policies contain limitations and conditions that greatly reduce the amount of money they will pay but often provide for reimbursement of such payments in certain situations.

A *reimbursement clause* in the medical payments coverage portion of an insurance policy means the carrier will pay the expenses initially but is entitled to reimbursement from the insured if he later receives an award of damages for medical expenses from the defendant or his insurance company. Policies with reimbursement clauses are often less expensive than those without but may offer fewer benefits.

An *excess only* clause in an insurance policy means the insurance carrier will pay only those medical costs still owed after other health insurance coverage has paid the maximum amount available under its policy. For example, if the insured has any collectible health insurance such as group medical, he must first submit expenses for payment by that carrier up to the maximum allowed. The vehicle insurance excess medical payments coverage then pays any balance owed.

*Liability insurance* protects the policyholder against financial loss in the event he is at fault in an accident. If someone files a claim against a policyholder, claiming that the accident was the policyholder's fault, the policyholder's liability insurance carrier will defend the claim. If it is determined that the policyholder was at fault, the insurance carrier will pay the claimant for any damages he suffered up to the limits of the policy. A person found to have been at fault in an accident may be held personally responsible for any damages above his policy limits.

Most states require drivers to have automobile liability insurance. In many states anyone who does not have automobile insurance can be fined and will have his driver's license suspended for at least one year (see Multistate compendium on Minimum Automobile Liability Insurance Requirements on page 167).

## CASE EVALUATION AND LIABILITY ASSESSMENT

The attorney responsible for processing a claim will examine all the facts of the accident and determine to what extent each person involved is at fault. This process, known as liability assessment, is an important part of determining the viability and value of any claim.

In addition to the statements that have been made by the claimant and the official police report, the attorney may have an investigator examine the accident site. The investigator will look for evidence that can be used to substantiate the claimant's case. He will measure skid marks, time the traffic signals, pick up debris left at the site, interview witnesses, check the speed limit, locate posted road signs, and check with the weather service for driving conditions at the time of the accident.

## DEFENSES TO A PERSONAL INJURY CLAIM

A person who has had a personal injury claim filed against him and is alleged to have been at fault in an automobile accident may rely on any legal defenses that are available. Some of the more common defenses used in personal injury claims are usually standard.

The *rule of avoidable consequences* is frequently applied in cases where the plaintiff causes further injury to himself above and beyond the initial damage caused by the defendant. For example, if the plaintiff suffers a strained back as the result of an automobile accident and then further aggravates the injury by performing excessively strenuous activities after he has been advised to rest, he may be denied recovery for the additional injuries. The law generally assumes that a person who has been injured must act reasonably to avoid or limit his losses or can be precluded from recovering damages for injuries that could have been avoided.

*Comparative negligence* has replaced the defense of contributory negligence in most states. Contributory negligence law would not allow a claimant to receive any compensation if he contributed in any way to causing the accident that resulted in his injury. This often caused extremely unfair results when a claimant who had been severely and permanently injured was not allowed to receive any compensation even if his negligence was only 1 percent responsible for causing the accident.

Comparative negligence allows a claimant partly responsible for causing the accident to receive a percentage of the value of his claim equal to the percentage of negligence of the other party. The claimant's compensation is reduced by the same percentage that his negligence contributed to the accident.

Each party has the right to claim compensation from the other, and sometimes a party who was more than 50 percent responsible for causing the accident receives much more money if the value of his claim is greater than that of the other party. For example, a claimant who was 40 percent at fault and whose case is worth ten thousand dollars would be entitled to receive only six thousand dollars while the other party, who was 60 percent at fault but whose case is worth one hundred thousand dollars, would be entitled to receive forty thousand dollars.

Comparative negligence is an affirmative defense, which means that the person who will benefit from using it has the burden of proving how and to what extent the other party contributed to causing the accident.

*Assumption of risk* is a defense in which the defendant claims that the plaintiff had advance knowledge of the condition or situation that caused him harm yet voluntarily exposed himself to the hazardous situation anyway. When it can be proved that a person voluntarily exposed himself to the risk that caused his injuries, the defendant will usually not be liable for any resulting injuries. For example, if someone is injured by a foul ball at a baseball game, the ball park owners could claim that this occurrence is common and well known to everyone and that the person hit by the foul ball assumed the risk of possible injury by attending the game. Assumption of risk arises regardless of the caution employed by the plaintiff and is based on his consent or willingness to participate in an activity.

The *statute of limitations* requires, in most states, that a personal injury lawsuit be filed within one year of the accident. If the plaintiff has not settled his case and fails to file a lawsuit within that time limit, the statute of limitations is an absolute defense to any suit filed later.

*Privilege* is immunity against self-incrimination and is the constitutional right of a person to refuse to answer questions or give testimony that would harm him or his case. However, the motor vehicle laws that require a driver to report an accident do not allow the concept of privilege to be used to avoid filing the report. An accident report is considered information only and is not deemed an admission of guilt.

*Immunity* in a civil case exonerates the defendant from liability because of his legal status or position. Most situations that once gave rise to assertion of the defense of immunity no longer exist.

## ATTORNEY'S FEES

In personal injury cases it is seldom necessary for a client to pay his attorney before his case is resolved. Usually the plaintiff's attorney is paid through a contingency fee. Under this arrangement a client pays nothing while the work is being done, and no fee is due the attorney unless the client collects damages from the opposing party. When the case is resolved, the client pays the attorney a portion of the amount received. Because an injured party entitled to compensation for his damages is often unable to bear the cost of extensive legal preparation, the contingency fee arrangement allows anyone with a valid claim to seek compensation.

Other fee arrangements are the fixed fee and the hourly fee. The fixed fee is seldom used in personal injury cases. It requires the client to pay a one-time fee, usually before legal services are provided. If the case is very small, an attorney may request this type of fee arrangement.

The hourly fee is usually reserved for corporate clients and is seldom applied to individual clients in personal injury cases. Under this arrangement the client is billed for the actual hours the attorney spends preparing and presenting the case. Most cases take many hours to prepare, so this fee arrangement is seldom advantageous for the client.

# Index

# About the Author

The United States was still recovering from the effects of World War II when Jess Araujo was born in El Paso, Texas. El Paso was then, and continues to be, a predominantly Hispanic, economically depressed city sprawling in the valley created by the Franklin Mountains. Large areas of El Paso are indistinguishable from its sister city of Juarez, across the Rio Grande in Mexico. Jess's father, Juan, a retired railroad worker, and mother, Dolores, still live in the home in which they raised a family of five. The neighborhood has seen very little change in the many years since he left home to join the United States Marine Corps.

Perhaps it was working in the cabbage fields and citrus orchards of the Central and Southern California agricultural belt as a youth that inspired Jess to seek a higher education and a better life for himself and his family. After receiving an honorable discharge at the rank of Sergeant, he obtained his associate in arts degree at Santa Ana College, receiving the Man of the Year award, and received his bachelor of arts degree at the University of California at Irvine, making the dean's honor roll and graduating *summa cum laude*. He obtained his law degree from Loyola University School of Law in 1976, which he attended on an academic scholarship.

He began practicing law in 1976 and in 1979 participated in establishing the law firm of DiMarco and Araujo with his present partners Andrew "Andy" J. DiMarco, Steven J. DiMarco, and John A. Montevideo. In 1997, the firm name was changed to DiMarco, Araujo & Montevideo, A Professional Law Corporation, to recognize the participation of John Montevideo. Subsequently, they established a second corporation, The Accident Law Center, specializing in personal injury and workers' compensation law. The list of Jess's professional affiliations is lengthy, including the American and California Bar Associations and the Orange County Hispanic Bar Association. He is certified to present cases in the California and United States Supreme Courts, as well as the Federal District and Circuit Courts in California and Washington, D.C.

A dedicated professional, Jess has served two terms as president of the Hispanic Bar Association and one term as vice president of the Orange County Fair-Housing Council. He is General Counsel to the Mexican Consulate in Orange County, California, and past president of the Orange County Bar Foundation. His commitment to his community is exemplified by his service on the board of Directors of the National Council on Alcoholism and as vice president of the Mexican-American Political Association (MAPA) of Orange County. He has made countless presentations in predominantly Mexican-American elementary and secondary schools and is often invited to lecture at the university level as well. In recent years, his daily radio talk show on legal issues aired on Radio XPRS, 1090 AM, whose signal reaches throughout Baja California, Mexico, and Southern California. In addition, Jess is a professor of legal subjects at California State University, Fullerton.

His avocations are almost as countless and varied as his professional credits. He is an avid amateur photographer and equestrian. His love of the sea compelled him to seek and obtain a Coast Guard Captain's license. But his greatest avocation is music. He plays piano and guitar and composed the song "La verdad," which he performs on an album of the same name.

Jess makes his home in San Clemente, California, together with his wife, Donna Marie. His son, Jess Jr., is an executive with a major California corporation, and his daughter, Kristina, is an elementary school teacher in Southern California.